"Those who cannot remember the past are condemned to repeat it."
-- George Santayana, Reason in Common Sense (1905)

INTRODUCTION

Pursuant to Title III of the Omnibus Diplomatic and Antiterrorism Act of 1986, 22 U.S.C. § 4831 *et seq.*, (the "Act"), Secretary of State Hillary Rodham Clinton convened an Accountability Review Board (ARB) for Benghazi to examine the facts and circumstances surrounding the September 11-12, 2012, killings of four U.S. government personnel, including the U.S. Ambassador to Libya, John Christopher Stevens, in Benghazi, Libya. A series of attacks on September 11-12, 2012 involving arson, small-arms and machine-gun fire, and use of rocket-propelled grenades (RPGs), grenades and mortars, focused on two U.S. facilities in Benghazi, as well as U.S. personnel en route between the two facilities. In addition, the attacks severely wounded two U.S. personnel, injured three Libyan contract guards and resulted in the destruction and abandonment of both facilities – the U.S. Special Mission compound (SMC) and Annex.

Four Board members were selected by the Secretary of State and one member from the intelligence community (IC) was selected by the Director for National Intelligence. Ambassador Thomas R. Pickering served as Chairman, with Admiral Michael Mullen as Vice Chairman. Additional members were Catherine Bertini, Richard Shinnick, and Hugh Turner, who represented the IC.

The criminal investigation of the September 11-12, 2012, Benghazi attacks, for which the statutory responsibility rests with the Federal Bureau of Investigation (FBI), was still underway at the time of this report. The Board enjoyed excellent cooperation with the Department of Justice and FBI throughout preparation of this report. The key questions surrounding the identity, actions and motivations of the perpetrators remain to be determined by the ongoing criminal investigation.

As called for by the Act, this report examines: whether the attacks were security related; whether security systems and procedures were adequate and implemented properly; the impact of intelligence and information availability; whether any other facts or circumstances in these cases may be relevant to appropriate security management of U.S. missions worldwide; and, finally, whether any U.S. government employee or contractor, as defined by the Act, breached her or his duty.

The Benghazi attacks represented the first murder of a U.S. ambassador since 1988, and took place 11 years to the day after the terrorist attacks of September 11, 2001. Ambassador Stevens personified the U.S. commitment to a free and democratic Libya. His knowledge of Arabic, his ability to move in all sectors of the population, and his wide circle of friends, particularly in Benghazi, marked him as an exceptional practitioner of modern diplomacy. The U.S. Special Mission in Benghazi, established in November 2011, was the successor to his highly successful endeavor as Special Envoy to the rebel-led government that eventually toppled Muammar Qaddafi in fall 2011. The Special Mission bolstered U.S. support for Libya's democratic transition through engagement with eastern Libya, the birthplace of the revolt against Qaddafi and a regional power center.

The Benghazi attacks took place against a backdrop of significantly increased demands on U.S. diplomats to be present in the world's most dangerous places to advance American interests and connect with populations beyond capitals, and beyond host governments' reach. With State Department civilians at the forefront of U.S. efforts to stabilize and build capacity in Iraq, as the U.S. military draws down in Afghanistan, and with security threats growing in volatile environments where the U.S. military is not present – from Peshawar to Bamako – the Bureau of Diplomatic Security (DS) is being stretched to the limit as never before. DS overall has done a fine job protecting thousands of employees in some 273 U.S. diplomatic missions around the world. No diplomatic presence is without risk, given past attempts by terrorists to pursue U.S. targets worldwide. And the total elimination of risk is a non-starter for U.S. diplomacy, given the need for the U.S. government to be present in places where stability and security are often most profoundly lacking and host government support is sometimes minimal to non-existent.

The Benghazi attacks also took place in a context in which the global terrorism threat as most often represented by al Qaeda (AQ) is fragmenting and increasingly devolving to local affiliates and other actors who share many of AQ's aims, including violent anti-Americanism, without necessarily being organized or operated under direct AQ command and control. This growing, diffuse range of terrorist and hostile actors poses an additional challenge to American security officers, diplomats, development professionals and decision-makers seeking to mitigate risk and remain active in high threat environments without resorting to an unacceptable total fortress and stay-at-home approach to U.S. diplomacy.

1.   State Dept. Accountability Review Board for Benghazi (12/20/2012)

For many years the State Department has been engaged in a struggle to obtain the resources necessary to carry out its work, with varying degrees of success. This has brought about a deep sense of the importance of husbanding resources to meet the highest priorities, laudable in the extreme in any government department. But it has also had the effect of conditioning a few State Department managers to favor restricting the use of resources as a general orientation. There is no easy way to cut through this Gordian knot, all the more so as budgetary austerity looms large ahead. At the same time, it is imperative for the State Department to be mission-driven, rather than resource-constrained – particularly when being present in increasingly risky areas of the world is integral to U.S. national security. The recommendations in this report attempt to grapple with these issues and err on the side of increased attention to prioritization and to fuller support for people and facilities engaged in working in high risk, high threat areas. The solution requires a more serious and sustained commitment from Congress to support State Department needs, which, in total, constitute a small percentage both of the full national budget and that spent for national security. One overall conclusion in this report is that Congress must do its part to meet this challenge and provide necessary resources to the State Department to address security risks and meet mission imperatives.

Mindful of these considerations, the ARB has examined the terrorist attacks in Benghazi with an eye towards how we can better advance American interests and protect our personnel in an increasingly complex and dangerous world. This Board presents its findings and recommendations with the unanimous conclusion that while the United States cannot retreat in the face of such challenges, we must work more rigorously and adeptly to address them, and that American diplomats and security professionals, like their military colleagues, serve the nation in an inherently risky profession. Risk mitigation involves two imperatives – engagement and security – which require wise leadership, good intelligence and evaluation, proper defense and strong preparedness and, at times, downsizing, indirect access and even withdrawal. There is no one paradigm. Experienced leadership, close coordination and agility, timely informed decision making, and adequate funding and personnel resources are essential. The selfless courage of the four Americans who died in the line of duty in Benghazi on September 11-12, 2012, as well as those who were injured and all those who valiantly fought to save their colleagues, inspires all of us as we seek to draw the right lessons from that tragic night.

1. State Dept. Accountability Review Board for Benghazi (12/20/2012)

EXECUTIVE OVERVIEW

A series of terrorist attacks in Benghazi, Libya, on September 11-12, 2012, resulted in the deaths of four U.S. government personnel, Ambassador Chris Stevens, Sean Smith, Tyrone Woods, and Glen Doherty; seriously wounded two other U.S. personnel and injured three Libyan contract guards; and resulted in the destruction and abandonment of the U.S. Special Mission compound and Annex.

FINDINGS

In examining the circumstances of these attacks, the Accountability Review Board for Benghazi determined that:

1. The attacks were security related, involving arson, small arms and machine gun fire, and the use of RPGs, grenades, and mortars against U.S. personnel at two separate facilities – the SMC and the Annex – and en route between them. Responsibility for the tragic loss of life, injuries, and damage to U.S. facilities and property rests solely and completely with the terrorists who perpetrated the attacks. The Board concluded that there was no protest prior to the attacks, which were unanticipated in their scale and intensity.

2. Systemic failures and leadership and management deficiencies at senior levels within two bureaus of the State Department (the "Department") resulted in a Special Mission security posture that was inadequate for Benghazi and grossly inadequate to deal with the attack that took place.

   Security in Benghazi was not recognized and implemented as a "shared responsibility" by the bureaus in Washington charged with supporting the post, resulting in stove-piped discussions and decisions on policy and security. That said, Embassy Tripoli did not demonstrate strong and sustained advocacy with Washington for increased security for Special Mission Benghazi.

   The short-term, transitory nature of Special Mission Benghazi's staffing, with talented and committed, but relatively inexperienced, American personnel often on temporary assignments of 40 days or less, resulted in diminished institutional knowledge, continuity, and mission capacity.

1. State Dept. Accountability Review Board for Benghazi (12/20/2012)

Overall, the number of Bureau of Diplomatic Security (DS) security staff in Benghazi on the day of the attack and in the months and weeks leading up to it was inadequate, despite repeated requests from Special Mission Benghazi and Embassy Tripoli for additional staffing. Board members found a pervasive realization among personnel who served in Benghazi that the Special Mission was not a high priority for Washington when it came to security-related requests, especially those relating to staffing.

The insufficient Special Mission security platform was at variance with the appropriate Overseas Security Policy Board (OSPB) standards with respect to perimeter and interior security. Benghazi was also severely under-resourced with regard to certain needed security equipment, although DS funded and installed in 2012 a number of physical security upgrades. These included heightening the outer perimeter wall, safety grills on safe area egress windows, concrete jersey barriers, manual drop-arm vehicle barriers, a steel gate for the Villa C safe area, some locally manufactured steel doors, sandbag fortifications, security cameras, some additional security lighting, guard booths, and an Internal Defense Notification System.

Special Mission Benghazi's uncertain future after 2012 and its "non-status" as a temporary, residential facility made allocation of resources for security and personnel more difficult, and left responsibility to meet security standards to the working-level in the field, with very limited resources.

In the weeks and months leading up to the attacks, the response from post, Embassy Tripoli, and Washington to a deteriorating security situation was inadequate. At the same time, the SMC's dependence on the armed but poorly skilled Libyan February 17 Martyrs' Brigade (February 17) militia members and unarmed, locally contracted Blue Mountain Libya (BML) guards for security support was misplaced.

Although the February 17 militia had proven effective in responding to improvised explosive device (IED) attacks on the Special Mission in April and June 2012, there were some troubling indicators of its reliability in the months and weeks preceding the September attacks. At the time of Ambassador Stevens' visit, February 17 militia members had stopped accompanying Special Mission vehicle movements in protest over salary and working hours.

1.   State Dept. Accountability Review Board for Benghazi (12/20/2012)

Post and the Department were well aware of the anniversary of the September 11, 2001 terrorist attacks but at no time were there ever any specific, credible threats against the mission in Benghazi related to the September 11 anniversary. Ambassador Stevens and Benghazi-based DS agents had taken the anniversary into account and decided to hold all meetings on-compound on September 11.

The Board found that Ambassador Stevens made the decision to travel to Benghazi independently of Washington, per standard practice. Timing for his trip was driven in part by commitments in Tripoli, as well as a staffing gap between principal officers in Benghazi. Plans for the Ambassador's trip provided for minimal close protection security support and were not shared thoroughly with the Embassy's country team, who were not fully aware of planned movements off compound. The Ambassador did not see a direct threat of an attack of this nature and scale on the U.S. Mission in the overall negative trendline of security incidents from spring to summer 2012. His status as the leading U.S. government advocate on Libya policy, and his expertise on Benghazi in particular, caused Washington to give unusual deference to his judgments.

Communication, cooperation, and coordination among Washington, Tripoli, and Benghazi functioned collegially at the working-level but were constrained by a lack of transparency, responsiveness, and leadership at the senior levels. Among various Department bureaus and personnel in the field, there appeared to be very real confusion over who, ultimately, was responsible and empowered to make decisions based on both policy and security considerations.

3. Notwithstanding the proper implementation of security systems and procedures and remarkable heroism shown by American personnel, those systems and the Libyan response fell short in the face of a series of attacks that began with the sudden penetration of the Special Mission compound by dozens of armed attackers.

The Board found the responses by both the BML guards and February 17 to be inadequate. The Board's inquiry found little evidence that the armed February 17 guards offered any meaningful defense of the SMC, or succeeded in summoning a February 17 militia presence to assist expeditiously.

The Board found the Libyan government's response to be profoundly lacking on the night of the attacks, reflecting both weak capacity and near absence of

1.   State Dept. Accountability Review Board for Benghazi (12/20/2012)

central government influence and control in Benghazi. The Libyan government did facilitate assistance from a quasi-governmental militia that supported the evacuation of U.S. government personnel to Benghazi airport. The Libyan government also provided a military C-130 aircraft which was used to evacuate remaining U.S. personnel and the bodies of the deceased from Benghazi to Tripoli on September 12.

The Board determined that U.S. personnel on the ground in Benghazi performed with courage and readiness to risk their lives to protect their colleagues, in a near impossible situation. The Board members believe every possible effort was made to rescue and recover Ambassador Stevens and Sean Smith.

The interagency response was timely and appropriate, but there simply was not enough time for armed U.S. military assets to have made a difference.

4. The Board found that intelligence provided no immediate, specific tactical warning of the September 11 attacks. Known gaps existed in the intelligence community's understanding of extremist militias in Libya and the potential threat they posed to U.S. interests, although some threats were known to exist.

5. The Board found that certain senior State Department officials within two bureaus demonstrated a lack of proactive leadership and management ability in their responses to security concerns posed by Special Mission Benghazi, given the deteriorating threat environment and the lack of reliable host government protection. However, the Board did not find reasonable cause to determine that any individual U.S. government employee breached his or her duty.

KEY RECOMMENDATIONS

With the lessons of the past and the challenges of the future in mind, the Board puts forward recommendations in six core areas: Overarching Security Considerations; Staffing High Risk, High Threat Posts; Training and Awareness; Security and Fire Safety Equipment; Intelligence and Threat Analysis; and Personnel Accountability.

OVERARCHING SECURITY CONSIDERATIONS

1. State Dept. Accountability Review Board for Benghazi (12/20/2012)

1. The Department must strengthen security for personnel and platforms beyond traditional reliance on host government security support in high risk, high threat[1] posts. The Department should urgently review the proper balance between acceptable risk and expected outcomes in high risk, high threat areas. While the answer cannot be to refrain from operating in such environments, the Department must do so on the basis of having: 1) a defined, attainable, and prioritized mission; 2) a clear-eyed assessment of the risk and costs involved; 3) a commitment of sufficient resources to mitigate these costs and risks; 4) an explicit acceptance of those costs and risks that cannot be mitigated; and 5) constant attention to changes in the situation, including when to leave and perform the mission from a distance. The United States must be self-reliant and enterprising in developing alternate security platforms, profiles, and staffing footprints to address such realities. Assessments must be made on a case-by-case basis and repeated as circumstances change.

2. The Board recommends that the Department re-examine DS organization and management, with a particular emphasis on span of control for security policy planning for all overseas U.S. diplomatic facilities. In this context, the recent creation of a new Diplomatic Security Deputy Assistant Secretary for High Threat Posts could be a positive first step if integrated into a sound strategy for DS reorganization.

3. As the President's personal representative, the Chief of Mission bears "direct and full responsibility for the security of [his or her] mission and all the personnel for whom [he or she is] responsible," and thus for risk management in the country to which he or she is accredited. In Washington, each regional Assistant Secretary has a corresponding responsibility to support the Chief of Mission in executing this duty. Regional bureaus should have augmented support within the bureau on security matters, to include a senior DS officer to report to the regional Assistant Secretary.

4. The Department should establish a panel of outside independent experts (military, security, humanitarian) with experience in high risk, high threat areas to support DS, identify best practices (from other agencies and other countries), and regularly evaluate U.S. security platforms in high risk, high threat posts.

---

[1] The Board defines "high risk, high threat" posts as those in countries with high to critical levels of political violence and terrorism, governments of weak capacity, and security platforms that fall well below established standards.

5. The Department should develop minimum security standards for occupancy of temporary facilities in high risk, high threat environments, and seek greater flexibility for the use of Bureau of Overseas Buildings Operations (OBO) sources of funding so that they can be rapidly made available for security upgrades at such facilities.

6. Before opening or re-opening critical threat or high risk, high threat posts, the Department should establish a multi-bureau support cell, residing in the regional bureau. The support cell should work to expedite the approval and funding for establishing and operating the post, implementing physical security measures, staffing of security and management personnel, and providing equipment, continuing as conditions at the post require.

7. The Nairobi and Dar es Salaam ARBs' report of January 1999 called for collocation of newly constructed State Department and other government agencies' facilities. All State Department and other government agencies' facilities should be collocated when they are in the same metropolitan area, unless a waiver has been approved.

8. The Secretary should require an action plan from DS, OBO and other relevant offices on the use of fire as a weapon against diplomatic facilities, including immediate steps to deal with urgent issues. The report should also include reviews of fire safety and crisis management training for all employees and dependents, safehaven standards and fire safety equipment, and recommendations to facilitate survival in smoke and fire situations.

9. Tripwires are too often treated only as indicators of threat rather than an essential trigger mechanism for serious risk management decisions and actions. The Department should revise its guidance to posts and require key offices to perform in-depth status checks of post tripwires.

10. Recalling the recommendations of the Nairobi and Dar es Salaam ARBs, the State Department must work with Congress to restore the Capital Security Cost Sharing Program at its full capacity, adjusted for inflation to approximately $2.2 billion in fiscal year 2015, including an up to ten-year program addressing that need, prioritized for construction of new facilities in high risk, high threat areas. It should also work with Congress to expand utilization of Overseas

1. State Dept. Accountability Review Board for Benghazi (12/20/2012)

Contingency Operations funding to respond to emerging security threats and vulnerabilities and operational requirements in high risk, high threat posts.

11. The Board supports the State Department's initiative to request additional Marines and expand the Marine Security Guard (MSG) Program – as well as corresponding requirements for staffing and funding. The Board also recommends that the State Department and DoD identify additional flexible MSG structures and request further resources for the Department and DoD to provide more capabilities and capacities at higher risk posts.

STAFFING HIGH RISK, HIGH THREAT POSTS

12. The Board strongly endorses the Department's request for increased DS personnel for high- and critical-threat posts and for additional Mobile Security Deployment teams, as well as an increase in DS domestic staffing in support of such action.

13. The Department should assign key policy, program, and security personnel at high risk, high threat posts for a minimum of one year. For less critical personnel, the temporary duty length (TDY) length should be no less than 120 days. The ARB suggests a comprehensive review of human resources authorities with an eye to using those authorities to promote sending more experienced officers, including "When Actually Employed" (WAE) personnel, to these high risk, high threat locations, particularly in security and management positions for longer periods of time.

14. The Department needs to review the staffing footprints at high risk, high threat posts, with particular attention to ensuring adequate Locally Employed Staff (LES) and management support. High risk, high threat posts must be funded and the human resources process prioritized to hire LES interpreters and translators.

15. With increased and more complex diplomatic activities in the Middle East, the Department should enhance its ongoing efforts to significantly upgrade its language capacity, especially Arabic, among American employees, including DS, and receive greater resources to do so.

TRAINING AND AWARENESS

1.   State Dept. Accountability Review Board for Benghazi (12/20/2012)

16. A panel of Senior Special Agents and Supervisory Special Agents should revisit DS high-threat training with respect to active internal defense and fire survival as well as Chief of Mission protective detail training.

17. The Diplomatic Security Training Center and Foreign Service Institute should collaborate in designing joint courses that integrate high threat training and risk management decision processes for senior and mid-level DS agents and Foreign Service Officers and better prepare them for leadership positions in high risk, high threat posts. They should consult throughout the U.S. government for best practices and lessons learned. Foreign Affairs Counter Threat training should be mandatory for high risk, high threat posts, whether an individual is assigned permanently or in longer-term temporary duty status.

SECURITY AND FIRE SAFETY EQUIPMENT

18. The Department should ensure provision of adequate fire safety and security equipment for safehavens and safe areas in non-Inman/SECCA[2] facilities, as well as high threat Inman facilities.

19. There have been technological advancements in non-lethal deterrents, and the State Department should ensure it rapidly and routinely identifies and procures additional options for non-lethal deterrents in high risk, high threat posts and trains personnel on their use.

20. DS should upgrade surveillance cameras at high risk, high threat posts for greater resolution, nighttime visibility, and monitoring capability beyond post.

INTELLIGENCE AND THREAT ANALYSIS

21. Post-2001, intelligence collection has expanded exponentially, but the Benghazi attacks are a stark reminder that we cannot over-rely on the certainty or even likelihood of warning intelligence. Careful attention should be given to factors showing a deteriorating threat situation in general as a basis for improving

---

[2] "Inman buildings" are diplomatic facilities that meet the mandatory minimum physical security standards established after the 1985 Inman Report about the 1983 Embassy and Marine barracks bombings in Lebanon. "SECCA" refers to the Secure Embassy Construction and Counterterrorism Act of 1999, passed by Congress after the 1998 Nairobi and Dar es Salaam Embassy bombings. SECCA mandated setback and other standards for newly acquired diplomatic facilities.

security posture. Key trends must be quickly identified and used to sharpen risk calculations.

22. The DS Office of Intelligence and Threat Analysis should report directly to the DS Assistant Secretary and directly supply threat analysis to all DS components, regional Assistant Secretaries and Chiefs of Mission in order to get key security-related threat information into the right hands more rapidly.

PERSONNEL ACCOUNTABILITY

23. The Board recognizes that poor performance does not ordinarily constitute a breach of duty that would serve as a basis for disciplinary action but is instead addressed through the performance management system. However, the Board is of the view that findings of unsatisfactory leadership performance by senior officials in relation to the security incident under review should be a potential basis for discipline recommendations by future ARBs, and would recommend a revision of Department regulations or amendment to the relevant statute to this end.

24. The Board was humbled by the courage and integrity shown by those on the ground in Benghazi and Tripoli, in particular the DS agents and Annex team who defended their colleagues; the Tripoli response team which mobilized without hesitation; those in Benghazi and Tripoli who cared for the wounded; and the many U.S. government employees who served in Benghazi under difficult conditions in the months leading up to the September 11-12 attacks. We trust that the Department and relevant agencies will take the opportunity to recognize their exceptional valor and performance, which epitomized the highest ideals of government service.

1.   State Dept. Accountability Review Board for Benghazi (12/20/2012)

POLITICAL AND SECURITY CONTEXT PRIOR TO THE ATTACKS

On April 5, 2011, then-Special Envoy to the Libyan Transitional National Council (TNC) Chris Stevens arrived via a Greek cargo ship at the rebel-held city of Benghazi to re-establish a U.S. presence in Libya. The State Department had been absent from Libya since the Embassy in Tripoli suspended operations and evacuated its American personnel on February 25, 2011, amidst an escalating campaign by Muammar Qaddafi to suppress violently a popular uprising against his rule.

Benghazi, the largest city and historical power center in eastern Libya, was the launching point for the uprising against Qaddafi and a long time nexus of anti-regime activism. It also served as the rebel-led Transitional National Council's base of operations. Eastern Libya (Cyrenaica) had long felt neglected and oppressed by Qaddafi, and there had been historic tensions between it and the rest of the country. Throughout Qaddafi's decades-long rule, eastern Libya consistently lagged behind Tripoli in terms of infrastructure and standard of living even as it was responsible for the vast majority of Libya's oil production. Stevens' presence in the city was seen as a significant sign of U.S. support for the TNC and a recognition of the resurgence of eastern Libya's political influence.

Benghazi was the seat of the Senussi monarchy until 1954, the site of a U.S. consulate, which was overrun by a mob and burned in 1967, and the place where Qaddafi began his 1969 revolution against the monarchy. Qaddafi's subsequent combination of oppression and neglect enhanced the city's sense of marginalization, and its after-effects were felt more widely in the eastern region where a Salafist jihadist movement took root. Jihadis from Benghazi engaged in Afghanistan against the Soviets and took up arms against U.S. forces in the post-2003 Iraq insurgency. Many of them reemerged in 2011 as leaders of anti-Qaddafi militias in eastern Libya.

Stevens initially operated from the Tibesti Hotel in downtown Benghazi. He was accompanied by a security contingent of 10 Diplomatic Security agents whose primary responsibilities were to provide personal protective services. Stevens' mission was to serve as the liaison with the TNC in preparation for a post-Qaddafi democratic government in Libya. By all accounts, he was extremely effective,

1.   State Dept. Accountability Review Board for Benghazi (12/20/2012)

earned the admiration of countless numbers of Libyans, and personified the U.S. government commitment to a free and democratic Libya.

Benghazi, however, was still very much a conflict zone. On June 1, 2011, a car bomb exploded outside the Tibesti Hotel, and shortly thereafter a credible threat against the Special Envoy mission prompted Stevens to move to the Annex. On June 21, 2011, he and his security contingent moved to what would become the Special Mission Benghazi compound (SMC). By the end of August 2011, the walled compound consisted of three sections (Villas A, B, and C) on 13 acres. (Use of Villa A was discontinued in January 2012, when the SMC footprint was consolidated into the Villas B and C compounds, some eight-acres total.)

On July 15, 2011, the United States officially recognized the TNC as Libya's legitimate governing authority although Qaddafi and his forces still retained control over significant portions of the country, including Tripoli. The TNC continued attacking the remaining Qaddafi strongholds, and Tripoli fell earlier than expected at the end of August. The TNC immediately began moving the government from Benghazi to Tripoli. By early September, 21 members of State Department Mobile Security Deployment teams were in Tripoli with the Deputy Chief of Mission (DCM) in preparation for the resumption of operations of the U.S. Embassy, which Ambassador Gene Cretz officially re-opened on September 22, 2011. From September 2011 onwards, Embassy Tripoli was open with a skeleton staff built on temporary duty (TDY) assignments, to include the DCM and Regional Security Officer (RSO). (The fall of Tripoli took place shortly after Embassy Tripoli lost its assigned staff and bureaucratically ceased to exist, pursuant to Department regulations regarding the length of time a post can remain open in evacuation status.)

Although the TNC declared that Tripoli would continue to be the capital of a post-Qaddafi Libya, many of the influential players in the TNC remained based in Benghazi. Stevens continued as Special Envoy to the TNC in Benghazi until he departed Libya on November 17, 2011, after which the Special Envoy position was not filled. Stevens was replaced by an experienced Civil Service employee who served for 73 days in what came to be called the "principal officer" position in Benghazi. After November 2011, the principal officer slot became a TDY assignment for officers with varying levels of experience who served in Benghazi anywhere from 10 days to over two months, usually without transiting Tripoli. In December 2011, the Under Secretary for Management approved a one-year continuation of the U.S. Special Mission in Benghazi, which was never a consulate

1.   State Dept. Accountability Review Board for Benghazi (12/20/2012)

and never formally notified to the Libyan government. Stevens arrived in Tripoli on May 26, 2012, to replace Cretz as Ambassador.

Throughout Libya, the security vacuum left by Qaddafi's departure, the continued presence of pro-Qaddafi supporters, the prevalence of and easy access to weapons, the inability of the interim government to reestablish a strong security apparatus, and the resulting weakness of those security forces that remained led to a volatile situation in which militias previously united in opposition to Qaddafi were now jockeying for position in the new Libya. Frequent clashes, including assassinations, took place between contesting militias. Fundamentalist influence with Salafi and al Qaeda connections was also growing, including notably in the eastern region. Public attitudes in Benghazi continued to be positive toward Americans, and it was generally seen as safer for Americans given U.S support of the TNC during the war. However, 2012 saw an overall deterioration of the security environment in Benghazi, as highlighted by a series of security incidents involving the Special Mission, international organizations, non-governmental organizations (NGOs), and third-country nationals and diplomats:

- March 18, 2012 – Armed robbery occurs at the British School in Benghazi.
- March 22, 2012 – Members of a militia searching for a suspect fire their weapons near the SMC and attempt to enter.
- April 2, 2012 – A UK armored diplomatic vehicle is attacked after driving into a local protest. The vehicle was damaged but occupants uninjured.
- April 6, 2012 – A gelatina bomb (traditional homemade explosive device used for fishing) is thrown over the SMC north wall.
- April 10, 2012 – An IED (gelatina or dynamite stick) is thrown at the motorcade of the UN Special Envoy to Libya in Benghazi.
- April 26, 2012 – Special Mission Benghazi principal officer is evacuated from International Medical University (IMU) after a fistfight escalated to gunfire between Tripoli-based trade delegation security personnel and IMU security.
- April 27, 2012 – Two South African nationals in Libya as part of U.S.-funded weapons abatement, unexploded ordnance removal and demining project are detained at gunpoint by militia, questioned and released.
- May 22, 2012 – Benghazi International Committee of the Red Cross (ICRC) building struck by rocket propelled grenades (RPGs).
- May 28, 2012 – A previously unknown organization, Omar Abdurrahman group, claims responsibility for the ICRC attack and issues a threat against the United States on social media sites.

- June 6, 2012 – IED attack on the SMC. The IED detonates with no injuries but blows a large hole in the compound's exterior wall. Omar Abdurrahman group makes an unsubstantiated claim of responsibility.
- June 8, 2012 – Two hand grenades target a parked UK diplomatic vehicle in Sabha (800 km south of Benghazi).
- June 11, 2012 – While in Benghazi, the British Ambassador's convoy is attacked with an RPG and possible AK-47s. Two UK security officers are injured; the UK closes its mission in Benghazi the following day.
- June 12, 2012 – An RPG attack is made on the ICRC compound in Misrata (400 km west of Benghazi).
- June 18, 2012 – Protestors storm the Tunisian consulate in Benghazi.
- July 29, 2012 – An IED is found on grounds of the Tibesti Hotel.
- July 30, 2012 – Sudanese Consul in Benghazi is carjacked and driver beaten.
- July 31, 2012 – Seven Iranian-citizen ICRC workers abducted in Benghazi.
- August 5, 2012 – ICRC Misrata office is attacked with RPGs. ICRC withdraws its representatives from Misrata and Benghazi.
- August 9, 2012 – A Spanish-American dual national NGO worker is abducted from the Islamic Cultural Center in Benghazi and released the same day.
- August 20, 2012 – A small bomb is thrown at an Egyptian diplomat's vehicle parked outside of the Egyptian consulate in Benghazi.

It is worth noting that the events above took place against a general backdrop of political violence, assassinations targeting former regime officials, lawlessness, and an overarching absence of central government authority in eastern Libya. While the June 6 IED at the SMC and the May ICRC attack were claimed by the same group, none of the remaining attacks were viewed in Tripoli and Benghazi as linked or having common perpetrators, which were not viewed as linked or having common perpetrators. This also tempered reactions in Washington. Furthermore, the Board believes that the longer a post is exposed to continuing high levels of violence the more it comes to consider security incidents which might otherwise provoke a reaction as normal, thus raising the threshold for an incident to cause a reassessment of risk and mission continuation. This was true for both people on the ground serving in Libya and in Washington.

While the June IED attack and the RPG attack targeting the UK convoy in Benghazi prompted the Special Mission to reduce movements off compound and have a one-week pause between principal officers, the successful nature of Libya's

1.   State Dept. Accountability Review Board for Benghazi (12/20/2012)

July 7, 2012, national elections – which exceeded expectations – renewed Washington's optimism in Libya's future. Nevertheless, the immediate period after the elections did not see the central government increase its capacity to consolidate control or provide security in eastern Libya, as efforts to form a government floundered and extremist militias in and outside Benghazi continued to work to strengthen their grip. At the time of the September attacks, Benghazi remained a lawless town nominally controlled by the Supreme Security Council (SSC) – a coalition of militia elements loosely cobbled into a single force to provide interim security – but in reality run by a diverse group of local Islamist militias, each of whose strength ebbed and flowed depending on the ever-shifting alliances and loyalties of various members. There was a notional national police presence, but it was ineffectual. By August 2012, Special Mission Benghazi would evaluate the worsening security situation and its implications.

1.   State Dept. Accountability Review Board for Benghazi (12/20/2012)

"I was at the foot of the wide marble staircase when the breakthrough occurred. Fanatical knife-carrying intruders, bleeding from cuts received as they were pushed through broken windows, ran down the hall. Putting on gas masks and dropping tear gas grenades, we engaged them on the stairs with rifle butts. In seconds tear gas saturated the area. We then moved into the vault, securing the steel combination door, locking in ten persons…. My greatest fear, which I kept to myself, was that gasoline for the generator would be found, sloshed under the vault door and ignited. When after minutes this did not happen, our hearts sank, nonetheless, as outside smoke wafted in and we knew the building had been set afire."

> *-- First-person account of the June 5, 1967 mob siege of the then-U.S. Consulate in Benghazi*

TIMELINE OF THE ATTACKS
September 11-12, 2012
*(All times are best estimates based on existing data
and should be considered approximate.)*

The Prelude – the Ambassador's Arrival

Ambassador Chris Stevens arrived in Benghazi, Libya on September 10, 2012, accompanied by two temporary duty (TDY) Assistant Regional Security Officers (ARSOs) from Tripoli. It was the Ambassador's first visit to Benghazi since he departed as then-Special Envoy in November 2011. With the Ambassador's arrival, there were eight Americans at the Special Mission compound (SMC) on September 10-11, 2012, including the Ambassador; Information Management Officer (IMO) Sean Smith, who arrived in Benghazi one week earlier to provide TDY communications and management support; and five Diplomatic Security (DS) agents (three assigned on short-term TDY to Benghazi – "TDY RSO", "ARSO 1" and "ARSO 2" – and the two who traveled from Tripoli to provide protection for the Ambassador during his visit – "ARSO 3" and "ARSO 4"). The eighth American, the TDY Benghazi principal officer, completed his 13-day assignment and returned to his full-time job in Tripoli the morning of September 11, leaving seven Americans at the compound. Ambassador Stevens was scheduled to remain in Benghazi until September 14, and his visit was timed in part to fill the staffing gaps between TDY principal officers as well as to open an American Corner at a local school and to reconnect with local contacts.

---

1. State Dept. Accountability Review Board for Benghazi (12/20/2012)

In the absence of an effective central government security presence, the Special Mission's Libyan security contingent was composed of four armed members of the February 17 Martyrs' Brigade (February 17) – a local umbrella organization of militias dominant in Benghazi (some of which were Islamist) and loosely affiliated with the Libyan government, but not under its control. They resided in a guest house building on compound. Normally four members resided on the Special Mission compound near the front gate, but on September 11 one had been absent for several days, reportedly due to a family illness. The Special Mission also had an unarmed, contract local guard force (LGF), Blue Mountain Libya (BML), which provided five guards per eight-hour shift, 24/7, to open and close the gates, patrol the compound, and give warning in case of an attack.

After the Ambassador's arrival at the Special Mission on September 10, ARSO 1 gave the Ambassador a tour of the SMC and pointed out the safe area and escape hatch windows in the Ambassador's room in Villa C. Later that afternoon, the Ambassador visited the Annex for a briefing. He then met with the City Council at a local hotel for dinner, an event at which local media invited by the Council showed up unexpectedly, despite U.S. efforts to keep the Ambassador's program and movements from being publicized.

Security Environment on September 11, Preceding Attacks

In consultation with the TDY RSO and mindful of the threat environment and the September 11 anniversary, Ambassador Stevens did not leave the SMC on September 11, but rather held meetings there. At approximately 0645 local that morning, a BML contract guard saw an unknown individual in a Libyan Supreme Security Council (SSC) police uniform apparently taking photos of the compound villas with a cell phone from the second floor of a building under construction across the street to the north of the SMC. The individual was reportedly stopped by BML guards, denied any wrongdoing, and departed in a police car with two others. This was reported to ARSOs 1 and 2. Later that morning they inspected the area where the individual was seen standing and informed the Annex of the incident. There had not been any related threat reporting. The local February 17 militia headquarters was informed of the incident and reportedly complained to the local SSC on the Special Mission's behalf. The Ambassador reviewed a Special Mission-drafted complaint to local authorities on the surveillance incident; however, it was not submitted due to the typically early closure of Libyan government offices. Later on September 11, the Ambassador was informed by his Deputy Chief of Mission (DCM) in Tripoli of the breach of the Embassy Cairo compound that had occurred that day and briefly discussed the news with ARSO 3. The TDY RSO was also informed of the Cairo compound breach by his Regional Security Officer counterpart in Tripoli and shared the information with colleagues at the Annex.

At approximately 1940 local, Ambassador Stevens and an accompanying ARSO escorted a Turkish diplomat to the SMC's main exit at the north C1 gate, where nothing out of the ordinary was noted. Some 30 minutes later, between 2010 and 2030 local, a UK security team supporting a day visit by British diplomats dropped off vehicles and equipment at the SMC (per arrangements made after the UK diplomatic office in Benghazi suspended operations in June 2012). When the UK security team departed via the C1 gate at about 2030 local, there were no signs of anything unusual, including no roadblocks outside of the compound, and traffic flowed normally.

Ambassador Stevens and IMO Sean Smith retired for the night to Villa C at about 2100 local, while ARSO 4 watched a video in the Villa C common space. ARSOs 1, 2, and 3 were sitting together outside and behind Villa C; the TDY RSO was working in the workspace building referred to as the "Office" or "TOC" (Tactical Operations Center), near the Villa B compound, which was connected to the Villa C compound by an alleyway. From the TOC, the TDY RSO could monitor a series of security cameras placed in and around the perimeter of the SMC. The ARSOs were each armed with their standard issue sidearm pistol; their "kits," generally consisting of body armor, radio and an M4 rifle, were in their bedroom/sleeping areas, in accord with Special Mission practice.

The Attack on the Special Mission Compound

An SSC police vehicle, which had arrived at the main compound gate (C1) at 2102 local, departed at 2142. The Special Mission had requested that a marked SSC police car be posted outside of the compound 24/7, but in practice a car was there only intermittently. The Special Mission had requested this presence again, specifically for the duration of the Ambassador's visit. A subsequent local press report quotes an SSC official as saying that he ordered the removal of the car "to prevent civilian casualties."

Around the same time, the TDY RSO working in the TOC heard shots and an explosion. He then saw via security camera dozens of individuals, many armed, begin to enter the compound through the main entrance at the C1 gate. He hit the duck and cover alarm and yelled a warning over the radio, and recalled no such warning from the February 17 or BML guards, who had already begun to flee to points south and east in the compound, towards the Villa B area. ARSOs 1 and 2 heard an attack warning from the BML guards passed on over the radio. The TDY RSO also alerted the Annex and Embassy Tripoli by cell phone.

The other three ARSOs behind Villa C also heard gunfire and explosions, as well as chanting, and responded immediately along with ARSO 4, who was inside Villa C. Following the SMC's emergency plan, ARSO 1 entered Villa C to secure the Ambassador and IMO in the safe area and to retrieve his kit; ARSOs 2, 3, and 4 moved to retrieve their kits, which were located in Villa B and the TOC. ARSO 1 in Villa C swiftly located the Ambassador and IMO Smith, asked them to don body armor, and led them into the safe area in Villa C, which ARSO 1 secured. He then reported their whereabouts by radio to the TDY RSO in the TOC. ARSO 1, armed with an M4 rifle, shotgun and pistol, took up a defensive position inside the Villa C safe area, with line of sight to the safe area gate and out of view of potential intruders. ARSO 1 gave his cell phone to the Ambassador, who began making calls to local contacts and Embassy Tripoli requesting assistance.

From Villa C, ARSO 4 ran to his sleeping quarters in Villa B to retrieve his kit, while ARSOs 2 and 3 ran to the TOC, where ARSO 3 had last seen the Ambassador, and where ARSO 2's kit was located. (ARSO 2's sleeping quarters were in the TOC, making him the designated "TOC Officer" in their emergency react plan.) ARSO 3, upon not finding the Ambassador in the TOC, ran to Villa B to get his kit; ARSO 2 remained in the TOC with the TDY RSO and shared notification and communication duties with him. At Villa B, ARSO 3 encountered ARSO 4, who was also arming and equipping himself, and the two then attempted to return to Villa C. They turned back, however, after seeing many armed intruders blocking the alley between Villas B and C. ARSOs 3 and 4, outnumbered and outgunned by the armed intruders in the alley, returned to Villa B and barricaded themselves in a back room, along with one LGF member whom they had encountered outside Villa B.

Attack Continues, Use of Fire as a Weapon

Sometime between 2145 and 2200 local, armed intruders appear to have used filled fuel cans that were stored next to new, uninstalled generators at the February 17 living quarters near the C1 entrance to burn that building. The crowd also lit on fire vehicles that were parked nearby. Members of the crowd then moved to Villa C.

In Villa C, ARSO 1, who was protecting Ambassador Stevens and IMO Smith in the safe area, heard intruders breaking through the Villa C front door. Men armed with AK rifles started to destroy the living room contents and then approached the safe area gate and started banging on it. ARSO 1 did not want to compromise their location in the safe area by engaging the intruders, and he warned the Ambassador and IMO Smith to prepare for the intruders to try to blast the safe area gate locks open. Instead the intruders departed, and the lights in Villa C appeared to dim. ARSO 1 realized that smoke from fires set inside the villa, away from his vantage point, was reducing the light and visibility. (There was no line of sight to Villa C from the Villa B/TOC compound where the TDY RSO and three ARSOs were barricaded. The TDY RSO in the TOC did not see smoke emerge on the view from the camera near Villa C until shortly after 2200 local.)

As smoke engulfed the Villa C safe area, ARSO 1 led Ambassador Stevens and IMO Smith into a bathroom with an exterior window. All three crawled into the bathroom, while the thick, black smoke made breathing difficult and reduced visibility to zero. ARSO 1 tried to seal the door with towels and provide some ventilation by opening the window. Instead, opening the window worsened conditions and drew more smoke into the bathroom, making it even more difficult to breathe. ARSO 1 determined that they could no longer stay in the safe area and yelled to the others, whom he could no longer see, to follow him to an adjacent bedroom, where there was an egress window. ARSO 1 crawled on his hands and knees through a hallway to the bedroom, unable to see, while yelling and banging on the floor to guide the Ambassador and IMO Smith to safety. ARSO 1 opened the window grill and exited the building, collapsing onto a small, partly enclosed patio, at which point he believed he was being fired upon. Immediately following his exit, ARSO 1 realized the Ambassador and IMO had not followed him out the window. He then re-entered Villa C through the egress window several times to search for his colleagues while under fire by the intruders outside. He was unable to locate the Ambassador or IMO Smith, and severe heat and smoke forced him to exit the building to recover between each attempt. After several attempts, he climbed a ladder to the roof where he radioed the TOC for assistance and attempted unsuccessfully to ventilate the building by breaking a skylight. Due to severe smoke inhalation, however, ARSO 1 was almost unintelligible, but the TDY RSO and ARSO 2 in the TOC finally understood him to be saying that he did not have the Ambassador or IMO Smith with him.

1.   State Dept. Accountability Review Board for Benghazi (12/20/2012)

While Villa C was under attack, armed individuals looted Villa B's interior and attempted to enter the area where ARSOs 3 and 4 were barricaded. The intruders carried jerry cans and were seen on security cameras trying to dump them on vehicles outside the TOC, but they were apparently empty. A group of intruders also attempted unsuccessfully to break down the TOC entrance.

Annex Responds, DS Agents Rally for Further Rescue Efforts

Just prior to receiving the TDY RSO's distress call shortly after 2142 local, the head of Annex security heard multiple explosions coming from the north in the direction of the SMC. The Annex security head immediately began to organize his team's departure and notified his superiors, who began to contact local security elements to request support. The Annex response team departed its compound in two vehicles at approximately 2205 local. The departure of the Annex team was not delayed by orders from superiors; the team leader decided on his own to depart the Annex compound once it was apparent, despite a brief delay to permit their continuing efforts, that rapid support from local security elements was not forthcoming.

While the TDY RSO continued to man the TOC and communicate with Tripoli, the Annex, and Washington, ARSO 2 used a smoke grenade to obscure his movements from the TOC to Villa B, where he joined ARSOs 3 and 4 who were barricaded inside. By this point, the first group of attackers appeared to have receded. The three ARSOs then drove an armored vehicle parked outside of the TOC to Villa C, where they assisted ARSO 1, who was in distress on the roof, vomiting from severe smoke inhalation and losing consciousness. ARSOs 2, 3, and 4 repeatedly entered Villa C through the egress window, at times crawling on their hands and knees through the safe area due to heavy smoke and the lack of air and visibility.

Near the SMC, the Annex team hoped to bring along friendly forces from militia compounds located along their route. The Annex team stopped at the intersection to the west of the C1 entrance and attempted to convince militia members there to assist. There was periodic, ineffective small arms fire in the team's location from the direction of the Special Mission.

Unable to secure additional assistance, the team moved on to the SMC. The February 17 living quarters and adjacent vehicles were burned, and heavy smoke was pouring out of the still smoldering Villa C. The Annex team made contact with the four ARSOs at Villa C. Some Annex team members went to retrieve the TDY RSO from the TOC, while other Annex team members joined the ARSOs in their search for the Ambassador.

During their searches of the Villa C safe area, the ARSOs found and removed the body of IMO Smith with Annex security team assistance. The team checked for vital signs and verified that IMO Smith was already deceased, apparently due to smoke inhalation. Other Annex security team members and the TDY RSO joined up with the ARSOs again to enter Villa C via the egress window but were unable to locate Ambassador Stevens despite multiple attempts. Heat and smoke continued to be limiting factors in their ability to move farther into the safe area. When the TDY RSO attempted to enter Villa C through the front door, the ceiling collapsed. During these rescue attempts, an ARSO received a severe laceration to his arm.

Second Phase Attack on the Compound, Evacuation to the Annex

At the urging of the Annex security team and friendly militia members, who warned that the compound was at risk of being overrun, the TDY RSO and four ARSOs departed for the Annex without having found Ambassador Stevens. As the Annex team provided cover fire, the five DS agents' fully armored vehicle departed and took hostile fire as they left the SMC and turned right out of the C1 entrance. The driver, ARSO 1, reversed direction to avoid a crowd farther down the street, then reverted back to the original easterly route towards the crowd after a man whom the DS agents believed to be with February 17 signaled them to do so. Farther ahead, another man in a small group of individuals then motioned to them to enter a neighboring compound, some 300 meters to the east of the C1 entrance of the Special Mission compound. The DS agents suspected a trap, ignored this signal, and continued past. The group along the route then opened fire at the vehicle's side, shattering and almost penetrating the armored glass and blowing out two tires. While the identities of the individuals who fired upon the DS agents is unknown, they may have been part of the initial wave of attackers who swarmed the SMC earlier that night. A roadblock was present outside this compound and groups of attackers were seen entering it at about the time this vehicle movement was taking place.

ARSO 1 accelerated past the armed crowd and navigated around another crowd and roadblock near the end of the road, driving down the center median and into the oncoming lane at one point to bypass stopped traffic. Two cars followed, with one turning off and the other following them with its lights off until it turned into a warehouse area not far from the Annex. The DS vehicle then proceeded to the Annex, arriving around 2330 local. There the ARSOs joined Annex personnel and took up defensive positions, to await the Annex security and Tripoli response team. The situation was relatively quiet. Wounded personnel received medical support.

Back at the SMC, the Annex security team at Villa C used small arms fire and took defensive positions to respond to an apparent second phase attack, which lasted about 15 minutes and included small arms fire and at least three rocket-propelled grenades (RPGs) launched from outside the C3 gate. With their many and repeated attempts to retrieve the Ambassador having proven fruitless and militia members warning them the SMC could not be held much longer, the Annex team departed the SMC, carrying with them the body of IMO Smith. They arrived back at the Annex and moved to take up additional defensive positions.

Embassy Tripoli Response

Upon notification of the attack from the TDY RSO around 2145 local, Embassy Tripoli set up a command center and notified Washington. About 2150 local, the DCM was able to reach Ambassador Stevens, who briefly reported that the SMC was under attack before the call cut off. The Embassy notified Benina Airbase in Benghazi of a potential need for logistic support and aircraft for extraction and received full cooperation. The DCM contacted the Libyan President and Prime Minister's offices to urge them to mobilize a rescue effort, and kept Washington apprised of post's efforts. The Embassy also reached out to Libyan Air Force and Armed Forces contacts, February 17 leadership, and UN and third country embassies, among others. Within hours, Embassy Tripoli chartered a private airplane and deployed a seven-person security team, which included two U.S. military personnel, to Benghazi.

At the direction of the U.S. military's Africa Command (AFRICOM), DoD moved a remotely piloted, unarmed surveillance aircraft which arrived over the SMC shortly before the DS team departed. A second remotely piloted, unarmed surveillance aircraft relieved the first, and monitored the eventual evacuation of personnel from the Annex to Benghazi airport later on the morning of September 12.

Uncertainty on Ambassador Stevens' Whereabouts

U.S. efforts to determine Ambassador Stevens' whereabouts were unsuccessful for several hours. At approximately 0200 local, Embassy Tripoli received a phone call from ARSO 1's cell phone, which he had given to the Ambassador while they were sheltered in the safe area. A male, Arabic-speaking caller said an unresponsive male who matched the physical description of the Ambassador was at a hospital. There was confusion over which hospital this might be, and the caller was unable to provide a picture of the Ambassador or give any other proof that he was with him. There was some concern that the call might be a ruse to lure American personnel into a trap. With the Benghazi Medical Center (BMC) believed to be dangerous for American personnel due to the possibility attackers were being treated there, a Libyan contact of the Special Mission was dispatched to the BMC and later confirmed the Ambassador's identity and that he was deceased.

BMC personnel would later report that at approximately 0115 local on September 12, an unidentified, unresponsive male foreigner – subsequently identified as Ambassador Stevens – was brought to the emergency room by six civilians. The identities of these civilians are unknown at the time of this report, but to the best knowledge of the Board these were "good Samaritans" among the hordes of looters and bystanders who descended upon the Special Mission after the DS and Annex teams departed. With the clearing of smoke, Ambassador Stevens' rescuers found him within a room in the safe area of Villa C, did not know his identity, pulled him out through an egress window, and sought medical attention for him. Although the Ambassador did not show signs of life upon arrival at the BMC, doctors attempted to resuscitate him for some 45 minutes before declaring him deceased, by apparent smoke inhalation.

Attacks on the Annex

Just before midnight, shortly after the DS and Annex security teams arrived from the SMC, the Annex began to be targeted by gunfire and RPGs, which continued intermittently for an hour. Annex security personnel engaged from their defensive positions, which were reinforced by DS agents. Other personnel remained in contact with Embassy Tripoli from the Annex.

The seven-person response team from Embassy Tripoli arrived in Benghazi to lend support. It arrived at the Annex about 0500 local. Less than fifteen minutes later, the Annex came under mortar and RPG attack, with five mortar rounds impacting close together in under 90 seconds. Three rounds hit the roof of an Annex building, killing security officers Tyrone Woods and Glen Doherty. The attack also severely injured one ARSO and one Annex security team member. Annex, Tripoli, and ARSO security team members at other locations moved rapidly to provide combat first aid to the injured.

At approximately 0630 local, all U.S. government personnel evacuated with support from a quasi-governmental Libyan militia. They arrived at the airport without incident. The DoD unarmed surveillance aircraft provided visual oversight during the evacuation. Embassy Tripoli lost communication with the convoy at one point during transit, but quickly regained it.

Evacuees, including all wounded personnel, departed Benghazi on the chartered jet at approximately 0730 local. Embassy Tripoli staff, including the Embassy nurse, met the first evacuation flight at Tripoli International Airport. Wounded personnel were transferred to a local hospital, in exemplary coordination that helped save the lives of two severely injured Americans.

Embassy Tripoli worked with the Libyan government to have a Libyan Air Force C-130 take the remaining U.S. government personnel from Benghazi to Tripoli. Two American citizen State Department contractors traveled to the airport and linked up with the remaining U.S. government personnel. While awaiting transport, the TDY RSO and Annex personnel continued to reach out to Libyan contacts to coordinate the transport of the presumed remains of Ambassador Stevens to the airport. The body was brought to the airport in what appeared to be a local ambulance at 0825 local, and the TDY RSO verified Ambassador Stevens' identity.

At 1130 local, September 12, 2012, the Libyan government-provided C-130 evacuation flight landed in Tripoli with the last U.S. government personnel from Benghazi and the remains of the four Americans killed, who were transported to a local hospital.

In coordination with the State Department and Embassy Tripoli, the Department of Defense sent two U.S. Air Force planes (a C-17 and a C-130) from Germany to Tripoli to provide medical evacuation support for the wounded. At 1915 local on September 12, Embassy Tripoli evacuees, Benghazi personnel, and

1. State Dept. Accountability Review Board for Benghazi (12/20/2012)

those wounded in the attacks departed Tripoli on the C-17 aircraft, with military doctors and nurses aboard providing en route medical care to the injured. The aircraft arrived at Ramstein Air Force Base at approximately 2230 (Tripoli time) on September 12, just over 24 hours after the attacks in Benghazi had commenced.

1.   State Dept. Accountability Review Board for Benghazi (12/20/2012)

FINDINGS AND DISCUSSION

1. The attacks in Benghazi were security-related, resulting in the deaths of four U.S. personnel after terrorists attacked two separate U.S. government facilities – the Special Mission compound (SMC) and the Annex.

Identification of the perpetrators and their motivations are the subject of an ongoing FBI criminal investigation. The Board concluded that no protest took place before the Special Mission and Annex attacks, which were unanticipated in their scale and intensity.

ADEQUACY OF SECURITY SYSTEMS AND PROCEDURES PRIOR TO SEPTEMBER 11, 2012

2. Systemic failures and leadership and management deficiencies at senior levels within two bureaus of the State Department resulted in a Special Mission security posture that was inadequate for Benghazi and grossly inadequate to deal with the attack that took place.

Through the course of its inquiry, the Board interviewed over 100 individuals, reviewed thousands of pages of documents, and viewed hours of video footage. On the basis of its comprehensive review of this information, the Board remains fully convinced that responsibility for the tragic loss of life, injuries, and damage to U.S. facilities and property rests solely and completely with the terrorists who perpetrated the attack.

Overriding Factors

This is not to say, however, that there are no lessons to be learned. A recurring theme throughout the Board's work was one also touched upon by the Nairobi and Dar es Salaam ARBs in 1999. Simply put, in the months leading up to September 11, 2012, security in Benghazi was not recognized and implemented as a "shared responsibility" in Washington, resulting in stove-piped discussions and decisions on policy and security. Key decisions, such as the extension of the State Department presence in Benghazi until December 2012, or non-decisions in Washington, such as the failure to establish standards for Benghazi and to meet them, or the lack of a cohesive staffing plan, essentially set up Benghazi as a

1.   State Dept. Accountability Review Board for Benghazi (12/20/2012)

floating TDY platform with successive principal officers often confined to the SMC due to threats and inadequate resources, and RSOs resorting to field-expedient solutions to correct security shortfalls.

Communication, cooperation, and coordination between Washington, Tripoli, and Benghazi occurred collegially at the working-level but were constrained by a lack of transparency, responsiveness, and leadership at senior bureau levels. The DS Bureau's action officers who worked on Libya are to be commended for their efforts within DS and across the Department to provide additional security resources to Benghazi. Action officers in the Bureau of Near Eastern Affairs' (NEA) Office of Maghreb Affairs and Executive Office showed similar dedication in collaborating on solutions with their DS counterparts and responding to TDY staffing demands. However, in DS, NEA, and at post, there appeared to be very real confusion over who, ultimately, was responsible and empowered to make decisions based on both policy and security considerations.

The DS Bureau showed a lack of proactive senior leadership with respect to Benghazi, failing to ensure that the priority security needs of a high risk, high threat post were met. At the same time, with attention in late 2011 shifting to growing crises in Egypt and Syria, the NEA Bureau's front office showed a lack of ownership of Benghazi's security issues, and a tendency to rely totally on DS for the latter. The Board also found that Embassy Tripoli leadership, saddled with their own staffing and security challenges, did not single out a special need for increased security for Benghazi.

Further shortfalls in Washington coordination were manifested by the flawed process by which Special Mission Benghazi's extension until the end of December 2012 was approved, a decision that did not take security considerations adequately into account. The result was the continuation of Special Mission Benghazi with an uncertain future and a one-year expiration date that made allocations of resources for security upgrades and personnel assignments difficult.

Another key driver behind the weak security platform in Benghazi was the decision to treat Benghazi as a temporary, residential facility, not officially notified to the host government, even though it was also a full time office facility. This resulted in the Special Mission compound being excepted from office facility standards and accountability under the Secure Embassy Construction and Counterterrorism Act of 1999 (SECCA) and the Overseas Security Policy Board (OSPB). Benghazi's initial platform in November 2011 was far short of OSPB standards and remained so even in September 2012, despite multiple field-expedient upgrades funded by DS. (As a temporary, residential facility, SMC was not eligible for OBO-funded security upgrades.) A comprehensive upgrade and risk-mitigation plan did not exist, nor was a comprehensive security review conducted by Washington for Benghazi in 2012. The unique circumstances surrounding the creation of the mission in Benghazi as a temporary mission outside the realm of permanent diplomatic posts resulted in significant disconnects and support gaps.

Personnel

The Board found the short-term, transitory nature of Benghazi's staffing to be another primary driver behind the inadequate security platform in Benghazi. Staffing was at times woefully insufficient considering post's security posture and high risk, high threat environment. The end result was a lack of institutional knowledge and mission capacity which could not be overcome by talent and hard work alone, although the Board found ample evidence of both in those who served there. The situation was exacerbated by the lack of Locally Employed Staff (LES) who would normally provide a backstop of continuity, local knowledge, and language ability. This staffing "churn" had significant detrimental effects on the post's ability to assess adequately both the political and security environment, as well as to provide the necessary advocacy and follow-through on major, essential security upgrades.

The Board determined that DS staffing levels in Benghazi after Embassy Tripoli re-opened were inadequate, decreasing significantly after then-Special Envoy Stevens' departure in November 2011. Although a full complement of five DS agents for Benghazi was initially projected, and later requested multiple times, Special Mission Benghazi achieved a level of five DS agents (not counting DoD-provided TDY Site Security Team personnel sent by Embassy Tripoli) for only 23 days between January 1-September 9, 2012.

As it became clear that DS would not provide a steady complement of five TDY DS agents to Benghazi, expectations on the ground were lowered by the daunting task of gaining approvals and the reality of an ever-shifting DS personnel platform. From discussions with former Benghazi-based staff, Board members concluded that the persistence of DS leadership in Washington in refusing to provide a steady platform of four to five DS agents created a resignation on the part of post about asking for more. The TDY DS agents resorted to doing the best they could with the limited resources provided.

Furthermore, DS's reliance on volunteers for TDY positions meant that the ARSOs in Benghazi often had relatively little or no prior DS program management or overseas experience. For a time, more experienced RSOs were sent out on longer term TDYs, but even that appeared to diminish after June 2012, exactly at the time the security environment in Benghazi was deteriorating further. It bears emphasizing, however, that the Board found the work done by these often junior DS agents to be exemplary. But given the threat environment and with very little operational oversight from more experienced, senior colleagues, combined with an under-resourced security platform, these agents were not well served by their leadership in Washington. The lack of Arabic-language skills among most American personnel assigned to Benghazi and the lack of a dedicated LES interpreter and sufficient local staff also served as a barrier to effective communication and situational awareness at the Special Mission.

Required security training for DS agents prior to service in Benghazi consisted of the High Threat Training Course (HTTC). However, domestically-based DS agents who had not served abroad did not have the opportunity to receive RSO training before serving in Benghazi. In addition, after April 2012 all personnel scheduled to serve in Libya for over 30 days were required to take the Foreign Affairs Counter Threat (FACT) training. IMOs, who also served as the "management officer" at post, did not, as a prerequisite, receive any basic management or General Services Officer (GSO) training to prepare them for their duties.

The Board determined that reliance on February 17 for security in the event of an attack was misplaced, even though February 17 had been considered to have responded satisfactorily to previous, albeit less threatening, incidents. The four assigned February 17 guards were insufficient and did not have the requisite skills and reliability to provide a reasonable level of security on a 24/7 basis for an eight-acre compound with an extended perimeter wall. In the days prior to the attack and on September 11, 2012, one was absent. Over the course of its inquiry, the Board also learned of troubling indicators of February 17's loyalties and its readiness to assist U.S. personnel. In the weeks preceding the Ambassador's arrival, February 17 had complained about salaries and the lack of a contract for its personnel. At the time of the attacks, February 17 had ceased accompanying Special Mission vehicle movements in protest. The Blue Mountain Libya (BML) unarmed guards, whose primary responsibilities were to provide early warning and control access to the SMC, were also poorly skilled.

Physical Security

Given the threat environment, the physical security platform in Benghazi was inadequate. It is incumbent upon the Board, however, to acknowledge that several upgrades and repairs took place over 2012. DS provided additional funding for the Local Guard Force (LGF), February 17, and residential security upgrades, including heightening the outer perimeter wall, safety grills on safe area egress windows that helped save the life of ARSO 1 on the night of September 11, concrete jersey barriers, manual drop-arm vehicle barriers, a steel gate for the Villa C safe area, some locally manufactured steel doors, sandbag fortifications, security cameras, some additional security lighting, guard booths, and an Internal Defense Notification System. Because OBO does not fund security upgrades for "temporary" facilities, DS also identified non-traditional funding streams to fund physical security upgrades and worked with the IMOs, NEA and Embassy Tripoli to move funds and supplies to Benghazi. The Engineering Security Office (ESO) in Cairo provided strong technical support and regularly visited. Following the June 2012 IED incident, which blew a large hole in the compound wall, DS, OBO, Tripoli, NEA and ESO Cairo immediately responded to Benghazi's request for assistance. Tripoli identified OBO funds that could be used to fix the wall, and ESO Cairo traveled to Benghazi on June 8 to provide technical support. The TDY IMOs worked tirelessly with the RSOs, Tripoli procurement and financial management staff, and Libyan professionals on statements of work, contracts and funding for the emergency repair of the SMC wall and for the other physical security upgrades, as well as ongoing electrical repairs. New upgrades remained a challenge, however, due to a lack of cash reserves and contract and procurement expertise, which meant Benghazi had to rely on Tripoli for further processing.

The Board found, however, that Washington showed a tendency to overemphasize the positive impact of physical security upgrades, which were often field-expedient improvements to a profoundly weak platform, while generally failing to meet Benghazi's repeated requests to augment the numbers of TDY DS personnel. The insufficient Special Mission compound security platform was at variance with the appropriate Overseas Security Policy Board (OSPB) standards with respect to perimeter, interior security, and safe areas. Benghazi was also under-resourced with regard to certain needed security equipment.

Security Planning

Post and the Department were well aware of the anniversary of the September 11, 2001, terrorist attacks, although DS did not issue a worldwide caution cable to posts related to the anniversary. Ambassador Stevens and his DS agents had taken the anniversary into account by deciding to hold all meetings at the SMC that day rather than making any moves outside.

The Ambassador chose to travel to Benghazi that week, independent of Washington, as per standard practice. Timing for his trip was driven in part by commitments in Tripoli, as well as a staffing gap between principal officers in Benghazi. His trip had been put off earlier in the summer, and the September 10-14 dates were not decided upon well in advance. The Board found that plans for the Ambassador's trip provided for minimal close protection security support, and that Embassy country team members were not fully aware of planned movements off compound. The Ambassador did not see a direct threat of an attack of this nature and scale on the U.S. Mission in the overall negative trendline of security incidents from spring to summer 2012. His status as the leading U.S. government advocate on Libya policy, and his expertise on Benghazi in particular, caused Washington to give unusual deference to his judgments.

IMPLEMENTATION OF SECURITY SYSTEMS AND PROCEDURES ON SEPTEMBER 11-12, 2012

3. **Notwithstanding the proper implementation of security systems and procedures and remarkable heroism shown by American personnel, those systems themselves and the Libyan response fell short in the face of a series of attacks that began with the sudden penetration of the Special Mission compound by dozens of armed attackers.** In short, Americans in Benghazi and their Tripoli colleagues did their best with what they had, which, in the end, was not enough to prevent the loss of lives of Ambassador Stevens, Sean Smith, Tyrone Woods, and Glen Doherty. At the same time, U.S. security professionals prevented a further loss of life and helped ensure the safe evacuation of remaining American personnel in Benghazi 12 hours after the attacks began.

As noted in the preceding section, physical security at the Special Mission was insufficient. The SMC perimeter was breached immediately, providing no reaction time to the five DS agents on compound. There was no advance warning regarding the group of attackers approaching outside the SMC prior to the attack, and no sign of them on surveillance cameras outside the C1 gate until the attack was underway. The Board learned that, as of the time of the attacks, the Special Mission compound had received additional surveillance cameras, which remained in boxes uninstalled, as technical support to install them had not yet visited post. In addition, the camera monitor in the local guard force booth next to the C1 gate was inoperable on the day of the attacks, a repair which also awaited the arrival of a technical team.

Some aspects of physical security upgrades did perform as intended – in particular, the safe area in Villa C, which prevented intruders from entering and the TOC door, which protected the DS agents from attackers trying to enter. Also, the installation of exits in the window grates of the Villa C safe area allowed ARSO 1 to escape the fire, and those exits were the entry point for him and other DS agents and Annex personnel to make multiple attempts to rescue and recover Sean Smith and Ambassador Stevens.

The Board found the responses by both BML and February 17 to be inadequate. No BML guards were present outside the compound immediately before the attack ensued, although perimeter security was one of their responsibilities, and there is conflicting information as to whether they sounded any alarms prior to fleeing the C1 gate area to other areas of the SMC. Although the unarmed BML guards could not be expected to repel an attack, they had core responsibility for providing early warning and controlling access to the compound, which they had not always performed well in the past. In the final analysis, the Board could not determine exactly how the C1 gate at the Special Mission compound was breached, but the speed with which attackers entered raised the possibility that BML guards left the C1 pedestrian gate open after initially seeing the attackers and fleeing the vicinity. They had left the gate unlatched before.

The Board's inquiry found little evidence that the armed February 17 guards alerted Americans at the SMC to the attack or summoned a February 17 militia presence to assist expeditiously once the attack was in progress – despite the fact that February 17 members were paid to provide interior security and a quick reaction force for the SMC and the fact that February 17 barracks were in the close vicinity, less than 2 km away from the SMC. A small number of February 17 militia members arrived at Villa C nearly an hour after the attack began. Although some February 17 members assisted in efforts to search for Ambassador Stevens in the smoke-filled Villa C building, the Board found little evidence that February 17

1.   State Dept. Accountability Review Board for Benghazi (12/20/2012)

contributed meaningfully to the defense of the Special Mission compound, or to the evacuation to the airport that took place on the morning of September 12.

In contrast, DS and Annex personnel on the ground in Benghazi performed with courage and an overriding desire to protect and rescue their colleagues, in a near impossible situation. The multiple trips that the DS agents and Annex security team members made into a burning, smoke-filled building in attempts to rescue Sean Smith and Ambassador Stevens showed readiness to risk life and limb to save others. They ultimately were unable to save Sean Smith and Ambassador Stevens, due to the intensity of the heat and smoke and a lack of resources, including breathing apparatus. The DS agents' decision to depart the SMC without the Ambassador came after they had all suffered smoke inhalation due to multiple rescue attempts, and amidst a renewed attack that continued as they departed the compound. The Board members believe every possible effort was made to protect, rescue, and recover Ambassador Stevens and Sean Smith, and that the bravery of the DS agents present in Benghazi helped prevent a further loss of life, particularly given their assistance in defending the Annex.

The Board found that the lack of non-lethal crowd control options also precluded a more vigorous defense of the SMC. The Board also determined that the lack of fire safety equipment severely impacted the Ambassador's and Sean Smith's ability to escape the deadly smoke conditions. On the other hand, the DS agents' tactical driving training, as well as their fully-armored vehicle, saved their lives when they were attacked by weapons fire en route from the SMC to the Annex. In addition, the DS emergency medical training and the DS-issued personal medical kit saved an ARSO's life after he was severely injured by a mortar attack at the Annex.

The Board found the Libyan government's response to be profoundly lacking on the night of the attacks, reflecting both weak capacity and a near total absence of central government influence in Benghazi. The Libyan government did facilitate assistance from a quasi-governmental militia that supported the evacuation of U.S. government personnel to Benghazi airport. It also facilitated the departure of the charter plane carrying the Tripoli rescue team to Benghazi, and provided a Libyan Air Force C-130 that was used to evacuate remaining personnel and the bodies of the deceased from Benghazi on the morning of September 12.

Washington-Tripoli-Benghazi communication, cooperation, and coordination on the night of the attacks were effective, despite multiple channels of communication among Washington, Tripoli, Benghazi, and AFRICOM headquarters in Stuttgart, as well as multiple channels of communication within Washington itself. Embassy Tripoli served as a lifeline to Benghazi throughout the attacks, marshalling support from Washington, Stuttgart and elsewhere, including quickly organizing the charter plane that sent the seven-person reinforcement team to Benghazi. At the direction of AFRICOM, DoD moved a remotely piloted, unarmed surveillance aircraft to Benghazi, which arrived over the SMC shortly before the DS team departed. A second remotely piloted, unarmed surveillance aircraft relieved the first, and monitored the eventual evacuation of personnel from the Annex to Benghazi airport later on the morning of September 12.

Embassy Tripoli staff showed absolute dedication and teamwork in mobilizing to respond to the crisis, with the DCM, DATT, Political, and other country team sections reaching out to a wide range of contacts in Tripoli and Benghazi to secure support; the Public Affairs team monitoring social media sites and recording a log of Mission calls; the Embassy nurse providing invaluable guidance on caring for the wounded evacuated from Benghazi; and a Consular officer donating blood that helped save the life of a wounded colleague. Throughout the crisis, the Acting NEA Assistant Secretary provided crucial leadership guidance to Embassy Tripoli's DCM, and Embassy Tripoli's RSO offered valuable counsel to the DS agents in Benghazi.

The interagency response was timely and appropriate, but there simply was not enough time given the speed of the attacks for armed U.S. military assets to have made a difference. Senior-level interagency discussions were underway soon after Washington received initial word of the attacks and continued through the night. The Board found no evidence of any undue delays in decision making or denial of support from Washington or from the military combatant commanders. Quite the contrary: the safe evacuation of all U.S. government personnel from Benghazi twelve hours after the initial attack and subsequently to Ramstein Air Force Base was the result of exceptional U.S. government coordination and military response and helped save the lives of two severely wounded Americans. In addition, at the State Department's request, the Department of Defense also provided a Marine FAST (Fleet Antiterrorism Security Team) as additional security support for Embassy Tripoli on September 12.

Overall, communication systems on the night of the attacks worked, with a near-constant information flow among Benghazi, Tripoli, and Washington. Cell phones were the main method of contact, but lacked redundancy. Radio

1.   State Dept. Accountability Review Board for Benghazi (12/20/2012)

communications between the Annex and the SMC also worked well, thanks to prior coordination between the two.

Shortly after receiving the initial notification from Embassy Tripoli at approximately 1545 EST, the State Department Operations Center notified the interagency, including the White House, of the Special Mission attack by secure conference call and email alerts. The Operations Center and the Diplomatic Security Command Center (DSCC) were exemplary in eliciting information from Tripoli- and Benghazi-based colleagues without overloading them.

IMPACT OF INTELLIGENCE AND INFORMATION AVAILABILITY

4. The Board found that intelligence provided no immediate, specific tactical warning of the September 11 attacks. Known gaps existed in the intelligence community's understanding of extremist militias in Libya and the potential threat they posed to U.S. interests, although some threats were known to exist.

Terrorist networks are difficult to monitor, and the Board emphasizes the conclusion of previous accountability review boards that vulnerable missions cannot rely on receiving specific warning intelligence. Similarly, the lack of specific threat intelligence does not imply a lessening of probability of a terrorist attack. The Board found that there was a tendency on the part of policy, security and other U.S. government officials to rely heavily on the probability of warning intelligence and on the absence of specific threat information. The result was possibly to overlook the usefulness of taking a hard look at accumulated, sometimes circumstantial information, and instead to fail to appreciate threats and understand trends, particularly based on increased violence and the targeting of foreign diplomats and international organizations in Benghazi. The latter information failed to come into clear relief against a backdrop of the lack of effective governance, widespread and growing political violence and instability and the ready availability of weapons in eastern Libya. There were U.S. assessments that provided situational awareness on the persistent, general threat to U.S. and Western interests in eastern Libya, including Benghazi. Board members, however, were struck by the lack of discussion focused specifically on Benghazi.

Benghazi's threat environment had been generally deteriorating since the "gelatina" bomb was thrown over the SMC fence on April 6, but was not judged to have reached a critical point before September 11. The July 7 elections, about

1.   State Dept. Accountability Review Board for Benghazi (12/20/2012)

which there had been some trepidation regarding the security situation, passed with less violence than expected and were followed by Ramadan, when incidents are usually lower. Before September 11, a patchwork of militias in Benghazi had assumed many, if not all, of the security functions normally associated with central government organs, as the government had little authority or reach in Benghazi. There seemed to be no attempt, however, to link formally the many anti-Western incidents in Benghazi, the general declarations of threat in U.S. assessments and a proliferation of violence-prone and little understood militias, the lack of any central authority and a general perception of a deteriorating security environment to any more specific and timely analysis of the threat to U.S. government facilities.

Board members found that there was little understanding of militias in Benghazi and the threat they posed to U.S. interests. One prime factor behind this knowledge gap was that eastern Libya is home to many militias, which are constantly dissolving, splitting apart and reforming. Furthermore, many individuals are associated with more than one militia. Understanding of February 17, in particular, was further limited by the fact that it is an umbrella organization, made up of many different militias with differing ideologies, some of which are extremist in nature.

The Board determined there were no warnings from Libyan interlocutors.

ACCOUNTABILITY OF PERSONNEL

5. **The Board found that certain senior State Department officials within two bureaus in critical positions of authority and responsibility in Washington demonstrated a lack of proactive leadership and management ability** appropriate for the State Department's senior ranks in their responses to security concerns posed by Special Mission Benghazi, given the deteriorating threat environment and the lack of reliable host government protection. However, the Board did not find that any individual U.S. Government employee engaged in misconduct or willfully ignored his or her responsibilities, and, therefore did not find reasonable cause to believe that an individual breached his or her duty so as to be the subject of a recommendation for disciplinary action.

1.   State Dept. Accountability Review Board for Benghazi (12/20/2012)

Flashing Red:
A Special Report On The Terrorist Attack At Benghazi

By
Joseph I. Lieberman, Chairman
Susan M. Collins, Ranking Member

United States Senate Committee On
Homeland Security And
Governmental Affairs

December 30, 2012

2. Senate Committee on Homeland Security and Governmental Affairs (12/30/2012)

While our country spent September 11, 2012, remembering the terrorist attacks that took place 11 years earlier, brave Americans posted at U.S. government facilities in Benghazi, Libya, were fighting for their lives against a terrorist assault. When the fight ended, U.S. Ambassador to Libya John C. (Chris) Stevens and three other Americans were dead and U.S. facilities in Benghazi were left in ruin. We must remember the sacrifice that these selfless public servants made to support the struggle for freedom in Libya and to improve our own national security. While we mourn their deaths, it is also crucial that we learn from how they died. By examining the circumstances of the attack in Benghazi on September 11th, we hope to gain a better understanding of what went wrong and what we must do now to ensure better protection for American diplomatic personnel who must sometimes operate in dangerous places abroad.

We are cognizant that the Congressionally-mandated Accountability Review Board (ARB) of the Department of State has now issued its important and constructive report and that other Congressional committees are investigating the Benghazi attack as well. Each makes significant contributions to our collective understanding of what transpired and what we must do going forward.

The Committee on Homeland Security and Governmental Affairs (HSGAC), pursuant to its authority under Rule XXV(k) of the Standing Rules of the Senate, Section 101 of S. Res 445 (108th Congress) and Section 12(e) of S. Res 81 (112th Congress), has a unique mandate to investigate the effectiveness and efficiency of governmental agencies, especially when matters that span multiple government agencies are involved. Over the years, HSGAC has spent much time and dedicated considerable resources to understanding the challenges inherent in national security interagency relationships, and it is through this lens that we have examined and drawn lessons from the attack in Benghazi.

Since the 112th Congress is drawing to a close, this investigation has necessarily been conducted with a sense of urgency and with focused objectives. Our findings and recommendations are based on investigative work that the Committee has conducted since shortly after the attack of September 11, 2012, including meetings of members and staff with senior and mid-level government officials; reviews of thousands of pages of documents provided by the Department of State, Department of Defense, and the Intelligence Community (IC); written responses to questions posed by the Committee to these agencies; and reading of publicly-available documents.

In the report that follows we provide a brief factual overview of the attacks in Benghazi and then discuss our findings and recommendations.

Brief Overview of the Benghazi Attacks

The attacks in Benghazi occurred at two different locations: a Department of State "Temporary Mission Facility" and an Annex facility ("Annex") approximately a mile away used by another agency of the United States Government. On September 11th, Ambassador Stevens was in Benghazi, accompanied by two Diplomatic Security (DS) agents who had traveled there with him. Also present were three other DS agents and a Foreign Service Officer, Sean Smith, who were posted at the Temporary Mission Facility ("facility" or "compound"). There were also three members of the February 17 Brigade, a Libyan militia deputized by the Libyan government but not under its direct control, and four unarmed local contract guards protecting the compound.

During the day on September 11th, the Ambassador held several meetings on the compound and retired to his room at approximately 9:00 p.m. local time. About 40 minutes later, several agents and guards heard loud shouting, noises coming from the gate, as well as gunfire, and an explosion. A closed-circuit television monitor at the facility's Tactical Operations Center ("TOC") showed a large number of armed people flowing unimpeded through the main gate. One of the DS agents in the compound's TOC triggered an audible alarm, and immediately alerted the U.S. Embassy in Tripoli and DS headquarters in Washington. These notifications were quickly transmitted from the Department of State to the Department of Defense. DS headquarters maintained open phone lines with the DS personnel throughout the attack. That same DS agent also called the Annex to request assistance from security personnel there, who immediately began to prepare to aid the U.S. personnel at the diplomatic facility.

When the attack commenced, four DS agents and Foreign Service Officer Smith were in or just outside the same building where the Ambassador was spending that night. A fifth DS agent was in the TOC when the terrorist attack began. Ambassador Stevens, Smith, and one DS agent sought shelter in the building's safe haven, a fortified area designed to keep intruders out, while the other three agents went to retrieve additional weapons and tactical gear such as body armor, helmets, and ammunition. After retrieving their gear, at least two of the DS agents sought to return to the building where the Ambassador was. On the way back, however, the DS agents encountered attackers. The lone DS agent with the Ambassador reported via radio that he was secure within the safe haven, allowing the two agents who had left in search of weapons to seek refuge in the same building where they had armed themselves. The third DS agent who had gone to the TOC to retrieve his gear, stayed there with the DS agent who had been manning the TOC since the beginning of the attack.

The attackers started to set several of the compound's structures on fire, using diesel fuel found on site, and groups of attackers tried to enter several buildings on the compound. The attackers did not succeed in entering the TOC, but did succeed in entering the building where Ambassador Stevens was staying and the building where the two DS agents were seeking refuge. No safe havens were breached during the initial assault. The attackers spread the diesel fuel throughout the building where the Ambassador was hiding, and ignited it, causing the building to fill with smoke.

When the smoke became so thick that breathing was difficult, the DS agent attempted to lead the Ambassador and Smith to escape through a nearby window. The agent opened the window to make sure it was safe to leave, and stepped out but then realized he had become separated from the Ambassador and Smith. The agent radioed the TOC, requesting assistance and returned numerous times to the building to look for the Ambassador and Smith. When the other agents arrived, they also took turns entering and searching the building. Though they were able to find and remove Smith's body, they were unable to find Ambassador Stevens.

After being notified about the attack, Annex personnel had attempted to contact the February 17 Brigade, other militias, and the Libyan government to ask for assistance. After gathering necessary weapons and gear, at approximately 10:04 p.m., six security personnel and a translator left the Annex en route to the facility. Prior to reaching the facility, they again attempted to contact and enlist assistance from the February 17 Brigade, other militias, and the Libyan government. By 10:25 p.m., the security personnel from the Annex had entered the compound and engaged in a 15-minute firefight with the armed invaders. The team reached the Ambassador's building at 10:40 p.m. but was unable to find him due to the intense fire and smoke.

At 11:15 p.m., the Annex security personnel sent the DS agents (who were all suffering from smoke inhalation from their continuous search for Ambassador Stevens and Smith) to the Annex, and followed there later, both groups taking fire while en route. By this time, an unmanned, unarmed surveillance aircraft began circling over the Benghazi compound, having been diverted by the Department of Defense from its previous surveillance assignment over another location. Soon after the Americans returned to the Annex, just before midnight, they were attacked by rocket-propelled grenade (RPG) and small arms fire. The sporadic attacks stopped at approximately 1:01 a.m.

U.S. government security personnel who were based in Tripoli had deployed to Benghazi by chartered aircraft after receiving word of the attack, arriving at the Benghazi airport at 1:15 a.m. They were held at the airport for at least three hours while they negotiated with Libyan authorities about logistics. The exact cause of this hours-long delay, and its relationship to the rescue effort, remains unclear and merits further inquiry. Was it simply the result of a difficult Libyan bureaucracy and a chaotic environment or was it part of a plot to keep American help from reaching the Americans under siege in Benghazi?

The team from Tripoli finally cleared the airport and arrived at the Annex at approximately 5:04 a.m., about ten minutes before a new assault by the terrorist began, involving mortar rounds fired at the Annex. The attack concluded at approximately 5:26 a.m., leaving Annex security team members Tyrone Woods and Glen Doherty dead and two others wounded. The decision was then made to leave the Annex. Libyan forces, not militia, arrived around 6:00 a.m. with 50 vehicles and escorted the Americans to the airport. Two planes carrying all remaining U.S. personnel then left Benghazi. The first flight departed between 7:00 a.m. and 7:40 a.m. (agency timelines vary on this point) and the second at 10:00 a.m.

*****

American government officials outside of Benghazi learned of the attack shortly after it started at 3:40 p.m. EST (9:40 p.m. Benghazi time). DS agents, in addition to notifying personnel at the Annex, immediately alerted officials at the U.S Embassy in Tripoli and the Department of State Headquarters in Washington, D.C. As noted earlier, the U.S. Africa Command (AFRICOM) at the Department of Defense (DOD) directed an unarmed surveillance aircraft to the skies over the Benghazi compound at 3:59 p.m. EST. It arrived there at 5:10 p.m. EST (11:10 p.m. Benghazi time). At 4:32 p.m., the National Military Command Center in the Pentagon alerted the Office of the Secretary of Defense and the Joint Staff, and the information was shared with Secretary of Defense Leon Panetta and Chairman of the Joint Chiefs of Staff, General Martin Dempsey. Secretary Panetta and General Dempsey were at the White House for a previously scheduled

3

meeting at 5:00 p.m. and so were able to brief the President on the developments in Benghazi as they were occurring.

From 6:00 to 8:00 p.m. EST, Secretary Panetta met with senior DOD officials to discuss the Benghazi attack and other violence in the region in reaction to the anti-Muslim video. The Secretary directed three actions: 1) that one Fleet Antiterrorism Security Team (FAST) platoon stationed in Rota, Spain, deploy to Benghazi and that a second FAST platoon in Rota prepare to deploy to Tripoli; 2) that U.S. European Command's In-extremis Force, which happened to be training in central Europe, deploy to a staging base in southern Europe; and 3) that a special operations force based in the United States deploy to a staging base in southern Europe. The National Command Center transmitted formal authorization for these actions at 8:39 p.m. A FAST platoon arrived in Tripoli the evening (local time) of September 12th, and the other forces arrived that evening at a staging base in Italy, long after the terrorist attack on the U.S. facilities in Benghazi had ended and four Americans had been killed.[1]

---

[1] The details of this narrative are based on briefings to the Committee in November 2012, as well as publicly available documents describing the narrative provided by the Department of State and the Department of Defense.

2. Senate Committee on Homeland Security and Governmental Affairs (12/30/2012)

Key Findings and Recommendations

Finding 1. In the months leading up to the attack on the Temporary Mission Facility in Benghazi, there was a large amount of evidence gathered by the U.S. Intelligence Community (IC) and from open sources that Benghazi was increasingly dangerous and unstable, and that a significant attack against American personnel there was becoming much more likely. While this intelligence was effectively shared within the Intelligence Community (IC) and with key officials at the Department of State, it did not lead to a commensurate increase in security at Benghazi nor to a decision to close the American mission there, either of which would have been more than justified by the intelligence presented.

Security decisions concerning U.S. facilities and personnel overseas are informed by several different types of information, including classified threat reporting from the IC; cables and spot reports from U.S. diplomatic posts, which describe local incidents and threats; and publicly available information. Prior to the attack, the IC and the Department of State were aware of the overall threat landscape in Libya and the challenges facing the new Libyan government in addressing those threats. This understanding evolved over time, consistent with broader changes in the nature of the threat, and also based on reported incidents and attacks in Benghazi and other parts of Libya in 2012.

The Committee has reviewed dozens of classified intelligence reports on the evolution of threats in Libya which were issued between February 2011 and September 11, 2012. We are precluded in this report from discussing the information in detail, but overall, these intelligence reports (as the ARB similarly noted) provide a clear and vivid picture of a rapidly deteriorating threat environment in eastern Libya—one that we believe should have been sufficient to inform policy-makers of the growing danger to U.S. facilities and personnel in that part of the country and the urgency of them doing something about it. This information was effectively shared by the IC with key officials at the Department of State. For example, both the Deputy Assistant Secretary of State for International Programs in the Bureau of Diplomatic Security, Charlene Lamb, who was responsible for the security at more than 275 diplomatic facilities, and former Regional Security Officer (RSO) for Libya Eric Nordstrom, who was the principal security adviser to the U.S. Ambassador in Libya from September 21, 2011 to July 26, 2012, told the Committee that they had full access to all threat information from the IC about eastern Libya during the months before the attack of September 11, 2012.[2] Yet the Department failed to take adequate action to protect its personnel there.

This classified intelligence reporting was complemented by open-source reporting on attacks and other incidents targeting western interests in Libya during the months prior to the September 11, 2012 attack. The RSO in Libya compiled a list of 234 security incidents in Libya between June 2011 and July 2012, 50 of which took place in Benghazi.[3] The document describes an array of incidents, including large-scale militia clashes, protests involving several hundred people, and the temporary detention of non-governmental organization (NGO) workers and of U.S. diplomatic personnel in Benghazi. Under Secretary for Management Patrick Kennedy noted in a

---

[2] Charlene Lamb and Eric Nordstrom, interviews with Committee staff, December 2012.
[3] U.S. Embassy Tripoli, Libya, Regional Security Office, "Security Incidents since June 2011."

briefing for the Committee, that Libya and Benghazi were "flashing red" around the time of the attack.[4]

The incident reporting shows that western facilities and personnel became an increasing focus of threats in the spring of 2012. For example, on April 2, 2012 in Benghazi, a British diplomatic vehicle was attacked by a mob of demonstrators. Four days later, on April 6th, a crude improvised explosive device (IED) was thrown over the wall of the U.S. facility in Benghazi, causing minimal damage. A spot report on the day of the event stated that shortly after the event two individuals were questioned. The suspects included one current and one former guard employed by Blue Mountain Group, the company which supplied the unarmed Libyan contract guards responsible for screening visitors to the U.S. compound—underscoring the potential risk of an insider threat in Benghazi.[5] Four days after that, on April 10th, also in Benghazi, a crude IED was thrown at the convoy of the United Nations Special Envoy to Libya.[6]

Other publicly reported incidents occurred during this time frame, but there are four that we believe are particularly noteworthy. Taken as a whole, they demonstrated the capability and intent of Benghazi-based Islamist extremist groups to conduct a significant attack against U.S. or other western interests in Libya:

- On May 22, 2012, the International Committee for the Red Cross/Red Crescent (ICRC) building in Benghazi was hit by two RPG rounds, causing damage to the building but no casualties. Several days later, the Brigades of the Imprisoned Sheikh Omar Abdel Rahman claimed responsibility for this attack, accusing the ICRC of proselytizing in Libya.[7]

- On June 6, 2012, the U.S. Temporary Mission Facility in Benghazi was targeted by an IED attack that blew a hole in the perimeter wall. Credit for this attack was also claimed by the Brigades of the Imprisoned Sheikh Omar Abdel Rahman, which said it carried out the attack in response to the reported drone strike on al Qaeda leader Abu Yahya al-Libi in Northern Waziristan.[8]

- On June 11, 2012, an attack was carried out in Benghazi on the convoy of the British Ambassador to Libya. Attackers fired an RPG on the convoy, followed by small arms fire. Two British bodyguards were injured in the attack. This attack was characterized afterwards in an incident report by the Department of State's Bureau of Diplomatic Security as a "complex, coordinated attack."[9]

---

[4] Committee Member briefing, November 14, 2012.
[5] REDACTED, e-mail message to DS-IP-NEA, April 6, 2012.
[6] U.S. Embassy Tripoli, Libya, Regional Security Office, "Security Incidents since June 2011."
[7] Ibid.
[8] Ibid.
[9] REDACTED, e-mail message to DS-IP-NEA; DSCC_E TIA/PII; DSCC_E TIA/TTA; DSCC_C DS Seniors, "Benghazi – SR – Attack on British Ambassador Motorcade – 06112012," June 11, 2012.

- On June 18, 2012, the Tunisian consulate in Benghazi was stormed by individuals affiliated with Ansar al-Sharia Libya (AAS), allegedly because of "attacks by Tunisian artists against Islam."[10]

Overall, the threat to western interests in eastern Libya and in Benghazi specifically was high even prior to the attack of September 11, 2012. Reviewing these incidents, an unclassified open source report by a contractor to AFRICOM noted in July 2012 that:

> "Nonetheless, Benghazi has seen a notable increase in violence in recent months, particularly against international targets. These events point to strong anti-Western sentiments among certain segments of the population, the willingness of Salafi-jihadi groups in the city to openly engage in violence against foreign targets, and their capacity to carry out these attacks."[11]

Taking classified reporting on the increasing dangers in eastern Libya together with the open source incidents should have provided a clear picture of the dangers for American personnel in Benghazi unless their security were greatly improved.

Finding 2. Notwithstanding the increasingly dangerous environment in eastern Libya in 2011 and 2012, the U.S. government did not have specific intelligence of an imminent attack on the U.S. mission in Benghazi. The lack of such actionable intelligence may reflect a failure in the IC to focus sufficiently on terrorist groups that have weak or no operational ties to core al Qaeda and its main affiliates.

While the IC had developed and adequately shared general threat information on terrorist groups and Islamist extremist militias in eastern Libya prior to the attack, it did not have specific warning that this attack was to take place on September 11, 2012. Intelligence capabilities that provide early, specific warnings have played a critical role in preventing terrorist attacks against U.S. facilities overseas and in the homeland in the last decade.[12] There were no such warnings available for Benghazi before the attack of September 11, 2012. Why?

First, there may not have been significant or elaborate advance planning for the attack. In a hearing before our Committee on September 19, 2012, National Counterterrorism Center (NCTC) Director Matthew Olsen described the attack as "opportunistic" and stated that the IC had no indication of "significant advanced planning or coordination for this attack."[13]

---

[10] Hadeel Al-Shalchi, "Gunmen attack Tunisian consulate in Benghazi," *Reuters*, June 18, 2012. http://www.reuters.com/article/2012/06/18/us-libya-gunmen-tunisia-idUSBRE85H1V620120618; Michel Cousins, "Tunisian Consulate in Benghazi attacked," *Libya Herald*, June 18, 2012. http://www.libyaherald.com/2012/06/18/tunisian-consulate-in-benghazi-attacked/

[11] Navanti Group, *Security Conditions in Benghazi, Libya*, July 12, 2012.

[12] However, as discussed later in this report, reliance solely on early warning intelligence is insufficient for making security improvement decisions.

[13] *Homeland Threats and Agency Responses:* Hearing before the Homeland Security and Governmental Affairs Committee, United States Senate, 112th Cong., September 19, 2012. (Statement of Matthew Olsen, Director, NCTC).

However, the activities of local terrorist and Islamist extremist groups in Libya may have received insufficient attention from the IC prior to the attack, partially because some of the groups possessed ambiguous operational ties to core al Qaeda and its primary affiliates. For example, public statements by Libyan officials and many news reports have indicated that Ansar al-Sharia Libya (AAS) was one of the key groups involved in carrying out this attack on the U.S. facility in Benghazi. The group took credit on its own Facebook page for the attack before later deleting the post. U.S. officials viewed AAS prior to the attack as a "local extremist group with an eye on gaining political ground in Libya."[14] AAS has not been designated as a foreign terrorist organization by the U.S. government, and apparently the IC was "not focused" on this group to the same extent as core al Qaeda and its operational affiliates.[15]

This finding has broader implications for U.S. counterterrorism activities in the Middle East and North Africa. With Osama bin Laden dead and core al Qaeda weakened, a new collection of violent Islamist extremist organizations and cells have emerged in the last two to three years. These groups are not all operationally linked to core al Qaeda or in some cases have only weak ties to al Qaeda. This trend is particularly notable in countries such as Libya, Egypt, Tunisia, and Syria that are going through political transition or military conflict as a result of the political upheavals referred to as the "Arab Spring."[16]

While such groups do not always have strong operational ties to al Qaeda, they adhere to a similar violent Islamist extremist ideology. As an unclassified August 2012 report by the Library of Congress noted, AAS in Libya shares common symbols (the black flag) and ideology with al Qaeda.[17] This Committee has spent several years focusing on the role that this ideology plays in motivating homegrown violent Islamist extremists, most of whom have no direct ties to al Qaeda. A similar phenomenon, though potentially much more dangerous, is at work with respect to many of these nascent terrorist groups, and is leading many of them to shift their focus from local grievances to foreign attacks against U.S. and other western facilities overseas.

Recommendation: U.S. intelligence agencies must broaden and deepen their focus in Libya, and beyond, on nascent violent Islamist extremist groups in the region that lack strong operational ties to core al Qaeda or its main affiliate groups.[18] One benefit of doing so would be improved tactical warning capabilities, the kind of which were not present at Benghazi, but might have been even for an "opportunistic" attack.

---

[14] Eli Lake, "Ansar al Sharia's Role in Benghazi Attacks still a Mystery," *The Daily Beast*, November 5, 2012, http://www.thedailybeast.com/articles/2012/11/05/ansar-al-sharia-s-role-in-benghazi-attacks-still-a-mystery.html
[15] Ibid.
[16] For a general discussion of this phenomenon: Robert F. Worth, "Al Qaeda-Inspired Groups, Minus Goal of Striking U.S.", *The New York Times*, October 27, 2012, http://www.nytimes.com/2012/10/28/world/middleeast/al-qaeda-inspired-groups-minus-goal-of-striking-us.html
[17] Federal Research Division, Library of Congress, *Al-Qaeda in Libya: A Profile*, August 2012. See, e.g., the discussion of two local Libyan Islamist-oriented militias—Ansar al-Sharia and al-A'hrar Libya—which are described as broadcasting "typical al-Qaeda–type propaganda on the Internet."(33), http://freebeacon.com/wp-content/uploads/2012/10/LOC-AQ-Libya.pdf
[18] As discussed further, infra, the State Department and the IC must also think beyond "warning" intelligence of specific attacks when making security decisions. This is one of the key lessons of the Accountability Review Board (ARB) Reports on the 1998 terrorist attacks on the U.S. embassies in Kenya and Tanzania.

Finding 3. The absence of specific intelligence about an imminent attack should not have prevented the Department of State from taking more effective steps to protect its personnel and facilities in Benghazi.

This finding reflects earlier conclusions of the 1985 Advisory Panel on Overseas Security ("Inman Report") and the 1999 Accountability Review Board report on the attacks on the U.S. embassies in Kenya and Tanzania, which both warned the Department of State against becoming too reliant on tactical intelligence to determine the level of potential terrorist threats. The Inman report points out that "it would be foolhardy to make security decisions on the basis of an expectation of advance warning of peril."[19]

Deputy Assistant Secretary Charlene Lamb stated that the level and kind of attack at Benghazi was something they had never seen before anywhere in the world.[20] However, given clear warnings that threats were increasing in the Benghazi area, the Department of State should not have waited for a specific incident to happen or expected the delivery of tactical intelligence of a specific, imminent threat before taking additional steps to protect its diplomats or, if that was not possible, to close the Benghazi facility.

Recommendation: In providing security for its personnel around the world, the Department of State must fully consider the types of attacks that could take place given the strategic threat environment, even in the absence of imminent warning intelligence.

Finding 4. Prior to the terrorist attacks in Libya on September 11, 2012, it was widely understood that the Libyan government was incapable of performing its duty to protect U.S. diplomatic facilities and personnel, as required by longstanding international agreements, but the Department of State failed to take adequate steps to fill the resulting security gap, or to invest in upgrading the Libyan security forces.

A host country's responsibility to protect and safeguard a foreign nation's diplomatic personnel and facilities in its country has been codified in several international treaties,[21] including the 1963 Vienna Convention on Consular Relations, which states that "[t]he receiving State is under a special duty to take all appropriate steps to protect the consular premises against any intrusion or damage and to prevent any disturbance of the peace of the consular post or impairment of its dignity."[22] The Treaty also states that "[t]he receiving State shall treat consular officers with due

---

[19] *Inman Report, Report of the Secretary of State's Advisory Panel on Overseas Security,* (June 1985). http://www.fas.org/irp/threat/inman/.

[20] Charlene Lamb, interview with Committee staff, December 6, 2012.

[21] *See Finzer v. Barry,* 798 F.2d 1450, 1455 (D.C. Cir. 1986) (Bork, J.), (*citing* 2 C. Hyde, International Law 1249 (1945)) ("The principle that host states have a special responsibility to ensure that foreign embassies and the personnel inside them are free from threats of violence and intimidation is 'solidly entrenched in the Law of Nations.'").

[22] Vienna Convention on Consular Relations, (Adopted April 24, 1963, entered into force, March 19, 1967) Art. 31; see also The 1961 Vienna Convention on Diplomatic Relations, Art. 22 (Adopted April 18, 1961, entered into force, April 29, 1964).

respect and shall take all appropriate steps to prevent any attack on their person, freedom or dignity."[23]

A host country's protection of an American embassy or other diplomatic facilities is one of the most important elements of security at that facility, but it is not the only one. A facility's own security, such as its U.S. Marine Corps Security Guards, DS agents, and in some cases, private security guards under contract, is also critical to its overall security posture. States whose governments do not exercise full control over their sovereign territory, or that have a limited security capability, cannot be counted on to safeguard U.S. diplomatic personnel and facilities. This is usually true, of course, in the aftermath of a revolution or civil war – as was the case in Libya – where the provision of protective services by the host nations is unpredictable at best. In those instances, the Department of State must improve one or more of the other three protectors of mission security within its control: Marine Corps Security Guards, Dipolmatic Security agents, or private security contractors.

In February 2011, the revolution began to end Colonel Muammar al-Qadhafi's autocratic rule of Libya. Between February and October of 2011, Libya was consumed with intense fighting between anti-government groups and Qadhafi's regime. On October 20, 2011, opposition forces conquered the last Qadhafi stronghold in Sirte and killed Qadhafi. Qadhafi's death ended the revolt but left open the question of who would govern Libya and how.

Just days after Qadhafi's death, Libyans turned to the interim Transitional National Council (TNC), established in the spring of 2011, to improve security and begin the process of reconstituting national institutions.[24] However, the TNC faced numerous challenges and "struggled to calm the incendiary regional and factional disputes or exert control even over its own militias."[25] Since no cohesive opposition group emerged from the civil war, the TNC had to contend with various armed factions that "remained a law unto themselves."[26]

On July 7, 2012, Libyan voters participated in the first national election since 1965 and elected 200 members to the General National Congress.[27] The election of the General National Congress represented a significant political achievement, but the formation of a new government was still under negotiation when the attacks in Benghazi occurred three months later in September. Civil order had not yet been restored. According to one expert review, "[a]ttacks on international targets, a series of aggressive attacks by armed Salafists on religious buildings around the country, and an assassination campaign against senior security officers have fueled widespread criticism of interim leaders since early 2012."[28]

Given the unstable political and security situation, particularly in eastern Libya, the Libyan government was unable to provide security protection to foreign diplomatic facilities in a manner

---

[23] Vienna Convention on Consular Relations, (Adopted April 24, 1963, entered into force, March 19, 1967) Art. 40.
[24] Christopher M. Blanchard, Congressional Research Service, *Libya: Transition and U.S. Policy*, October 18, 2012 (16).
[25] Adam Nossiter and Kareem Fahim, "Revolution Won, Top Libyan Official Promises Elections and a More Pious State," *New York Times*, October 24, 2011, A10.
[26] Ibid.
[27] Blanchard (17).
[28] Blanchard (6).

consistent with international law. That is why the Department of State relied in part on a local militia, the February 17 Brigade, to provide protection for the Benghazi facility, as well as unarmed Libyan guards under contract with a private security firm. Throughout 2012, Department of State officials questioned the February 17 Brigade's competence and expressed concerns about its abilities.[29] U.S. Department of State personnel were also concerned about the involvement of members of the February 17 Brigade in the extrajudicial detention of U.S. diplomatic personnel in at least one incident in Benghazi.[30] Eric Nordstrom, told the Committee that while the February 17 Brigade did provide some protection and would likely respond to an attack, they clearly needed additional training.[31] Only limited training ever occurred.

Some U.S. personnel also questioned the Brigade's loyalty to the Libyan government and their capacity or desire to safeguard American interests.[32] In June 2012, an RSO in Benghazi wrote, "Unfortunately, given the current threat to the diplomatic mission, the militia members not currently on the [four-man team stationed at the facility] have expressed concern with showing active open support for the Americans in Benghazi."[33] Notably, the contract between the State Department and the February 17 Brigade had expired by the time of the attack. In a handoff email to his replacement on August 29, 2012, the principal U.S. diplomatic officer in Benghazi wrote that the contract with the militia "lapsed several weeks ago" but that they were still operating under its terms. He said that "[t]his is a delicate issue, as we are relying on a militia in lieu of the central authorities and [Feb 17 Brigade] has been implicated in several of the recent detentions. We also have the usual concerns re their ultimate loyalties. But they are competent, and give us an added measure of security. For the time being, I don't think we have a viable alternative."[34] In early September, a member of the February 17 Brigade told another RSO in Benghazi that it could no longer support U.S. personnel movements. The RSO also asked specifically if the militia could provide additional support for the Ambassador's pending visit and was told no.[35]

The ability of the Libyan government to provide surge forces to rescue or evacuate personnel from the Benghazi facility was also extremely limited. The Department of State recognized this limitation.[36] As early as February 1, 2012, RSO Nordstrom stated in a memo to his superiors that the political situation in post-revolution Libya "was fragile" and that "[m]any basic state institutions, including emergency services and tourist facilities are not yet fully operational."[37]

---

[29] See, for example, REDACTED, e-mail message to REDACTED, January 4, 2012; or REDACTED, e-mail message to REDACTED, April 1, 2012.
[30] "Security Incidents since June 2011," U.S. Embassy Tripoli, Libya, Regional Security Office and REDACTED, email to DS-IP-NEA, "Benghazi RSO Spot Report," March 15, 2012.
[31] Eric Nordstrom, interview with Committee staff, December 7, 2012. The State Department did provide some training to members of the Brigade.
[32] See, for example, REDACTED, e-mail message to REDACTED, January 4, 2012; or REDACTED, e-mail message to REDACTED, April 1, 2012. See also, REDACTED, email to REDACTED, June 17, 2012.
[33] REDACTED, e-mail message to REDACTED, June 17, 2012.
[34] REDACTED, e-mail message to REDACTED, "Benghazi Hand-off Notes," August 29, 2012.
[35] REDACTED, e-mail message to Charlene Lamb, "Ambassador's protective detail in Benghazi," September 20, 2012.
[36] *The Security Failures of Benghazi*: Hearing before the Committee on Oversight and Government Reform, U.S. Congress, 112th Cong., October 10, 2012. (Eric Allan Nordstrom, Regional Security Officer, Tripoli, Libya from 9/21/11 – 7/26/12).
[37] RSO Eric Nordstrom, Memorandum to DS/DSS/T1A/OSAC, "OSAC Crime and Safety Report," February 1, 2012.

Nordstrom noted that "various factions and militias continue to vie for power in the absence of a stable political and security environment, often resulting in violence."[38]

This view of the Libyan government's inadequate security capabilities persisted through the attack on September 11, 2012. Communications from U.S. personnel in Libya continued to repeat the same conclusions stated by Nordstrom earlier in February. For instance, an early August cable from the Tripoli Embassy to the Department of State in Washington, states that even though the TNC had established a Supreme Security Council (SSC) to stabilize the security situation in Benghazi, its own commander had said that the SSC had "not coalesced into an effective, stable security force."[39] Further, the cable warned that the "absence of a significant deterrence, has contributed to a security vacuum that is being exploited by independent actors."[40] Similarly, an August 20, 2012 security update reported that other diplomats believed the SSC was "'fading away,' unwilling to take on 'anyone with powerful patrons from powerful tribes.'"[41] That same month, DS personnel reviewing tripwires for an ordered departure[42] of the post – that is, political, security, and intelligence benchmarks which would prompt diplomatic officials to close a facility or modify its operations – stated that "[m]ission opinion is that Libyan security forces are indifferent to the safety needs of the U.S. mission."[43] On September 11, 2012, the day of the attack, the "Weekly Report" prepared by Department of State officers on the security situation in Benghazi described the frustrations of an SSC commander that the police and security forces were "too weak to keep the country secure."[44]

Prior to Ambassador Stevens' visit to Benghazi in September 2012, the U.S. mission in Benghazi had made a request to the Libyan Ministry of Foreign Affairs for additional security in Benghazi to support the visit. At a minimum, these requests included appeals for a 24/7 police presence consisting of a vehicle and personnel at each of the compound's three gates.[45] The only Libyan government response appears to have been an SSC police vehicle parked in front of the front gate (which, as the ARB noted, sped away as the attack began).

Though a few members of the February 17 Brigade and the Libya Shield militia assisted the Americans on the night of the attack, the security that these militias and the local police provided to U.S. personnel was woefully inadequate to the dangerous security environment in Benghazi.

The unarmed local contract guards also provided no meaningful resistance to the attackers. The Department of State's Inspector General had previously found that concerns about local security guards were not limited to Libya. A February 2012 Department of State Inspector General (IG) report found that more than two-thirds of 86 diplomatic posts around the world surveyed

---

[38] Ibid.

[39] REDACTED, e-mail message to REDACTED, "The Guns of August: security in eastern Libya," August 8, 2012.

[40] Ibid.

[41] REDACTED, e-mail message to REDACTED, "Benghazi Weekly Report, Special Eid al-Fitr Edition," August 20, 2012.

[42] Under an ordered departure, all U.S. diplomatic personnel and their families are instructed by the Chief of Mission to leave the post.

[43] *Benghazi Assessment of Tripwires Breached as of August 13, 2012.*

[44] REDACTED, e-mail message to REDACTED, "Benghazi Weekly Report," September 11, 2012. (1).

[45] REDACTED, e-mail message to Charlene Lamb, "Ambassador's protective detail in Benghazi," September 20, 2012.

reported problems with their local guard contractors. Of those posts that reported problems with their contractors, 37 percent said there was an insufficient number of local guards and 40 percent said there was insufficient training.[46] The IG found that overseas diplomatic posts, particularly those in high-threat situations beyond Iraq, Afghanistan, and Pakistan urgently needed best-value contracting, which takes into account the past performance of contractors.[47]

Recommendation: When it becomes clear that a host nation cannot adequately perform its functions under the Vienna Convention, the Department of State must provide additional security measures of its own, urgently attempt to upgrade the host nation security forces, or decide to close a U.S. Diplomatic facility and remove U.S. personnel until appropriate steps can be taken to provide adequate security. American personnel who serve us abroad must often work in high risk environments, but when they do, we must provide them with adequate security. That clearly was not the case in Benghazi on September 11, 2012.

Recommendation: The Department must conduct a review of its local guard programs and particularly the use of local guard contractors at high-risk posts who do not meet appropriate standards necessary for the protection of our personnel or facilities.

Finding 5. The Benghazi facility's temporary status had a detrimental effect on security decisions, and that fact was clearly known by DS personnel in Benghazi and to their superiors who nevertheless left the American personnel in Benghazi in this very dangerous situation. The Department of State did not take adequate measures to mitigate the facility's significant vulnerabilities in this high-threat environment.

The Department of State opened the temporary mission in Benghazi in 2011 after the revolution against the Qadhafi government began because eastern Libya was the headquartes of the opposition to Qadhafi, and the embassy in Tripoli had been closed due to security concerns. The temporary mission was first located in a hotel and then moved, based on security concerns, to the compound referred to as the Temporary Mission Facility.[48] After the U.S. Embassy was reopened in Tripoli when Qadhafi was overthrown, the Department of State initially planned to close the Benghazi facility in late 2011.[49] However, in December 2011, the Department decided to extend its presence in Benghazi until December 2012. In the memo approving this decision, the Department stated that the facility would be a "smaller operation" but noted its importance to eastern Libyans and the assistance it could provide to the embassy in Tripoli.[50]

The temporary status of the Benghazi facility contributed to its vulnerability. For example, DS agents stationed in Benghazi were always on temporary duty assignments, remaining there for relatively short periods, often no longer than a month. As Nordstrom noted, having temporary

---

[46] State Department, Office of Inspector General, *Review of Best-Value Contracting for the Department of State Local Guard Program and the Utility of Expanding the Policy Beyond High-Threat Posts in Iraq, Afghanistan, and Pakistan*, February, 2012 (9).

[47] Ibid. (5).

[48] Alex Tiersky and Susan Epstein, Congressional Research Service, *Securing U.S. Diplomatic Facilities and Personnel Abroad: Background and Policy Issues*, November 26, 2012, (3).

[49] REDACTED, e-mail message to DS-IP-NEA and REDACTED, September 13, 2012.

[50] NEA–Jeffrey Feltman, Action Memo to Under Secretary Kennedy, December 27, 2011, (2).

duty agents made "developing security procedures, policies, and relationships more difficult."[51]
The temporary status also made it difficult to procure funds for security upgrades. A briefing
paper prepared for a meeting of Assistant Secretary of State for Diplomatic Security Eric
Boswell and then-Ambassador to Libya Gene Cretz noted, "Due to the ambiguity surrounding
the duration of the U.S. Mission in Benghazi, RSO Benghazi has encountered funding issues for
projects that are commonplace at most U.S. missions."[52] The Committee received conflicting
evidence with regard to whether the temporary Benghazi facility was on the Security
Environment Threat List— a semiannual document that aids DS management in the allocation of
overseas security resources and programs.[53] In any event, it is hard to imagine there were more
than a few Department of State missions anywhere in the world that were in a more dangerous
environment than Benghazi.

In the December 2011 memo approving the Temporary Mission Facility in Benghazi, the
Department of State noted the need for corrective security measures for the facility. According to
RSO Nordstrom, the Department of State never consulted with him about the security
requirements of the facility before the December 2011 action memo was sent to Under Secretary
Kennedy for approval.[54] The memo approved by Kennedy indicated that the Department of State
would " rapidly implement a series of corrective security measures as part of the consolidation of
the State footprint."[55] However, the memo lacked details as to the security standards to be
followed and the resources required to implement the security measures. The absence of
dedicated resources contributed to the constraints under which those in Washington and
Benghazi would operate throughout 2012.

During 2012, however, the Department did make a variety of field expedient security
enhancements, including:

- The installation of concrete jersey barriers;
- The installation of four vehicle barriers for access control and anti-ram protection;
- Increased compound lighting;
- The installation of barbed wire on top of the existing perimeter wall to raise height and on
  top of the interior chain link fence to create secondary barrier;
- The installation of platforms for property and street surveillance;
- The construction of four guard booths;
- The installation of steel grillwork on windows;
- The installation of emergency releases on select windows grills for fire/emergency exit;
- The replacement of several wooden doors with steel doors with appropriate locking
  hardware;
- Sandbag emplacements for internal defense purposes; and

---

[51] *The Security Failures of Benghazi*: Hearing before the Committee on Oversight and Government Reform, U.S.
Congress, 112th Cong., October 10, 2012. (Eric Allan Nordstrom, Regional Security Officer, Tripoli, Libya from
9/21/11 – 7/26/12).
[52] Diplomatic Security Issues Only Briefing paper for March 6, 2012 meeting of Assistant Secretary Boswell and
Ambassador Cretz.
[53] Eric Nordstrom, interview with Committee staff, December 7, 2012.
[54] Ibid.
[55] NEA-Jeffrey Feltman, Action Memo to Under Secretary Kennedy, December 27, 2011, (2).

- Hardening villas with safe rooms with a steel door. [56]

But these physical security upgrades were insufficient to deter or repel the dozens of armed attackers that swarmed the compound, unimpeded, on September 11, 2012. As discussed in more detail below, the facility lacked the type of pedestrian barriers that could have slowed the attackers, even though the Department of State Inspector General and an earlier Accountability Review Board had each recommended the installation of such barriers at diplomatic posts in high-risk places like Benghazi.

Because the Benghazi facility was temporary, no security standards applied to it.[57] While existing security standards require meaningful physical barriers to slow pedestrian access for permanent U.S. diplomatic facilities, there were few meaningful physical barriers at the Benghazi facility that would slow pedestrian access other than the closed gate. Once the gate was opened, there were no other physical impediments at that access point to keep anyone out of the facility's grounds or slow their assault.

Having additional physical barriers to reinforce the gate might have delayed the breach of the compound, giving those inside more time to prepare for the attack. For example, some permanent diplomatic facilities have a compound access control (CAC) point, a "mantrap," or both. Both of these types of barriers act as gates or enclosures that are used to limit the movement of pedestrians entering a diplomatic facility. While a CAC is primarily installed in conjunction with a pedestrian entrance, a mantrap is typically installed in conjunction with a vehicle gate or barrier. According to Deputy Assistant Secretary Charlene Lamb, a CAC was not in place at Benghazi due to time and money constraints. She estimated a CAC there would have cost hundreds of thousands of dollars.[58] No mantrap was in place either, though the reason for that is less clear. Unfortunately, we will never know if the additional investment in either a CAC or mantrap would have provided the time needed to save the lives of Ambassador Chris Stevens and Foreign Service Officer Sean Smith because of the fires set by the terrorists.

The absence of mantraps has been identified as a security vulnerability at least twice in the last ten years by the Department of State. According to a 2009 Department of State Inspector General Report, the 2004 Accountability Review Board regarding the attack on the U.S. consulate in Jeddah, Saudi Arabia recommended the installation of pedestrian barriers at U.S. diplomatic facilities overseas.[59] During that attack, terrorists exited their vehicle and quickly breached the perimeter after being stopped by the entrance's anti-vehicle barrier. The attackers killed six and wounded several others.[60]

Five years later, the Department of State Inspector General found that the absence of approved security standards or recent directives from the Bureau of Diplomatic Security regarding the installation of mantraps resulted in a fewer number of mantraps at overseas posts than required

---

[56] REDACTED, e-mail message to DS-IP-NEA and REDACTED, September 13, 2012.

[57] Charlene Lamb and Eric Nordstrom, interviews with Committee staff, December 2012.

[58] Charlene Lamb, interview with Committee staff, December 6, 2012.

[59] Department of State, Inspector General, *Review of the Department's Implementation of Mantraps*, Report Number ISP-I-09-29, February 2009, (2-3).

[60] Attack on U.S. Consulate General in Jeddah, James C. Oberwetter, U.S. Ambassador to Saudi Arabia, On-the-Record Briefing, Jeddah, Saudi Arabia, December 7, 2004 http://2001-2009.state.gov/p/nea/rls/rm/39516.htm

worldwide. At the time, 25 percent of critical threat posts that responded to the IG's survey did not have or request a mantrap and 39 percent of posts rated as a high threat post that responded to the survey also had no mantraps, plans for a mantrap, or were unable to accommodate mantraps. The numbers were worse for low and medium threat posts. According to the Department of State IG report, the average cost of installing mantraps at a U.S. diplomatic post (including related infrastructure) is approximately $55,000.[61]

In determining the amount of additional security to provide to the Benghazi facility, the Department of State did not conduct a joint analysis or confer with other agencies, such as DOD or members of the IC. For U.S. diplomatic facilities at greatest risk, such as Benghazi, more interagency analysis of security needs must be done to identify gaps in security and take the steps to address them. Since the attack in Benghazi, the Department of State and the Department of Defense have jointly begun this important work, focusing initially on the highest threat facilities around the globe,[62] but that should have happened before the attack.

Resourcing for security is a joint responsibility of the Executive Branch and the Legislative Branch. The Department of State's decisions regarding security at the Benghazi facility were made in the context of its budget and security requirements for diplomatic facilities around the world. Overall, the Department of State's base requests for security funding have increased by 38 percent since Fiscal Year (FY) 2007, and base budget appropriations have increased by 27 percent in the same time period. Other security funding provided beyond that in supplemental appropriations bills has been nearly entirely for diplomatic facilities in just three countries—Iraq, Afghanistan, and Pakistan.[63] Less has gone elsewhere and very little is available to the temporary facilities such as the one in Benghazi.

Importantly, funding requests for baseline diplomatic security programs[64] have not been fully funded in any year since FY 2010. These accounts fund local guards, security technology, DS agents, and maintenance, construction and security upgrades for facilities. The Administration requested almost $2.4 billion for the Worldwide Security Protection (WSP) and Embassy Security, Construction and Maintenance (ESCM) accounts in fiscal year 2011 (the Department of State's two largest diplomatic security accounts), but the House of Representatives recommended a funding level that was $127.5 million less than the President's Budget request. The Senate restored $38 million of the funding in the final enacted appropriations bill for that year. In fiscal year 2012, the gap was larger: Congress enacted appropriations for diplomatic security that were $275 million less than was requested.[65]

---

[61] Department of State, Inspector General, *Review of the Department's Implementation of Mantraps*, Report Number ISP-I-09-29, February 2009, (3).

[62] Committee member briefing, November 14, 2012.

[63] Congressional Research Service (CRS), e-mail message to Committee staff, December 20, 2012. For example, CRS noted all Overseas Contingency Operations enacted and requested for the Worldwide Security Protection account in Fiscal Years 2012 and 2013 were for facilities in Afghanistan and Pakistan. Additionally, there was approximately $1.5 billion funding for Iraq embassy "security and overhead cover" in FY 2012.

[64] According to CRS, these include State Department accounts for Worldwide Security Protection (WSP); Embassy Security, Construction and Maintenance (ESCM); Diplomatic Security, Counterterrorism within the Diplomatic and Consular Programs; and Diplomatic Security within the Border Security Program.

[65] Department of State, *Congressional Budget Justification Volume 1: Department of State Operations Fiscal Year 2013* (February 13, 2012), and the Consolidated Appropriations Act, 2012, P.L. 112-74.

2. Senate Committee on Homeland Security and Governmental Affairs (12/30/2012)

At the same time, Congress has generally been responsive in providing supplemental and Overseas Contingency Operations (OCO) funds to the Department of State – more than $1.7 billion since 2007 – in response to emergent, security-driven funding requests, although primarily for facilities in Iraq, Afghanistan and Pakistan. However, there was no supplemental or OCO request made by the President for additional diplomatic security enhancements in FY2010 or FY2011.[66] Neither the Department of State nor Congress made a point of providing additional funds in a supplemental request for Libya, or more specifically, Benghazi.

Congress' inability to appropriate funds in a timely manner has also had consequences for the implementation of security upgrades. RSO Nordstrom stated that Continuing Resolutions had two detrimental effects on efforts to improve security in Benghazi. First, the Department of State would only allow funds to be expended at a rate of 80 percent of the previous year's appropriations level, so as not to risk a violation of the Anti-Deficiency Act. Second, in the absence of a supplemental appropriations or reprogramming request, security funds for Benghazi had to be taken "out of hide" from funding levels for Libya because Benghazi was not included in previous budget requests.[67]

Recommendation: The Department of State should establish a mandatory process to determine what security standards are applicable to temporary facilities to ensure that they are adequately protected.

Recommendation: In the future, more interagency joint assessments or analyses of security needs must be done for U.S. diplomatic facilities at greatest risk. A joint assessment could not only improve our government's ability to identify security gaps, it would make all agencies more aware of assets available to meet security challenges and those available to respond to a crisis.

Recommendation: The Administration and Congress must work together to provide sufficient, steady, and timely funding resources to secure diplomatic facilities and personnel worldwide.

Finding 6. The Department of State did not adequately support security requests from its own security personnel in Benghazi.

Throughout 2012, the number of DS agents temporarily deployed to Benghazi fluctuated, decreasing to as low as *one* agent for a six week period in March and April 2012 due to visa problems.[68] At the time of the attack, there were three DS agents who were stationed in Benghazi and two more who accompanied the Ambassador there from Tripoli. RSO Nordstrom said that security personnel in Tripoli were sometimes used to augment Benghazi security when necessary.[69]

---

[66] Alex Tiersky and Susan Epstein, Congressional Research Service, *Securing U.S. Diplomatic Facilities and Personnel Abroad: Background and Policy Issues*, November 26, 2012, (15).
[67] Eric Nordstrom, interview with Committee staff, December 7, 2012.
[68] REDACTED, e-mail message to REDACTED, October 1, 2012.
[69] Eric Nordstrom, interview with Committee staff, December 7, 2012.

As conditions changed in late spring and early summer, officers in Tripoli and in Washington had good situational awareness of the growing threats in Libya and especially in Benghazi. However, the Department of State did not provide enough security to address the increased threats and did not adequately support field requests for additional security. For example, in March 2012 the Tripoli Embassy had requested five full-time security positions for Benghazi. However, a day after sending this request, Nordstrom was told that Washington had capped the number of agents in Benghazi at three, even though the request for five agents was consistent with the December 2011 action memo approved by Under Secretary Kennedy to extend the duration of the Benghazi facility.[70] In addressing the March request for five DS agents, Deputy Assistant Secretary Lamb questioned RSO Nordstrom about the fact that two of those five requested positions would be used for non-personnel security related duties—one for driving and one to secure a computer.[71] Deputy Assistant Secretary Lamb asked that local employees be hired for these positions since they were arguably not related to security.[72] Later, two local nationals were hired to fulfill these duties. In July Embassy officials in Tripoli requested a *minimum* of three DS agents for Benghazi.

Nordstrom also testified that he would have preferred to extend a DOD support team, which DOD provided to the Department of State on a non-reimbursable basis, that was scheduled to depart in August 2012. The 16-person Site Security Team (SST) was stationed in Tripoli, but on occasion some of its members also helped with security in Benghazi. The team's deployment had previously been extended twice. Nordstrom said he though that requesting an extension would have "too much political cost," and he was not told to do so.[73] In July 2012, Nordstrom had sent a request, via cable approved by Ambassador Stevens, for a minimum of 13 temporary U.S. security personnel—which he said could be either DS employees or SST personnel, or a combination of both—to support needs in Tripoli.[74] Nordstrom said he never received a response to that request.[75] Though the Department of State never formally asked DOD to extend the SST team, at the time of the attack several members of the SST were still in Tripoli for other purposes, and two participated in the rescue effort the night of the attack.

In the Department's late 2011 plan describing a transition to "locally staffed operations," one of the reasons given for that transition was that "DS does not have sufficient resources to sustain the current level of the security assets in Libya."[76] Lamb commented on this issue in her interview with the Committee, stating that it was hard to sustain large numbers of DS agents on short-term tours because there is not a floating pool of agents so that to fill a gap in Libya she needed to create a gap elsewhere.[77]

---

[70] Eric Nordstrom, e-mail message to REDACTED, March 29, 2012.

[71] Charlene Lamb, interview with Committee staff, December 6, 2012.

[72] Ibid.

[73] *The Security Failures of Benghazi*: Hearing before the Committee on Oversight and Government Reform, U.S. Congress, 112th Cong., October 10, 2012. (Eric Allan Nordstrom, Regional Security Officer from September 21 – July 26, 2012).

[74] 12 Tripoli 690, July 9, 2012.

[75] *The Security Failures of Benghazi*: Hearing before the Committee on Oversight and Government Reform, U.S. Congress, 112th Cong., October 10, 2012. (Eric Allan Nordstrom, Regional Security Officer from September 21 – July 26, 2012).

[76] DS/IP/OPO/FPD, Proposal for Security Support to RSO Tripoli.

[77] Charlene Lamb, interview with Committee staff, December 6, 2012.

2. Senate Committee on Homeland Security and Governmental Affairs (12/30/2012)

Finding 7. Despite the inability of the Libyan government to fulfill its duties to secure the facility, the increasingly dangerous threat assessments, and a particularly vulnerable facility, the Department of State officials did not conclude the facility in Benghazi should be closed or temporarily shut down. That was a grievous mistake.

The Department of State kept the Benghazi facility open despite the inability of the Libyan government to fulfill its duties to secure the facility and the increasingly dangerous threat environment that American intelligence described. Though diplomatic security officials in Libya repeatedly considered and discussed the adequacy of security at the Benghazi facility, we found no evidence that any official ever recommended closing the facility even though the facility's vulnerability remained high, particularly in relation to the limited number and quality of the security personnel on site including the militia, the contracted guards, and DS agents on short-term assignments.

In the months leading up to the September 11, 2012 attack, U.S. personnel sitting on the Benghazi Emergency Action Committee (EAC)—the interagency entity responsible for assessing the security of the facility—met several times to discuss the growing threats in eastern Libya, and whether additional actions to protect U.S. personnel ought to be taken. As late as August 15, 2012, an EAC was convened and resolved to update the "tripwires" for the facility. The updates were to include a new category, "suspension of operations," under which diplomatic personnel remain present at a post but limit activity off U.S. grounds. Notes from that meeting show that joint security exercises were carried out with Annex security personnel that same month, and that conditional manpower requests and the revised set of tripwires were sent to the Embassy in Tripoli for review. A Department of State document shared between officials in Tripoli show various "tripwires" in Benghazi were, in fact, set off weeks before September 11, 2012.[78] Following a bomb attack on a Libyan Army colonel in August, the principal U.S. diplomatic officer in Benghazi wrote that "[g]iven our small size, there is really no distinction between authorized and ordered departure from Benghazi: if we lose one more person, we will be ineffective… we are already at a skeleton crew."[79]

Still, no additional security was provided to the facility in Benghazi and there was no ordered evacuation. RSO Nordstrom said the inability of the host nation to provide security is a significant tripwire. Yet neither he nor, to his knowledge anyone else at the Department of State, recommended the Benghazi post be closed.[80]

Despite the Department of State's initial determination that the facility in Benghazi would be a temporary one, as time progressed, some Department of State officials believed U.S. diplomats needed to remain there longer than they initially expected. Just weeks before his death and even

---

[78] REDACTED, e-mail message to REDACTED, August 30, 2012. Subject: "Latest tripwires for Tripoli and Benghazi," which included an attached document entitled "Benghazi assessment of tripwires breached as of 8/31/2012"

[79] REDACTED, e-mail message to REDACTED, August 6, 2012, "Security Incident Involving Embassy Vehicle Driven by DOD Personnel."

[80] Eric Nordstrom, interview with Committee staff, December 7, 2012.

after there had been attacks against the facility and other western targets in Benghazi, Ambassador Stevens continued to make the case that the Department of State needed a long term presence in Benghazi.[81]

A number of other western governments also continued to maintain a presence in Benghazi throughout the summer and fall of 2012. Under Secretary Kennedy noted that diplomats for Italy, France, Turkey and the United Nations remained in Benghazi during that time period. [82]

One option American officials did consider was co-locating the American government facilities in Benghazi. By December 27, 2011, officials had "come to the conclusion that co-location is the best and most economical option for" a continued presence in Benghazi. They also recognized that there were administrative hurdles to this—such as finding a suitable location large enough for the presence of all personnel.[83] The ARB report on the 1998 Nairobi and Dar es Salaam attacks recommended that, "When building new chanceries abroad, all U.S. government agencies, with rare exceptions, should be located in the same compound."[84] The Department of State should also examine whether similar standards should be adopted for the co-location of temporary facilities.

Finding 8. The Department of Defense and the Department of State had not jointly assessed the availability of U.S. assets to support the Temporary Mission Facility in Benghazi in the event of a crisis and although DOD attempted to quickly mobilize its resources, it did not have assets or personnel close enough to reach Benghazi in a timely fashion.

The Department of Defense (DOD) has a longstanding cooperative relationship with the Department of State, providing support for evacuation and security of diplomatic facilities.[85] For Libya, responsibility for DOD support for diplomatic missions primarily rested with AFRICOM and its Combatant Commander, General Carter F. Ham, headquartered in Stuttgart, Germany. AFRICOM is one of DOD's six geographic combatant commands and is responsible for all DOD operations, exercises, and security cooperation on the African continent (with the exception of Egypt), its island nations, and surrounding waters. The command is also responsible to the Secretary of Defense for military relations with 54 African nations, the African Union, and African regional security organizations. It was established in February 2007 and became a stand-alone command in October 2008. The reason for establishing AFRICOM grew out of concerns about DOD's division of responsibility for Africa among three geographic commands—European Command (EUCOM), Central Command (CENTCOM), and Pacific Command (PACOM)—and worries that security in Africa was receiving less attention than it required based on the increasing presence of Islamist extremists and terrorists there.

---

[81] "Benghazi.docx," document attached to email of August 31, 2012.
[82] Committee member briefing, November 29, 2012.
[83] NEA –Jeffrey Feltman, Action Memo to Under Secretary Kennedy, December 27, 2011. Re: "Future of Operations in Benghazi, Libya"
[84] Accountability Review Board, *Bombings of the US Embassies in Nairobi, Kenya and Dar es Salaam, Tanzania on August 7, 1998,* (January 8, 1999). NB: The facility in Benghazi was a lease and not new construction.
[85] Committee member briefing, November 14, 2012.

2. Senate Committee on Homeland Security and Governmental Affairs (12/30/2012)

Since its creation, AFRICOM has been involved in a number of operations in Africa, with a focus on training African forces and engaging in counterterrorism activities in the Horn of Africa. Unlike many of the other geographical combatant commands, AFRICOM was developed to maintain a light footprint.[86] It maintains a single base on the entire continent, in Djibouti,. In the spring of 2011, AFRICOM directed U.S. support to the NATO military operations in Libya, and in October 2011, it established a joint task force to command and control post-conflict U.S. operations related to Libya. Since DOD assumes responsibility for evacuation of diplomatic personnel, U.S. citizens, and designated host nation and third country nationals in crises, AFRICOM was responsible for working with Department of State officials in Libya to develop and coordinate Noncombatant Evacuation Operations (NEO) plans for the diplomatic facilities within the region.[87] But the Department of State did not know how long it would take DOD to evacuate personnel at the Benghazi facility in the case of a crisis, naturally making it more difficult for the Department of State to ensure it had adequate security at the facility.

In addition, General Ham did not have complete visibility of the extent and number of government personnel in Benghazi in the event that a NEO was required.[88] If sufficient time had been available for such an evacuation, we are concerned that this limitation could have impeded AFRICOM's ability to respond and fulfill its mission responsibility.

AFRICOM's lack of operational assets near Benghazi hindered its capacity to evacuate U.S. personnel during the attacks. The Djibouti base was several thousand miles away. There was no Marine expeditionary unit, carrier group or a smaller group of U.S. ships closely located in the Mediterranean Sea that could have provided aerial or ground support or helped evacuate personnel from Benghazi. AFRICOM also lacked a dedicated Commander's In-extremis Force (CIF)—a specially trained force capable of performing no-notice missions. As a result, General Ham was forced to call on the European Command's CIF whose location in Eastern Europe prevented it from getting to Benghazi before the four Americans were killed and all other U.S. personnel were evacuated. We note that AFRICOM later received an independent CIF in October, 2012.[89] DOD and AFRICOM tried to provide effective support on September 11th, but given the nature of the attack in Benghazi and the distance of their assets from Benghazi, they were tragically unable to do so.

Recommendation: DOD and the Department of State must jointly perform comprehensive crisis defense and evacuation planning for personnel at U.S. diplomatic facilities worldwide, particularly in high risk environments to determine whether DOD can provide timely support and evacuation capabilities, and assist the Department of State in deciding whether to keep facilities open.

---

[86] *Fiscal Year 2013 National Defense Authorization Budget Request from U.S. European Command and U.S. Africa Command:* Armed Services Committee, United States House of Representatives, 112th Congress, February 29, 2012. (General Carter Ham, Commander, United States Africa Command).
http://www.africom.mil/getArticle.asp?art=4133
[87] Joint Chiefs of Staff, *Noncombatant Evacuation Operations*, Report 3-68, December 23, 2010, I-1.
http://www.dtic.mil/doctrine/new_pubs/jp3_68.pdf.
[88] General Carter Ham, Combatant Commander for Africa Command, briefing Chairman and Ranking Member, December 6, 2012.
[89] General Carter Ham, *Counterterrorism in Africa*, Homeland Security Policy Institute event, December 3, 2012. According to General Ham, DOD had been developing this force since 2011.

2. Senate Committee on Homeland Security and Governmental Affairs (12/30/2012)

Recommendation: Because Africa has increasingly become a haven for terrorist groups in places like Libya and Mali, DOD should provide more assets and personnel within range on land and sea to protect and defend both Americans and our allies on the African continent.

Finding 9. Although the September 11, 2012 attack in Benghazi was recognized as a terrorist attack by the Intelligence Community and personnel at the Department of State from the beginning, Administration officials were inconsistent in stating publicly that the deaths in Benghazi were the result of a terrorist attack.

One of the key lessons of this Committee's six-year focus on the threat of violent Islamist extremism is that, in order to understand and counter the threat we face, we must clearly identify that threat. During the Committee's investigation into the Fort Hood massacre, for example, we found systemic problems with the way the military addressed violent Islamist extremism in its policies and procedures (treating this specific threat within the broader context of "workplace violence").[90] Similarly, while we welcomed the Administration's release last year of a national strategy and implementation plan for countering radicalization domestically,[91] we expressed our disappointment in the Administration's continued refusal to identify violent Islamist extremism as our enemy.[92] The enemy is not a vague catchall of violent extremism, but a specific violent Islamist extremism. It is unfair to the vast majority of law-abiding Muslims not to distinguish between their peaceful religion and a twisted corruption of that religion used to justify violence.

There are related lessons to be learned from the Administration's public comments about Benghazi, which we believe contributed to the confusion in the public discourse after the attack about exactly what happened.

The NCTC and U.S. law define terrorism as the "premeditated, politically motivated violence perpetrated against noncombatant targets by subnational groups or clandestine agents."[93] Senior officials from the IC, the Department of State, and the FBI who participated in briefings and interviews with the Committee said they believed the attack on the mission facility in Benghazi to be a terrorist attack immediately or almost immediately after it occurred.[94] The ODNI's

---

[90] U.S. Senate, Homeland Security and Government Affairs Committee, *A Ticking Time Bomb: Counterterrorism Lessons From the U.S. Government's Failure to Prevent the Fort Hood Attack*, 112th Cong., 1st sess, February 3, 2011, 7,9.

[91] The White House, *Strategic Implementation Plan for Empowering Local Partners to Prevent Violent Extremism in the United States*, December 2011.

[92] "Lieberman, Collins React to Administration's Countering Violent Extremism Strategic Implementation Plan," Homeland Security and Government Affairs Committee, press release, December 8, 2011.
http://www.hsgac.senate.gov/media/majority-media/lieberman-collins-react-to-administrations-countering-violent-extremism-strategic-implementation-plan

[93] The National Counterterrorism Center, *Terrorism Definitions*, August 27, 2010.
http://www.nctc.gov/site/other/definitions.html

[94] Committee member briefings, November 14, 2012 and November 29, 2012.

spokesman also has publicly said, "The intelligence community assessed from the very beginning that what happened in Benghazi was a terrorist attack."[95]

In short, regardless of questions about whether there had been a demonstration or protest outside the Temporary Mission Facility in advance of the attack, the extent to which the attacks were preplanned, or the role of an anti-Islamic video which had sparked protests at the U.S. embassy in Cairo and elsewhere earlier on September 11th, there was never any doubt among key officials, including officials in the IC and the Department of State, that the attack in Benghazi was an act of terrorism.

For example, two emails from the State Department Diplomatic Security Operations Center on the day of the attack, September 11, and the day after, September 12, 2012, characterized the attack as an "initial terrorism incident" and as a "terrorist event."[96] Agencies and offices responsible for terrorism, including the National Counterterrorism Center (NCTC), the CIA's Office of Terrorism Analysis, and the FBI's Counterterrorism Division, were immediately involved with gathering information about the attack. Indeed, how could there have been any doubt in anyone's mind that, when a large number of armed men break into a U.S. diplomatic facility, set fire to its buildings, and fire mortars at Americans, that it is by definition a terrorist attack?

However, the IC's assessment was not reflected consistently in the public statements made by Administration officials, several of whom cited the ongoing investigation, in the week following the attack:

> On September 12th, Secretary of State Hillary Clinton attributed the attack to "heavily armed militants" who assaulted the compound…" Her suspicion was that the people involved in this "were looking to target Americans from the start." She also noted that we "continue to apply pressure on Al Qaeda and other elements that are affiliated…"[97]
>
> Also that September 12th President Obama, referring to the anti-Islamic video, said "we reject all efforts to denigrate the religious beliefs of others. But there is absolutely no justification to this type of senseless violence…" He went on to add, "Of course, yesterday was already a painful day for our nation as we marked the solem memory of the 9/11 attacks," and that "No acts of terror will ever shake the resolve of this great nation, alter that character, or eclipse the light of the values that we stand for."[98]

However, that same day, the President had the following exchanges with Steve Kroft in a taping for the CBS news program *60 Minutes*:

---

[95] "Sources: Office of the DNI cut "al Qaeda" reference from Benghazi talking points, and CIA, FBI signed off," *CBS News*, November 20, 2010. http://www.cbsnews.com/8301-505263_162-57552328/sources-office-of-the-dni-cut-al-qaeda-reference-from-benghazi-talking-points-and-cia-fbi-signed-off/

[96] See, for example, REDACTED on behalf of the DS Command Center, email message, "Terrorism Event Notification – Libya," September 12, 2012.

[97] Secretary Hillary Clinton, "Remarks on the Deaths of American Personnel in Benghazi, Libya," Treaty Room, September 12, 2012.

[98] President Barack Obama, "Remarks by the President on the Deaths of U.S. Embassy Staff in Libya," Rose Garden, September 12, 2012.

Mr. Kroft: Do you believe that this was a terrorist attack?

The President: Well, it's too early to know exactly how this came about, what group was involved, but obviously it was an attack on Americans and we are going to be working with the Libyan government to make sure that we bring these folks to justice one way or the other.."

Mr. Kroft: That doesn't sound like your normal demonstration.

The President: As I said, we're still investigating exactly what happened, I don't want to jump the gun on this. But – you're right that this is not a situation that was – exactly the same as what happened in Egypt. And – my suspicion is- is that there are folks involved in this who were looking to target Americans from the start. So we're gonna- make sure that our first priority is to get our folks out safe, make sure that our embassies are secured around the world. And then we are gonna go after – those folks who carried this out…

This is also obviously a reminder that for all the progress that we've made in fighting terrorism, that we're living in a volatile world. And, you know, our troops, but also our diplomats and our intelligence officers they're putting their lives on the line every single day in some very dangerous circumstances…

But I think we also also have to understand that, we have to remain vigilant. And that even as we – continue to apply pressure on Al Qaeda and – other elements that are affiliated—that in big chunks of the world, in Northern Africa and the Middle East, you've got – a lot of dangerous characeters. And we've got to make sure that we're continuing to apply pressure on them…[99]

Two days later, during a September 14, 2012, White House press briefing, Press Secretary Jay Carney was asked to respond to senators' characterizations of the incident as a terrorist attack following a briefing by Secretary Panetta and others:

[Unidentified Reporter]: Jay, one last question -- while we were sitting here -- Secretary Panetta and the Vice Chair of the Joint Chiefs briefed the Senate Armed Services Committee. And the senators came out and said their indication was that this, or the attack on Benghazi was a terrorist attack organized and carried out by terrorists, that it was premeditated, a calculated act of terror. Levin said -- Senator Levin -- I think it was a planned, premeditated attack. The kind of equipment that they had used was evidence it was a planned, premeditated attack. Is there anything more you can -- now that the administration is briefing senators on this, is there anything more you can tell us?

Mr. Carney: Well, I think we wait to hear from administration officials. Again, it's actively under investigation, both the Benghazi attack and incidents elsewhere. And my point was that we don't have and did not have concrete evidence to suggest that this was not in reaction to the film. But we're obviously investigating the matter, and I'll certainly -- I'm sure both the Department of Defense and the White House and other places will have more to say about that as more information becomes available.

---

[99] President Barack Obama, interview by Steve Kroft, *60 Minutes*, CBS, September 12, 2012, transcript.

Then, on September 16th, during one of several similar appearances on the Sunday news programs, Ambassador Susan Rice had the following exchange with David Gregory of *NBC's Meet the Press*:

> **Gregory:** Can you say definitively that the attacks on – on our consulate in Libya that killed Ambassador Stevens and others there security personnel, that was spontaneous, was it a planned attack? Was there a terrorist element to it?
>
> **Ms. Rice:** Well, let us-- let me tell you the-- the best information we have at present. First of all, there's an FBI investigation which is ongoing. And we look to that investigation to give us the definitive word as to what transpired. But putting together the best information that we have available to us today our current assessment is that what happened in Benghazi was in fact initially a spontaneous reaction to what had just transpired hours before in Cairo, almost a copycat of-- of the demonstrations against our facility in Cairo, which were prompted, of course, by the video. What we think then transpired in Benghazi is that opportunistic extremist elements came to the consulate as this was unfolding. They came with heavy weapons which unfortunately are readily available in post revolutionary Libya. And it escalated into a much more violent episode. Obviously, that's-- that's our best judgment now. We'll await the results of the investigation…[100]

On September 18th, President Obama said on the Late Show with David Letterman that "extremists and terrorists used this (referring again to the anti-Islamist video) as an excuse to attack a variety of our embassies, including the consulate in Libya."

A definitive response to the question of whether Benghazi was a terrorist attack was given by NCTC Director Matthew Olsen during a hearing before this Committee on September 19, 2012. Olsen was asked by the Chairman whether he "would say that Ambassador Stevens and the three other Americans died as a result of a terrorist attack."[101] Director Olsen responded that, "[c]ertainly, on that particular question, I would say yes. They were killed in the course of a terrorist attack" on our diplomatic mission in Benghazi.[102]

After Olsen's September 19th appearance before the Committee, other Administration officials stated with more certainty that Benghazi was a terrorist attack. For example:

> On September 19th, referring to Matthew Olsen's statements that Benghazi was a terrorist attack, Victoria Nuland stated "We stand by comments made by our intelligence

---

[100] Benjamin Netanyahu, Susan Rice, Keith Ellison, Peter King, Bob Woodward, Jeffrey Goldberg, Andrea Mitchell, interview by David Gregory, *Meet the Press*, NBC, September 16, 2012, transcript. http://www.msnbc.msn.com/id/49051097/ns/meet_the_press-transcripts/t/september-benjamin-netanyahu-susan-rice-keith-ellison-peter-king-bob-woodward-jeffrey-goldberg-andrea-mitchell/

[101] *Homeland Threats and Agency Responses:* Hearing before the Homeland Security and Governmental Affairs Committee, United States Senate, 112th Cong., September 19, 2012. (Statement of Matthew Olsen, Director, NCTC).

[102] Ibid.

community who has first responsibility for evaluating the intelligence and what they believe we are seeing."[103]

On September 20th, Jay Carney said, "It is, I think, self-evident that what happened in Benghazi was a terrorist attack. Our embassy was attacked violently, and the result was four deaths of American officials. So again, that's self evident..."[104]

On September 21st, Secretary Clinton said, "What happened in Benghazi was a terrorist attack, and we will not rest until we have tracked down and brought to justice the terrorist who murdered four Americans."[105]

On September 24th, however, when one of the co-hosts of the television program *The View* asked the President to clarify what she perceived to be discrepancies in the public record regarding the Administration's position about whether Benghazi attack was an act of terrorism, the President's answer was not as definitive:

> **Joy Behar**: It was reported that people just went crazy and wild because of this anti-Muslim movie, or anti-Muhammad, I guess, movie. But then I heard Hillary Clinton say that it was an act of terrorism. Is it? What do you say?
>
> **The President**: Well, we're still doing an investigation. There's no doubt that the kind of weapons that were used, the ongoing assault, that it wasn't just a mob action. Now, we don't have all the information yet, so we're still gathering it. But what's clear is that around the world, there's still a lot of threats out there. And that's why we have to maintain the strongest military in the world. That's why we can't let down our guard when it comes to the intelligence work that we do, and staying on top of not just al Qaeda – the traditional al Qaeda in Pakistan and Afghanistan – but all these various fringe groups that have started to develop...[106]

*****

Director Olsen's statement on September 19, 2012 before this Committee was also significant because he mentioned ties to al Qaeda. He said:

> At this point, what I would say is that a number of different elements appear to have been involved in the attack, including individuals connected to militant groups that are prevalent in eastern Libya, particularly in the Benghazi area. As well, we are looking at

---

[103] Department of State Spokesperson Victoria Nuland, Press Briefing, September 19, 2012, transcript.

[104] Press Secretary Carney, press briefing, The White House, September 20, 2012, transcript.

[105] Secretary of State Hillary Clinton, "Remarks With Pakistani Foreign Minister Hina Rabbani Khar Before Their Meeting," Treaty Room, September 21, 2012.

[106] President Obama, interview by Joy Behar, *The View*, September 24, 2012. http://www.youtube.com/watch?v=Hdn1iX1a528

26

indications that individuals involved in the attack may have had connections to al Qaeda or al Qaeda's affiliates, in particular al Qaeda in Islamic Maghreb.[107]

Olsen's acknowledgement was important because, in talking points that were prepared the previous week by the IC for Congress, a line saying "we know" that individuals associated with al Qaeda or its affiliates participated in the attacks had been changed to say: "There are *indications* that *extremists* participated," dropping the reference to al Qaeda and its affiliates altogether.[108] Members of the IC differed over whether or not this information should remain classified. It is nevertheless noteworthy that the analyst who drafted the original talking points – a veteran career analyst in the intelligence community believed it was appropriate to include a reference to al Qaeda in the unclassified talking points. The senior analyst concluded that the information could be made public because of the claims of responsibility made by Ansar al-Sharia, which has been publicly linked to al Qaeda. [109]

In addition to the change deleting al-Qaeda, a reference to "attacks" in Benghazi was changed to "demonstrations." [110] Director of National Intelligence (DNI) James Clapper and representatives from the CIA, the State Department, NCTC and the FBI told this Committee that the changes characterizing the attacks as "demonstrations" and removing references to al-Qaeda or its affiliates were made within the CIA and the IC, while the change from "we know" to "indications" was made in response to an FBI request. They also testified that no changes were made for political reasons, that there was no attempt to mislead the American people about what happened in Benghazi, and that the only change made by the White House was to change a reference of "consulate" to "mission."[111]

To provide a full account of the changes made to the talking points, by whom they were made and why, DNI Clapper offered to provide the Committee with a detailed timeline regarding the development of the talking points. At the time of writing this report, despite repeated requests, the Committee had yet to receive this timeline. According to a senior IC official, the timeline has not been delivered as promised because the Administration has spent weeks debating internally whether or not it should turn over information considered "deliberative" to the Congress. The September 28, 2012 public statement from the ODNI confirmed the IC's judgment "that some of those involved were linked to groups affiliated with, or sympathetic to al Qa'ida."[112]

---

[107] Homeland Threats and Agency Responses: Hearing before the Homeland Security and Governmental Affairs Committee, United States Senate, 112th Cong., September 19, 2012. (Statement of Matthew Olsen, Director, NCTC). The ODNI also released a statement on September 28, 2012 which confirmed that the IC had "assess[ed] that some of those involved were linked to groups affiliated with, or sympathetic to al-Qa'ida." *See* Statement by the Director of Public Affairs for the Director of National Intelligence, Shawn Turner, on the intelligence related to the terrorist attack on the U.S. Consulate in Benghazi, Libya, September 28, 2012.

[108] Committee member briefing, November 29, 2012.

[109] Committee member briefing, November 29, 2012.

[110] Sources: Office of the DNI cut "al Qaeda" reference from Benghazi talking points, and CIA, FBI signed off, CBS News, November 20, 2010

[111] Committee member briefing, November 29, 2012.

[112] "Statement by the Director of Public Affairs for the Director of National Intelligence, Shawn Turner, on the intelligence related to the terrorist attack on the U.S. Consulate in Benghazi, Libya," Office of the Director of National Intelligence, press release, September 28, 2012.

27

We anticipate that the ongoing investigation into these attacks by the FBI will provide important new details about exactly which violent Islamist extremists carried out the attack, the extent to which it was planned, and their precise motivations. But as everyone now acknowledges, there is no doubt that Benghazi was indeed a deliberate and organized terrorist attack on our nation. If the fact that Benghazi was indeed a terrorist attack had been made clear from the outset by all Administration and Executive Branch spokespeople, there would have been much less confusion and division in the public response to what happened there on September 11, 2012.

Much of the public discussion about the Benghazi attack has focused on whether a protest took place in Benghazi prior to the attack. While the IC worked feverishly in the days after the attack to identify the perpetrators of the attack, they did not place a high priority on determining with certainty whether a protest had in fact occurred. The IC's preliminary conclusion was that there had been a protest outside of the mission prior to the attack, making this assessment based on open source news reports and on other information available to intelligence agencies. The IC later revised its assessment and the Accountability Review Board has since "concluded that no protest took place before the Special Mission and Annex attacks."[113]

The unnecessary confusion in public statements about what happened that night with regards to an alleged protest should have ended much earlier than it did. Key evidence suggesting the absence of a protest was not widely shared as early as it could have been, creating or contributing to confusion over whether this was a peaceful protest that evolved into something more violent or a terrorist attack by an opportunistic enemy looking for the most advantageous moments to strike.

As early as September 15th, the Annex team that had been in Benghazi during the attack reported there had been no protest.[114] This information was apparently not shared broadly, and to the extent that it was shared, it apparently did not outweigh the evidence decribed above that there was a protest. The next day, the President of Libya's General National Congress, Mohamed Yousef el-Magariaf, also stated on the CBS News show *Face the Nation* that the attack was planned and involved Al Qaeda elements.

On September 15th and 16th, officials from the FBI conducted face-to-face interviews in Germany of the U.S. personnel who had been on the compound in Benghazi during the attack. The U.S. personnel who were interviewed saw no indications that there had been a protest prior to the attack. Information from those interviews was shared on a secure video teleconference on the afternoon of the 16th with FBI and other IC officials in Washington; it is unclear whether the question of whether a protest took place was discussed during this video conference.[115]

Information from those interviews was written into FBI FD-302 interrogation reports and sent back to the FBI headquarters. Nearly a week later, on or around September 22nd, key information from those interrogation reports was disseminated by the FBI in Intelligence Information Reports (IIRs) to other agencies within the IC.[116] By that date, however, the IC had

---

[113] Accountability Review Board, Department of State, December 19, 2012, 4.
[114] Acting Director Michael Morell, briefing Senator Collins, November 28, 2012.
[115] Committee member briefing, November 29, 2012.
[116] Ibid.

already received conclusive proof via other means that there had been no protest prior to the attack, in the form of video evidence from the facility's CCTV cameras.

We also found documentation that one DS agent apparently concluded there had been no protest as early as September 18th.[117] On that date, a State Department DS agent who had seen national press reporting about the attacks asked an agent at the DS Command Center in an email, "Was there any rioting in Benghazi reported prior to the attack?" The reply from the Command Center agent: "Zip, nothing, nada."

Recommendation: When terrorists attack our country, either at home or abroad, Administration officials should speak clearly and consistently about what has happened. While specific details and a full accounting cannot be provided until the government has completed its investigation, the fact that a terrorist attack occurred must be communicated with clarity.

Finding 10. As discussed earlier, the talking points about the September 11th attack in Benghazi which were issued by the Intelligence Community on September 14th in response to a request by the House Permanent Select Committee on Intelligence, were the subject of much of the confusion and division in the discussion of the attack. That confusion and division were intensified by the fact that the talking points were issued before the IC had a high degree of confidence about what happened in Benghazi and in the midst of a national political campaign.

Recommendation: While the Intelligence Community's primary mission is to inform the appropriate officials of the executive and legislative branches of our government about events that affect our security, it is not the responsibility of the IC to draft talking points for public consumption – especially in the heat of a political campaign – and we therefore recommend that the IC decline to do so in the future.

Conclusion

The deaths of Ambassador Stevens and three other Americans at the hands of terrorists is a tragic reminder that the fight our country is engaged in with Islamist extremists and terrorists is not over. U.S. and Western diplomats, and other personnel operating in the Middle East and other countries where these terrorists use violence to further their extremist agenda and thwart democratic reforms are increasingly at risk.

We hope this report will help contribute to the ongoing discussion that our nation must have about how best to protect the brave men and women who serve our country abroad and how to win this war that will continue for years to come. We owe it to our public servants abroad to protect them as they work to protect us. The government of the U.S. failed tragically to fulfill that responsibility in Benghazi on September 11, 2012. We hope the findings and recommendations we have made in this Special Report will help ensure that such a failure never happens again.

---

[117] REDACTED, e-mail message on September 18, 2012.

INTERIM PROGRESS REPORT *for the*
Members of the House Republican Conference
on the Events Surrounding the September 11, 2012
Terrorist Attacks in Benghazi, Libya

Chairman Howard P. "Buck" McKeon, Committee on Armed Services
Chairman Ed Royce, Committee on Foreign Affairs
Chairman Bob Goodlatte, Committee on the Judiciary
Chairman Darrell Issa, Committee on Oversight & Government Reform
Chairman Mike Rogers, Permanent Select Committee on Intelligence

April 23, 2013

EXECUTIVE SUMMARY

An ongoing Congressional investigation across five House Committees concerning the events surrounding the September 11, 2012, terrorist attacks on U.S. facilities in Benghazi, Libya has made several determinations to date, including:

- Reductions of security levels prior to the attacks in Benghazi were approved at the highest levels of the State Department, up to and including Secretary Clinton. This fact contradicts her testimony before the House Foreign Affairs Committee on January 23, 2013.

- In the days following the attacks, White House and senior State Department officials altered accurate talking points drafted by the Intelligence Community in order to protect the State Department.

- Contrary to Administration rhetoric, the talking points were not edited to protect classified information. Concern for classified information is never mentioned in email traffic among senior Administration officials.

These preliminary findings illustrate the need for continued examination and oversight by the five House Committees. The Committees will continue to review who exactly was responsible for the failure to respond to the repeated requests for more security and for the effort to cover up the nature of the attacks, so that appropriate officials will be held accountable.

TABLE OF CONTENTS

I.   Prior to the Benghazi attacks, State Department officials in Libya made repeated requests for additional security that were denied in Washington despite ample documentation of the threat posed by violent extremist militias.

II.   The volatile security environment erupted on September 11, 2012, when militias composed of al-Qa'ida-affiliated extremists attacked U.S. interests in Benghazi.

III.   After the attacks, the Administration perpetuated a deliberately misleading and incomplete narrative that the violence grew out of a demonstration caused by a YouTube video. The Administration consciously decided not to discuss extremist involvement or previous attacks against Western interests in Benghazi.

IV.   The Administration's investigations and reviews of the Benghazi attacks highlight its failed security policies leading to the attacks while undermining the ability of the United States government to bring the perpetrators to justice.

V.   The Benghazi attacks revealed fundamental flaws in the Administration's approach to securing U.S. interests and personnel around the world.

<u>**Introduction**</u>

On September 11, 2012, armed militias with ties to terrorist organizations attacked U.S. facilities in Benghazi, Libya, killing four U.S. personnel: Ambassador Christopher Stevens; State Department Information Officer Sean Smith; and two American security officers – and former U.S. Navy SEALs – Tyrone Woods and Glen Doherty. Given the gravity of these attacks and the loss of American life, the House Committees on Armed Services, Foreign Affairs, Intelligence, Judiciary, and Oversight and Government Reform initiated immediate inquiries into issues within each Committee's jurisdiction concerning the events surrounding the attacks.

In the course of their investigations, the Committees have interviewed dozens of officials and individuals with first-hand knowledge of the events, met with members of the military and diplomatic corps overseas, and reviewed tens of thousands of classified and unclassified documents, cables, emails, and reports. Members of Congress traveled on fact-finding missions to foreign countries, including Libya. The Committees paid particular attention to investigating allegations receiving public attention after the attacks and the associated findings are included in this report.

At the direction of the Speaker of the House of Representatives and the Majority Leader, the coordinated oversight work and assessments made to date are being presented to the Members of the House Republican Conference in this interim progress report. The Committees will continue to review available information, and to interview sources as they come forward. This progress report will be updated as warranted.

<u>**Findings**</u>

This progress report reveals a fundamental lack of understanding at the highest levels of the State Department as to the dangers presented in Benghazi, Libya, as well as a concerted attempt to insulate the Department of State from blame following the terrorist attacks. The Committees' majority staff summarizes findings to date as follows:

Before the Attacks:

- After the U.S.-backed Libyan revolution ended the Gadhafi regime, **the U.S. government did not deploy sufficient U.S. security elements to protect U.S. interests and personnel that remained on the ground.**

- **Senior State Department officials knew that the threat environment in Benghazi was high and that the Benghazi compound was vulnerable and unable to withstand an attack, yet the Department continued to systematically withdraw security personnel.**

- **Repeated requests for additional security were denied at the highest levels of the State Department.** For example, an April 2012 State Department cable bearing Secretary Hillary Clinton's signature acknowledged then-Ambassador Cretz's formal request for additional security assets but ordered the withdrawal of security elements to proceed as planned.

- **The attacks were not the result of a failure by the Intelligence Community (IC) to recognize or communicate the threat.** The IC collected considerable information about the threats in the region, and disseminated regular assessments to senior U.S. officials warning of the deteriorating security environment in Benghazi, which included threats to American interests, facilities, and personnel.

- **The President, as Commander-in-Chief, failed to proactively anticipate the significance of September 11 and provide the Department of Defense with the authority to launch offensive operations beyond self-defense.** Defense Department assets were correctly positioned for the general threat across the region, but the assets were not authorized at an alert posture to launch offensive operations beyond self-defense, and were provided no notice to defend diplomatic facilities.

During the Attacks:

- On the evening of September 11, 2012, **U.S. security teams on the ground in Benghazi exhibited extreme bravery** responding the attacks by al-Qa'ida-affiliated groups against the U.S. mission.

- **Department of Defense officials and military personnel reacted quickly to the attacks in Benghazi.** The effectiveness of their response was hindered on account of U.S. military forces not being properly postured to address the growing threats in northern Africa or to respond to a brief, high-intensity attack on U.S. personnel or interests across much of Africa.

2

After the Attacks:

- **The Administration willfully perpetuated a deliberately misleading and incomplete narrative that the attacks evolved from a political demonstration caused by a YouTube video.** U.S. officials on the ground reported – and video evidence confirms – that demonstrations outside the Benghazi Mission did not occur and that the incident began with an armed attack on the facility. Senior Administration officials knowingly minimized the role played by al-Qa'ida-affiliated entities and other associated groups in the attacks, and decided to exclude from the discussion the previous attempts by extremists to attack U.S. persons or facilities in Libya.

- **Administration officials crafted and continued to rely on incomplete and misleading talking points.** Specifically, after a White House Deputies Meeting on Saturday, September 15, 2012, the Administration altered the talking points to remove references to the likely participation of Islamic extremists in the attacks. The Administration also removed references to the threat of extremists linked to al-Qa'ida in Benghazi and eastern Libya, including information about at least five other attacks against foreign interests in Benghazi. Senior State Department officials requested – and the White House approved – that the details of the threats, specifics of the previous attacks, and previous warnings be removed to insulate the Department from criticism that it ignored the threat environment in Benghazi.

- **Evidence rebuts Administration claims that the talking points were modified to protect classified information or to protect an investigation by the Federal Bureau of Investigation (FBI).** Email exchanges during the interagency process do not reveal any concern with protecting classified information. Additionally, the Bureau itself approved a version of the talking points with significantly more information about the attacks and previous threats than the version that the State Department requested. Thus, the claim that the State Department's edits were made solely to protect that investigation is not credible.

- **The Administration deflected responsibility by blaming the IC for the information it communicated to the public in both the talking points and the subsequent narrative it perpetuated.** Had Administration spokesmen performed even limited due diligence inquiries into the intelligence behind the talking points or requested reports from personnel on the ground, they would have quickly understood that the situation was more complex than the narrative provided by Ambassador Susan Rice and others in the Administration.

- **The Administration's decision to respond to the Benghazi attacks with an FBI investigation, rather than military or other intelligence resources, contributed to the government's lack of candor about the nature of the attack.**

- **Responding to the attacks with an FBI investigation significantly delayed U.S. access to key witnesses and evidence and undermined the government's ability to bring those responsible for the attacks to justice in a timely manner.**

<u>**Policy Considerations**</u>

- **The events in Benghazi reflect the Administration's lack of a comprehensive national security strategy or a credible national security posture in the region.** The United States continues to maintain an inadequate defensive posture in North Africa and the Middle East as a result of the Administration's under-appreciation of the threat that al-Qa'ida and related terrorist groups pose in the region.

- **This singular event will be repeated unless the United States recognizes and responds to the threats we face around the world, and properly postures resources and security assets to counter and respond to those threats.** Until that time, the United States will remain in a reactionary mode and should expect more catastrophes like Benghazi, in which U.S. personnel on the ground perform bravely, but are not provided with the resources for an effective response. As those opposed to U.S. interests will continue to take advantage of perceived U.S. weaknesses, the United States will continue to lose credibility with its allies and face the worst of all possible outcomes in strategically important locations around the world.

- **Congress must maintain pressure on the Administration to ensure the United States takes all necessary steps to find the Benghazi attackers.** It has been more than seven months since the FBI investigation began, and there is very little progress. The risks of treating the Benghazi terrorist attacks as a law enforcement matter rather than a military matter are becoming increasingly clear. The failure to respond more assertively to the attacks and to impose meaningful consequences on those who planned and perpetrated them has contributed to a perception of U.S. weakness and retreat. Al-Qa'ida grew emboldened when the U.S. failed to respond forcibly and effectively to the terrorist attacks on the World Trade Center (1993), U.S. Embassies in East Africa (1998), and the U.S.S. Cole (2000). Active terrorist organizations and potential recruits will also be emboldened to attack U.S. interests if the U.S. fails to hold those responsible for this attack accountable.

- **Congress must also provide an effective counterweight to the Administration's failure to adequately communicate the nature and the extent of the threats our country faces today.** The Administration must do more to develop a coherent and robust national security strategy, and Congress must hold it accountable to do so.

3. House Republican Conference (4/23/2013)

I.   **Prior to the Benghazi attacks, State Department officials in Libya made repeated requests for additional security that were denied in Washington despite ample documentation of the threat posed by violent extremist militias.**

> *I said, "Jim, you know what [is] most frustrating about this assignment? It's not the hardship, it's not the gunfire, it's not the threats. It's dealing and fighting against the people, programs, and personnel who are supposed to be supporting me … For me, the Taliban is on the inside of the building."*
>
> **Testimony of Regional Security Office for the U.S. Mission to Libya Eric Nordstrom before the House Oversight & Government Reform Committee, October 12, 2012**

Setting Up the Benghazi Mission

The Libyan revolution, which led to the overthrow of brutal dictator Muammar Gadhafi, was supported by the United States, most directly in the form of NATO air operations which lasted from March through October of 2011. After Gadhafi was killed in October of that year, the revolution's interim Transitional National Council (TNC) declared the country liberated, and began attempting to establish a democratically-elected government. Around this time, the TNC relocated its center of operations from Benghazi to Tripoli.

A State Department memorandum circulated at the end of 2011 recommended U.S. personnel remain in Benghazi.[1] It explained many Libyans were "strongly" in favor of a U.S. outpost in Benghazi, in part because they believed a U.S. presence in eastern Libya would ensure that the new Tripoli-based government fairly considered eastern Libyan interests.

The memorandum also outlined conditions for a U.S. mission in Benghazi (the "Benghazi Mission,") which were approved by Under Secretary for Management Patrick F. Kennedy.[2] These **conditions included the staffing of five Diplomatic Security (DS) agents**. Diplomatic Security agents manage embassy security programs for the State Department and generally serve as the first line of defense for diplomatic personnel when stationed abroad.[3] They include the Regional Security Officers (RSOs) who serve as each U.S. embassy's principal security advisor.

The Deteriorating Security Environment in Benghazi

In spite of the TNC's efforts after the revolution, U.S. officials were aware that Libya remained volatile. U.S. officials were particularly concerned with the numerous armed militias that operated freely throughout the country, including those in Benghazi with ties to al-Qa'ida

---

[1] (SBU) Action Memorandum for Under Secretary for Management Patrick F. Kennedy, "Future Operations in Benghazi, Libya." December 27, 2011.

[2] *Id.*

[3] "Securing Our Embassies Overseas." U.S. Department of State. Retrieved at: http://www.state.gov/m/ds/about/overview/c9004.htm.

and Ansar Al Sharia.[4] In August 2012, the State Department warned U.S. citizens against traveling to Libya, explaining that "inter-militia conflict can erupt at any time or any place."[5]

The deteriorating security environment in Benghazi throughout 2012 mirrored the declining situation in the rest of Libya. From June 2011 to July 2012, then-Regional Security Officer (RSO) for Libya Eric Nordstrom compiled a **list of more than 200 security incidents in Libya, 50 of which took place in Benghazi**.[6] These incidents included violent acts directed against diplomats and diplomatic facilities, international organizations, and third-country nationals, as well as large-scale militia clashes.[7] U.S. diplomatic facilities in Benghazi came under direct fire twice in the months leading up to September 11, 2012: first in April 2012, when disgruntled Libyan contract guards allegedly threw a small improvised explosive device (IED) over the perimeter wall; and in June 2012, when unknown assailants used an IED to blow a hole in the perimeter wall.

The decisions by the British Embassy, United Nations, and the International Committee of the Red Cross to withdraw their personnel from Benghazi after armed assailants launched directed attacks against each organization were additional major indicators of the increasingly threatening environment. These developments caused Lieutenant Colonel Andrew Wood, who led the U.S. military's efforts to supplement diplomatic security in Libya, to recommend that the State Department consider pulling out of Benghazi altogether. Lieutenant Colonel Wood explained that after the withdrawal of these other organizations, "it was apparent to me that we were the last [Western] flag flying in Benghazi. We were the last thing on their target list to remove from Benghazi."[8]

---

[4] Transcribed interview of Benghazi Assistant Regional Security Officer David Oliveira, October 9, 2012. *See also* "Al-Qaeda in Libya: A Profile," A Report Prepared By The Federal Research Division, Library Of Congress, Under An Interagency Agreement With The Combating Terrorism Technical Support Office's Irregular Warfare Support Program, August 2012, at p. 4.

[5] Travel Warning, U.S. Department of State, Bureau of Consular Affairs. Libya. August 27, 2012. Retrieved at: http://travel.state.gov/travel/cis_pa_tw/tw/tw_5762.html.

[6] U.S. Embassy Tripoli, Libya, Regional Security Office, "Security Incidents since June 2011."

[7] *Id.* See also, the State Department's Accountability Review Board Report for a list of security incidents in Benghazi, Libya during 2012 that were directed at western interests. These include: a March 2012 event in which members of a militia searching for a suspect fire weapons near the U.S. diplomatic compound and attempt to enter; an April 2012 incident in which a U.K. armored diplomatic vehicle is attacked after driving into a local protest; an April 2012 event in which a homemade explosive device is thrown over the U.S. diplomatic compound's north wall; an April 2012 event in which an IED was thrown at the motorcade of the U.N. Special Envoy to Libya in Benghazi; an April 2012 event in which a Special Mission Benghazi principal officer is evacuated from International Medical University (IMU) after a fistfight escalated to gunfire between Tripoli-based trade delegation security personnel and IMU security; a May 2012, event in which the Benghazi International Committee of the Red Cross (ICRC) building was struck by rocket propelled grenades; a June 2012 IED attack on the U.S. diplomatic compound; a June 2012, event in Benghazi where the British Ambassador's convoy was attacked with a rocket propelled grenade and possible AK-47s; a June 2012, event in which a rocket propelled grenade attack is made on the ICRC compound in Misrata (400 km west of Benghazi); a June 2012, attack in which protestors storm the Tunisian consulate in Benghazi; an August 2012 event in which a small bomb is thrown at an Egyptian diplomat's vehicle parked outside of the Egyptian consulate in Benghazi.

[8] Testimony of Lieutenant Colonel Andrew Wood before the House Committee on Oversight and Government Reform, October 10, 2012.

<u>**Security Arrangements for the Benghazi Mission**</u>

Despite mounting security concerns, for most of 2012 the Benghazi Mission was forced to rely on fewer than the approved number of DS agents. Specifically, while the State Department memorandum signed by Under Secretary Kennedy stated that five agents would be provided, this was the case for only 23 days in 2012.[9] Reports indicate the Benghazi Mission was typically staffed with only three DS agents, and sometimes as few as one DS agent.[10]

For its security, the Benghazi Mission used a combination of these few DS agents, as well as a U.S. Military Security Support Team (SST), and two Mobile Security Detachment (MSD) teams provided by the State Department. The SST consisted of 16 Defense Department special operations personnel. As commander of the SST, Lieutenant Colonel Wood reported to the U.S. Chief of Mission in Libya.[11] The MSD teams each consisted of six DS agents, all of whom underwent advanced training to augment security at high-threat posts.[12]

In addition to the security provided by U.S. agencies, the Benghazi Mission used local, unarmed guards, who were responsible for activating the alarm in the event of an attack, as well as four armed members of the February 17 Martyrs Brigade, who were to serve as a quick reaction force. The February 17 Martyrs Brigade was one of the militias that fought for Gadhafi's overthrow. Numerous reports have indicated that the Brigade had extremist connections, and it had been implicated in the kidnapping of American citizens as well as in the threats against U.S. military assets. In addition, on September 8, 2012, just days before Ambassador Stevens arrived in Benghazi, the February 17 Martyrs Brigade told State Department officials that the group would no longer support U.S. movements in the city, including the Ambassador's visit.[13]

<u>**Internal State Department Communications on Security**</u>

State Department officials in Washington acknowledged that the Benghazi Mission lacked sufficient resources to protect its personnel in a deteriorating security environment. However, in a cable signed by Secretary Clinton in April 2012, the State Department settled on a plan to scale back security assets for the U.S. Mission in Libya, including Benghazi. Specifically, despite acknowledging Ambassador Cretz's March 2012 cable requesting additional security assets, the April plan called for the removal of the two remaining MSD teams, the third initially deployed MSD team having been previously removed. This

---

[9] Department of State, Accountability Review Board for Benghazi Attack of September 2012, December 19, 2012, at p. 31; Interview of Regional Security Officer Eric Nordstrom, October 1, 2012.

[10] Interview of Regional Security Officer Eric Nordstrom, October 1, 2012. See also, email from James Bacigalupo to Brian Papanu and David Sparrowgrove, May 7, 2012, 1:01 p.m., Subject: FW: Special Agent Tony Zamudio's TDY Performance in Benghazi.

[11] Testimony of Lieutenant Colonel Andrew Wood before the House Committee on Oversight and Government Reform, October 10, 2012.

[12] "Securing Our Embassies Overseas." U.S. Department of State. Retrieved at: http://www.state.gov/m/ds/about/overview/c9004.htm.

[13] Email from Alec Henderson to John B. Martinec, "RE: Benghazi QRF agreement," (Sep. 9, 2012 11:31 PM).

reduced security footprint was of significant concern to U.S. Ambassador to Libya Gene Cretz, who had requested the continued deployment of both MSD teams, or at least additional DS agents to replace them, and the full five DS agents for the Benghazi Mission that the December 2011 Kennedy memorandum documented would be stationed in Benghazi. His successor, Ambassador Christopher Stevens – who replaced him in May 2012 – shared Ambassador Cretz's concerns.

Critical Cables

During 2012, in numerous communications with the State Department, officials from the U.S. Mission in Libya stress both the inadequacy of security as well as the need for additional personnel. Two critical cables warrant specific mention:

• On **March 28, 2012**, Ambassador Cretz sends a cable to Secretary Clinton requesting additional security assets.

• On **April 19, 2012**, the response cable from the Department of State to Embassy Tripoli, bearing Secretary Clinton's signature, acknowledges Ambassador Cretz's request for additional security but instead articulates a plan to scale back security assets for the U.S. Mission in Libya, including the Benghazi Mission.

In addition, the April 2012 cable from Secretary Clinton recommended that the State Department's Bureau of Diplomatic Security and the U.S. Mission in Libya conduct a "joint re-assessment of the number of DS agents requested for Benghazi."[14] This prompted one frustrated Embassy Tripoli employee to remark to her colleagues that it "looks like no movement on the full complement of [five DS] personnel for Benghazi, but rather a reassessment to bring the numbers lower."[15]

In May 2012, Ambassador Stevens replaced Ambassador Cretz and continued to make requests for additional security. In an email in early June, he told a State Department official that with national elections occurring in Libya in July and August, the U.S. Mission in Libya **"would feel much safer if we could keep two MSD teams with us through this period [to support] our staff and [personal detail] for me and the [Deputy Chief of Mission] and any VIP visitors."**[16] The State Department official replied that due to other commitments and limited resources, "unfortunately, MSD cannot support the request."[17]

---

[14] 12 STATE 38939, April 19, 2012, Signature: CLINTON.
[15] Email from Jennifer A. Larson to Eric Nordstrom, Ambassador Gene Cretz, et al., April 21, 2012, 1:57 p.m., Subject: Re: Tripoli – Request for DS DTY and FTE Support.
[16] Email chain between Ambassador Chris Stevens and John Moretti, June 7, 2012, 3:34 a.m., Subject: MSD/Tripoli.
[17] *Id.*

Despite the denial of Ambassador Stevens' request, Embassy Tripoli officials persisted in their requests for additional security. In July 2012, for example, RSO Eric Nordstrom alerted DS officials in Washington that he intended to submit a formal cable request for an extension of the SST and MSD teams. DS personnel in Washington alerted Mr. Nordstrom that Ms. Charlene Lamb, the Deputy Assistant Secretary for Diplomatic Security, was "reluctant to ask for an SST extension, apparently out of concern that it would be embarrassing to the [State Department] to continue to have to rely on [Defense Department] assets to protect our Mission."[18] Moreover, in response to Mr. Nordstrom's intent to request an MSD extension, Ms. Lamb responded, "NO, I do not [I repeat] not want them to ask for the MSD team to stay!"[19]

Critical Emails

June 7, 2012: Ambassador Stevens asks the State Department to keep the two MSD teams the Clinton April cable ordered removed from Libya. This request is denied.

July 6, 2012: Deputy Assistant Secretary for Diplomatic Security Lamb strongly asserts that Embassy Tripoli should not make a formal request for an extension of the SST and MSD teams.

On July 9, 2012, Ambassador Stevens responded with a cable that stressed that the security conditions in Libya had not met the requisite benchmarks established by the State Department and the U.S. Mission in Libya to warrant initiating a security drawdown.[20] He requested that a sufficient number of security personnel, whether DS agents, or SST or MSD team members, be permitted to stay.[21] Under Secretary Kennedy rejected the request for the SST extension, and both the SST and MSD teams were subsequently withdrawn.[22] Although the State Department made some modest physical security upgrades to the Benghazi Mission, the systematic withdrawal of existing security personnel resulted in a security posture for the Benghazi Mission that the State Department's Accountability Review Board later determined was "inadequate for Benghazi."[23]

Multiple Committees have reviewed the State Department documents cited in the previous sections and remain concerned that the documents do not reconcile with public comments Secretary Clinton made regarding how high in the State Department the security

---

[18] Email from David C. McFarland to Ambassador Chris Stevens, et al., July 9, 2012, 12:24 p.m., Subject: (SBU) Tripoli O-I July 9.

[19] (SBU) Email from Charlene Lamb to State Department personnel. July 6, 2012, 2:59 p m. Subject: Re: Tripoli – Request for extension of TDY Security Personnel.

[20] 12 TRIPOLI 690, July 9, 2012. Signature: STEVENS.

[21] *Id.*

[22] Briefing by Under Secretary for Management Patrick F. Kennedy to Congressional staff, January 2013.

[23] Department of State, Accountability Review Board for Benghazi Attack of September 2012, December 19, 2012, at p. 4.

9

situation and requests were discussed. Despite acknowledging a security request made on April 19, 2012, Secretary Clinton made the following statements before the House Foreign Affairs Committee on January 23, 2013:

- "I have made it very clear that the security cables did not come to my attention or above the assistant secretary level where the ARB [Accountability Review Board] placed responsibility. Where, as I think Ambassador Pickering said, 'the rubber hit the road.'"[24]

- "You know, Congressman, it was very disappointing to me that the [Accountability Review Board] concluded there were inadequacies and problems in the responsiveness of our team here in Washington to the security requests that were made by our team in Libya. And I was not aware of that going on, it was not brought to my attention, but obviously it's something we're fixing and intend to put into place protocols and systems to make sure it doesn't happen again. … Well if I could – 1.43 million cables a year come to the State Department. They are all addressed to me. They do not all come to me. They are reported through the bureaucracy."[25]

In addition, it remains unclear why the State Department chose to reduce security in the face of such a challenging security environment and chose to deny multiple requests from Embassy Tripoli for more assistance. It is clear that funding – or a lack thereof – is not the reason for the reductions in security, as Deputy Assistant Secretary for Diplomatic Security Lamb testified and as emails reviewed by the Committees attest.[26]

Moreover, a lack of funding would not have been at issue with respect to the rejection of the request to extend the deployment of the SST, as that team was provided via the Defense Department at no expense to the State Department. The Administration owes the American people an explanation regarding these unanswered questions, which must be explored in greater depth in the weeks and months ahead.

---

[24] Testimony of Secretary Hillary Clinton before the House Foreign Affairs Committee on January 23, 2013.
[25] Id.
[26] Testimony of Deputy Assistant Secretary of State for Diplomatic Security Charlene Lamb before the House Committee on Oversight and Government Reform, October 10, 2012; email exchange between Assistant Secretary Eric Boswell and Diplomatic Security Chief Financial Officer Robert Baldre, September 28, 2012 ("I do not feel that we have ever been at a point where we sacrificed security due to a lack of funding...Typically Congress has provided sufficient funding.")

3. House Republican Conference (4/23/2013)

II. **The volatile security environment erupted on September 11, 2012, when militias composed of al-Qa'ida-affiliated extremists attacked U.S. interests in Benghazi.**

The Committees have concluded that U.S. security personnel on the ground exhibited extreme bravery in conducting defensive actions and rescue operations in the face of coordinated and sophisticated attacks on the U.S. presence in Benghazi.

Ambassador Stevens' Visit to Benghazi

Ambassador Stevens previously served in Libya as Deputy Chief of Mission (2007 – 2009) and as Special Representative to the Transitional National Council (March 2011 – November 2011). He became U.S. Ambassador to Libya in May 2012. Ambassador Stevens traveled to Benghazi on September 10, 2012, to fill staffing gaps between principal officers in Benghazi and to allow him to reconnect with local contacts. He also planned to attend the establishment of a new American Corner at a local Benghazi school.[27] It has been reported to multiple Committee staff - but not confirmed - that an additional purpose of his visit was to personally assess the security situation in Benghazi in order to lend more urgency to his planned request for additional security resources from Washington.

The Attack on the Benghazi Mission Begins

On September 11, 2012, there were a total of 28 U.S. personnel on the ground at the Benghazi Mission and at the Annex in Benghazi, including Ambassador Stevens.[28]

At appropriately 9:40 PM,[29] dozens of armed men approached the Benghazi Mission and quickly breached the front gate, setting fire to the guard house and main diplomatic building. The attackers were members of extremist groups, including the Libya-based Ansar al-Sharia (AAS) and al-Qa'ida in the Lands of the Islamic Maghreb (AQIM). A State Department officer in the Benghazi Mission's Tactical Operations Center (TOC) immediately notified the Annex, Embassy Tripoli, and State Department Headquarters that the Benghazi Mission was under attack and requested assistance. At no point did U.S. officials on the ground report a protest.[30]

At the time of the attack, Ambassador Stevens, Information Officer Sean Smith, and a DS agent were located in Villa C, the main building of the Benghazi Mission. At approximately 10:00 PM, within 20 minutes of the attack, Ambassador Stevens, Mr. Smith, and the DS agent suffered debilitating effects from smoke inhalation due to the heavy smoke as the main diplomatic building burned. All three tried to escape by crawling along the floor towards a window. Due to the thick smoke, the DS agent unknowingly lost contact with Ambassador

---

[27] American Corners are partnerships between the Public Affairs sections of United States Embassies and host institutions. They provide access to current and reliable information from and about the United States via book collections, the Internet, and through local programming to the general public overseas or abroad.

[28] As described in this timeline, as the attacks were ongoing, seven additional personnel arrived from Tripoli to assist, **bringing the total to 35 U.S. personnel on the ground that night**.

[29] All times local.

[30] Emails from State Department Operations Center to various recipients, September 11, 2012, at 4:05 p.m. Eastern and 6:08 p.m. Eastern.

Stevens and Mr. Smith at some point along the smoke-filled escape route. After crawling out of a window and realizing the Ambassador and Mr. Smith were not with him, the DS agent, under gunfire, repeatedly re-entered the burning building to search for them. As he was doing so, the DS agent also used his radio to call for help. Security officers from other parts of the Benghazi Mission responded and joined the DS agent's search for the missing individuals.

Within 25 minutes of the initial assault, a security team at the Annex was notified and departed for the Benghazi Mission. The security team tried unsuccessfully to secure heavy weapons from militia members encountered along the way, and the team faced some resistance, including gunfire, in getting to the Benghazi Mission. Over the course of the next hour, the Annex security team joined the Benghazi Mission team in searching for Ambassador Stevens and Mr. Smith. Together, the teams repelled sporadic gunfire and RPG fire while assembling all the remaining U.S. personnel at the facility.

While the security officers were able to retrieve the body of Mr. Smith, they were unable to locate Ambassador Stevens. After 90 minutes of repeated attempts to enter the burning main diplomatic building to search for the Ambassador, the teams assessed the security situation had deteriorated to the point that they were forced to abandon their search. The Annex security team loaded all U.S. personnel into vehicles and started the process of departing for the Annex, with the first vehicle departing at 11:15 PM and the second vehicle departing at 11:30 PM. Meanwhile, at approximately 11:10 PM, Defense Department unarmed surveillance aircraft arrived overhead. As the vehicles exited the Benghazi Mission, they encountered heavy gunfire and at least one roadblock in their route to the Annex.

Escalation at the Annex

At approximately 12:30 AM, a team of seven U.S. personnel departed Tripoli. This team arrived in Benghazi at 1:30 AM. At around 5:15 AM, within 15 minutes of the Tripoli team's arrival at the Annex, a short but deadly and coordinated terrorist attack began on the annex.[31] The attack, which included small arms, RPG, and well-aimed mortar fire, mortally wounded two American security officers, Mr. Tyrone Woods and Mr. Doherty, and severely wounded two other U.S. personnel. At 6:05 AM, the 31 survivors from the initial attack on the Benghazi Mission departed the Annex for the Benghazi airport. The surviving Americans departed Benghazi along with three of the four fallen Americans at 7:40 AM on September 12, 2012. The C-17 deployed from Germany departed Tripoli at 7:17 PM, carrying the American survivors and the remains of Mr. Smith, Mr. Woods, and Mr. Doherty. The plane arrived in Ramstein, Germany at 10:19 PM on September 12, 2012.

---

[31] The Tripoli team spent the hours between the arrival at the airport and the arrival at the Annex focused on gaining situational awareness about its main mission, which at the time was locating Ambassador Stevens, who they thought might have been kidnapped.

<u>**Timeline for Ambassador Stevens**</u>

Due to the deteriorating security situation and exhaustive, but unsuccessful search for Ambassador Stevens, the security teams made the decision to evacuate the survivors of the attack on the Benghazi Mission and the remains of Mr. Smith about 90 minutes after the attack began. The evacuation began at approximately 11:30 PM.

At approximately 1:00 AM on September 12, 2012, local Libyans found the remains of Ambassador Stevens in the main diplomatic building at the Benghazi Mission and transported him to the hospital. The Libyans apparently did not realize who the Ambassador was, but they alerted the State Department of his location by using the cell phone that was in the Ambassador's pocket. Libyan doctors tried unsuccessfully to resuscitate Ambassador Stevens upon his arrival at the hospital. At 8:15 PM that evening, his remains were transported from the hospital to the Benghazi airport to begin the journey to Tripoli, to Germany, and then finally home.

<u>**The Defense Department's Timeline**</u>

At 9:59 PM,[32] within twenty minutes of the initial attack, Defense Department officials directed an unarmed, unmanned surveillance aircraft to reposition overhead of the Benghazi Mission. The aircraft arrived at 11:10 PM, approximately 20 minutes before the evacuation of the Benghazi Mission began.

In Washington, at 10:32 PM, an officer in the National Military Command Center at the Pentagon,[33] after receiving initial reports of the incident from the State Department, notified the Office of the Secretary of Defense and the Joint Staff. The information was quickly passed to Secretary of Defense, Mr. Leon E. Panetta, and the Chairman of the Joint Chiefs of Staff, General Martin E. Dempsey. Secretary Panetta and General Dempsey attended a previously scheduled meeting with the President at the White House at 11:00 PM, approximately 80 minutes after the attack began. The Defense Department reported that principals discussed potential responses to the ongoing situation.[34]

Following the White House meeting, Secretary Panetta returned to the Pentagon and convened a series of meetings from 12:00 AM to 2:00 AM with senior officials, including General Dempsey and General Carter F. Ham, the Commander of U.S. Africa Command (AFRICOM), which is the Geographic Combatant Command responsible for U.S. military activities in Libya. They discussed additional response options for Benghazi and the potential outbreak of further violence throughout the region, particularly in Tunis, Tunisia; Cairo, Egypt; and Sana'a, Yemen.

---

[32] Again all times local

[33] The purpose of the National Military Command Center (NMCC) is to support military command and control for the Commander in Chief and the Secretary of Defense (often referred to as the National Command Authority). It is operated by the Joint Staff, to coordinate joint actions and coordinate with the supported Combatant Command. Principally located at the Pentagon, the NMCC broadly consists of multiple people, organizations, command and control systems, procedures, and facilities.

[34] Unclassified timeline, Department of Defense.

To help expedite the movement of forces after the receipt of formal authorization, Pentagon officials verbally conveyed orders to other Combatant Commands.

Specifically, Secretary Panetta verbally directed the deployment of:

1. two Marine Fleet Antiterrorism Security Team (FAST) platoons from Rota, Spain to the Benghazi Mission and Embassy Tripoli;
2. a U.S. European Command (EUCOM) Commander's in-Extremis Force (CIF) to an intermediate staging base in southern Europe; and
3. a special operations force based in the United States to an intermediate staging base in southern Europe.

Concurrently, at 12:30 AM, a six-man security team and one linguist stationed at Embassy Tripoli departed for Benghazi; the team landed in Benghazi at 1:30 AM. At 2:39 AM, officers in the National Military Command Center transmitted the formal authorizations for the deployments of the two Marine FAST platoons and the EUCOM special operations force. At 2:53 AM, the U.S-based special operations force received formal authorization to deploy.

<u>**Analysis of the Defense Department's Response**</u>

Despite the brave and honorable efforts of the individuals on the ground in Benghazi – reinforced by the team from Tripoli – serious concerns regarding the Defense Department's systemic response required extensive review. **Combined with the failure of the President to anticipate the significance of the day and to proactively authorize the Defense Department with an alert posture to launch offensive operations beyond self-defense, forces were provided no notice to defend diplomatic facilities.** Fundamentally, the progress report finds that the Benghazi Mission did not have a sufficient, layered defense designed to fend off an attack until a military response could be deployed to provide a decisive conclusion to an assault. The oversight review of the Defense Department's response, however, has highlighted serious deficiencies in the military's strategic posture in Africa – and the region – which require corrective action and necessitate further examination by congressional committees of jurisdiction.

The military command responsible for this region is U.S. Africa Command (AFRICOM), which officially became one of the Defense Department's six geographic commands in 2008. The Command is responsible for all Department of Defense operations, exercises, and security cooperation efforts on the Continent of Africa, its island nations, and surrounding waters. AFRICOM faces serious resource deficiencies: it does not have any Army or Marine Corps units formally assigned to the command; it shares Air Force and Navy components with U.S. European Command (EUCOM); and it did not have a Commander's in-Extremis Force (CIF) assigned to the command at the time of the attack on September 11, 2012. Moreover,

AFRICOM still lacks a fully constituted CIF with vital and unique enabling capabilities.[35] As a result, when the U.S. needed to respond swiftly to the attacks in Benghazi, the Defense Department did not task AFRICOM. Instead, it was forced to task EUCOM's CIF to respond, which was engaged in a training mission in Croatia.

In addition, because AFRICOM does not have assigned Marine FAST platoons – which are limited-duration, expeditionary security forces capable of responding to emergencies – it had to rely on elements of a FAST unit assigned to EUCOM for response in Benghazi. The Marine FAST platoon in Rota, Spain was hindered in its response because it lacked dedicated airlift at its location; the airlift was in Germany. Even if the airlift had been co-located with the platoon, the platoon would not have been able to arrive in time to save the lives of the four Americans killed in the attack.

The House Armed Services Committee also examined the deployment of stateside-based response forces. The special operations force deployed from the continental United States (CONUS) reached the staging based in southern Europe approximately 24 hours after the initial attack, even though the force was forward-leaning in its preparations as it awaited formal authorization to deploy. The Benghazi attack highlights significant drawbacks of policy options that solely rely on a CONUS-based response force, and the Committee will continue its vigorous oversight of the global disposition of military forces to determine whether the Department of Defense is appropriately postured to more rapidly respond to similar incidents in the future.

In addition, the House Armed Services Committee conducted a review of air assets available to respond to Benghazi. No U.S. government element refused or denied requests for emergency assistance during the crisis. The evidence also does not show there were armed air assets above Benghazi at any time or that any such assets were called off from assisting U.S. personnel on the ground. According to witness testimony, the security officials on the ground did use laser sights, but they did so as an escalatory demonstration of force in an effort to deter some attackers. They were not lasing targets for air assets.[36]

The House Armed Services Committee also examined the question of whether the Defense Department failed to deploy assets to Benghazi because it believed the attack was over after the first phase. The progress report finds that officials at the Defense Department were monitoring the situation throughout and kept the forces that were initially deployed flowing into the region. No evidence has been provided to suggest these officials refused to deploy resources because they thought the situation had been sufficiently resolved.

Similarly, the evidence does not show that military commanders involved in the U.S. military's response to the terrorist attacks in Benghazi were relieved of command, transferred, or encouraged to seek early retirement as a result of their actions in response to the attacks. In the

---

[35] U.S. Africa Command Posture Hearing testimony at the House Armed Services Committee. March 15, 2013.
[36] House Intelligence Community staff briefing with key surviving personnel and U.S. security officials. December 14, 2012.

15

case of General Carter Ham, Commander of U.S. Africa Command (AFRICOM), House Armed Services Committee staff were aware of General Ham's plans to retire well in advance of September 11, 2012.

The disposition of military forces is a reflection of policy, strategy, and resources. Because of a number of factors -- including the lack of a coherent Administration policy toward North Africa; an ad hoc and reactive Administration strategy for addressing threats to U.S. interests in the region; a lack of resources for AFRICOM; and the short duration of the attack -- the Department of Defense was unable to provide an effective military response to the Benghazi attacks. Although responsible military officers and civilian officials within the Department of Defense reacted quickly to the attacks in Benghazi, **the effectiveness of their response was hindered because U.S. military forces were not properly postured** to address the growing threats in northern Africa or to respond to a brief, high-intensity attack on U.S. personnel or interests across much of Africa.

<u>**Analysis of the Intelligence Community's Role**</u>

The Benghazi terrorist attacks did not constitute an intelligence failure. The Intelligence Community collected considerable information about the threat and disseminated regular assessments warning of the deteriorating security environment in Benghazi and risks to American interests, facilities, and personnel.

The House Intelligence Committee examined the question of why the U.S. Intelligence Community (IC) did not provide an immediate and specific tactical warning of the attack in Benghazi. **A review of relevant documents confirmed that the intelligence community did not possess intelligence indicating planning or intentions for an attack on the Benghazi facility on or about September 11, 2012.** The review, however, also demonstrated that any official responsible for security at a U.S. facility or for personnel in Benghazi or the region would have had **sufficient warning of the deteriorating security situation, the corresponding increasing threat, and the expressed intent of anti-U.S. extremists in the region to attack Western and specifically U.S. targets.**

Throughout 2012, there were more than 20 attacks against Western and international interests in Benghazi. The IC monitored these and other extremist activities in North Africa and published hundreds of reports and assessments related to threats to these interests in the region before the September 11 attacks.[37] These reports and assessments, which were available to senior policymakers in the government, including those at the State Department and the White House, made clear that there were serious and credible threats to American interests and facilities in the region and in Benghazi specifically.[38] In addition, these reports and assessments made

---

[37] HPSCI review of intelligence assessments, cables, and reports.
[38] *Id.*

clear that the Benghazi Mission was the subject of credible threats, although no reporting warned of the attack on September 11, 2012.[39]

Other U.S. facilities were raided in September 2012, and known al-Qa'ida-affiliated terrorists were involved in each of the incidents. Also on September 11, Egyptian protesters scaled the walls of the U.S. Embassy in Cairo, Egypt, which at least four senior jihadists with well-documented ties to al-Qa'ida helped instigate.[40] On September 13th, hundreds of Yemenis – including some al-Qa'ida-linked individuals – stormed the U.S. Embassy in Sana'a, Yemen, but were repelled by local security forces. On September 14th, Ansar-al-Sharia-Tunisia (an al-Qa'ida-affiliated group) participated in an attack on the U.S. Embassy in Tunis, Tunisia, and set fire to the nearby American school.

---

[39] Id.
[40] Id.

III.   **After the attacks, the Administration perpetuated a deliberately misleading and incomplete narrative that the violence grew out of a demonstration caused by a YouTube video. The Administration consciously decided not to discuss extremist involvement or previous attacks against Western interests in Benghazi.**

> *The U.S. government immediately had information that the attacks were conducted by al-Qa'ida-affiliated terrorists, yet Administration officials downplayed those connections, and focused on the idea that provocation for violence resulted from a YouTube video.*

<u>Analysis At the Time of the Attack</u>

The U.S. government knew immediately that the attacks constituted an act of terror. In an "Ops Alert" issued shortly after the attack began, the State Department Operations Center notified senior Department officials, the White House Situation Room, and others, that the Benghazi compound was under attack and that "approximately 20 armed people fired shots; explosions have been heard as well."[41] Two hours later, the Operations Center issued an alert that al-Qa'ida linked Ansar al-Sharia (AAS) claimed responsibility for the attack and had called for an attack on Embassy Tripoli.[42] **Neither alert mentioned that there had been a protest at the location of the attacks.**[43] Further, Administration documents provided to the Committees show that there was ample evidence that the attack was planned and intentional. **The coordinated, complex, and deadly attack on the Annex – that included sophisticated weapons – is perhaps the strongest evidence that the attacks were not spontaneous. The question of why a deliberately misleading and incomplete narrative to the contrary was initially perpetuated by the Administration despite the existence of this information has not yet been fully answered and must be addressed as oversight efforts continue.**

<u>Timeline of the Administration's Narrative</u>

In the days after the events, the White House and senior Administration officials sought to portray the attacks as provoked by a YouTube video.[44] The President, Secretary Clinton, White House Press Secretary Jay Carney, and United States Ambassador to the United Nations Susan Rice each made statements denouncing the video and condemning those who purportedly used it to justify their behavior.[45] The President and Secretary Clinton also appeared in a $70,000 advertisement campaign in Pakistan to disavow the video.[46]

---

[41] Email from State Department Operations Center to various recipients, September 11, 2012, 4:05 p.m. Eastern.

[42] Email from State Department Operations Center to various recipients, September 11, 2012, 6:08 p.m. Eastern.

[43] The ARB also concluded that "there was no protest prior to the attacks, which were unanticipated in their scale and intensity."

[44] "Administration Statements on the Attack in Benghazi," The New York Times, September 27, 2012. See also, Remarks by the President to the UN General Assembly, United Nation Headquarters, New York, New York, September 25, 2012, 10:22 a.m.

[45] *Id.*

[46] Found at: http://www.youtube.com/watch?v=6akGlF6g-Zw.

On Sunday, September 16, 2012, Ambassador Rice appeared on five morning television programs to discuss the Administration's account of the attack. In nearly identical statements, she stated that the attack was a spontaneous protest in response to a "hateful video," similar to what transpired in Cairo, Egypt, earlier that day.[47] Rice asserted that "we do not have information at present that leads us to conclude that this was premeditated or preplanned."[48] Her interviews stand in sharp contrast to interviews given on the same morning talk shows by the President of the Libyan National Congress, Mohamad Magarif, who characterized the attack as criminal and preplanned.[49] Further, on that same day and prior to Ambassador Rice's scheduled appearances on the Sunday morning programs, a senior official on the ground in Libya informed senior leaders at the State Department that there was no demonstration prior to the attack.[50]

The Administration echoed Ambassador Rice's statements until September 19 when National Counterterrorism Center (NCTC) Director Matt Olsen testified before the Senate Homeland Security and Government Affairs Committee that our diplomats died "in the course of a terrorist attack on our embassy."[51]

Director Olsen's testimony marked a significant shift in the Administration's rhetoric. Immediately afterward, Administration officials began referring to the event as a terrorist attack. On September 20, 2012, Mr. Carney stated that, "it is, I think, self-evident that what happened in Benghazi was a terrorist attack."[52] Similarly, on September 21, Secretary Clinton stated, "What happened in Benghazi was a terrorist attack, and we will not rest until we have tracked down and brought to justice the terrorists who murdered four Americans."[53] On October 9, the State Department held a conference call briefing for reporters in which Department officials publicly acknowledged that there had been no protest outside the Benghazi diplomatic facility prior to the assault. Members should note that the following day, senior State Department officials were scheduled to appear before the House Oversight and Government Reform Committee.

<u>Analysis of the Evolving Drafts of the Talking Points</u>

To protect the State Department, the Administration deliberately removed references to al-Qa'ida-linked groups and previous attacks in Benghazi in the talking points used by Ambassador Rice, thereby perpetuating the deliberately misleading and incomplete narrative that the attacks evolved from a demonstration caused by a YouTube video.

---

[47] "Timeline: How Benghazi attack, probe unfolded," CBS News, November 2, 2012.

[48] *Id.*

[49] Transcript of Meet the Press interview found at: http://www.cbsnews.com/8301-3460_162-57513819/face-the-nation-transcripts-september-16-2012-libyan-pres-magariaf-amb-rice-and-sen-mccain/.

[50] Email from William V. Roebuck to Beth Jones, "Update: 9-16-12," (Sept. 16, 2012 8:38 AM).

[51] Testimony of National Counterterrorism Center Director Matt Olsen before the Senate Committee on Homeland Security and Governmental Affairs, September 19, 2012.

[52] "Timeline: How Benghazi attack, probe unfolded," CBS News, November 2, 2012.

[53] *Id.*

The Administration's talking points were developed in an interagency process that focused more on protecting the reputation and credibility of the State Department than on explaining to the American people the facts surrounding the fatal attacks on U.S. diplomatic facilities and personnel in Libya. Congressional investigators were given access to email exchanges, in which White House and senior Department officials discussed and edited the talking points. **Those emails clearly reveal that Administration officials intentionally removed references in the talking points to the likely participation by Islamic extremists, to the known threat of extremists linked to al-Qa'ida in Benghazi and eastern Libya, and to other recent attacks against foreign interests in Benghazi.**

The talking points in question were initially created for the House Intelligence Committee, after a briefing by then-Director of the CIA, David Petraeus.[54] Members of the Committee sought guidance on how to discuss the attacks publicly and in an unclassified manner. The CIA generated the initial drafts of the unclassified talking points and provided them to other officials within the Executive Branch for clearance. The initial CIA draft circulated to the interagency group included references to:

1. previous notifications provided to Embassy Cairo of social media reporting encouraging jihadists to break into the Embassy;
2. indications that Islamic extremists participated in the events in Benghazi;
3. potential links to Ansar al-Sharia;
4. information about CIA-produced assessments of the threat from extremists linked to al-Qa'ida in Benghazi and eastern Libya; and
5. information about five previous attacks against foreign interests in Benghazi since April 2012.[55]

When draft talking points were sent to officials throughout the Executive Branch, senior State Department officials requested the talking points be changed to avoid criticism for ignoring the threat environment in Benghazi. Specifically, State Department emails reveal senior officials had "serious concerns" about the talking points, because Members of Congress might attack the State Department for "not paying attention to Agency warnings" about the growing threat in Benghazi.[56] This process to alter the talking points can only be construed as a deliberate effort to mislead Congress and the American people.

After slight modifications were made on Friday, September 14, a senior State Department official again responded that the edits did not "resolve all my issues or those of my building leadership," and that the Department's leadership was "consulting with [National Security Staff]."[57] Several minutes later, White House officials responded by stating that the State

---

[54] House Intelligence Committee classified briefing with Director Petraeus, September 14, 2012.
[55] Draft talking points circulated via email within interagency at 6:52 p.m., September 14, 2012.
[56] Email from Senior State Department official to interagency team at 7:39 p.m., Friday, September 14, 2012.
[57] Email from Senior State Department official to interagency team at 9:24 p.m., Friday, September 14, 2012.

20

Department's concerns would have to be taken into account and asserted further discussion would occur the following morning at a Deputies Committee Meeting.[58]

After the Deputies Committee Meeting on Saturday, September 15, 2012, at which any interagency disagreement would be resolved by the White House,[59] a small group of officials from both the State Department and the CIA worked to modify the talking points to their final form to reflect the decision reached in the Deputies meeting.[60] The actual edits were made by a current high-ranking CIA official.[61] **Those edits struck any and all suggestions that the State Department had been previously warned of threats in the region, that there had been previous attacks in Benghazi by al-Qa'ida-linked groups in Benghazi and eastern Libya, and that extremists linked to al-Qa'ida may have participated in the attack on the Benghazi Mission.**[62] The talking points also excluded details about the wide availability of weapons and experienced fighters in Libya, an exacerbating factor that contributed to the lethality of the attacks.[63]

Administration officials have said that modification of **the talking points was an attempt to protect classified information and an investigation by the FBI,**[64] but the evidence refutes these assertions. Administration officials transmitted and reviewed different drafts of the talking points - many of which included reference to al-Qa'ida-associated groups, including Ansar al-Sharia - over unsecure email systems. Also, **there were no concerns about protecting classified information in the email traffic.** Finally, the FBI approved a version of the talking points with significantly more information about the attacks and previous threats than the version requested by the State Department. Claims that the edits were made to protect the FBI investigation are not credible.[65]

---

[58] A Deputies meeting is an interagency gathering – often done in person or over a secure video conferencing system (SVTC) -- at which deputies of all relevant departments advocate for their departments' positions. Deputies typically reach a consensus, or the White House will provide a decision if there is continued dispute. In this case, the Deputies met by (SVTC) on the morning of Saturday, September 15, 2012. While Congress has not yet been given minutes of that meeting, it appears to have included representatives of the State Department, the CIA, DOD, the FBI/DOJ, and the White House, represented by National Security Staff.

[59] This appears to directly contradict White House Spokesman Jay Carney's comments at the Daily Press Briefing on November 28, 2012: "The White House and the State Department have made clear that the single adjustment that was made to those talking points by either of those two -- of these two institutions were changing the word 'consulate' to 'diplomatic facility,' because 'consulate' was inaccurate. Those talking points originated from the intelligence community. They reflect the IC's best assessments of what they thought had happened."

[60] Email to Ambassador Rice, Saturday, September 15, 2012, discussing the results of the Deputies meeting.

[61] Final version of talking points circulated at 9:52 a.m., September 15, 2012.

[62] Id.

[63] Id.

[64] CIA Acting Director Michael Morrell suggested at a hearing before the Senate Select Committee on Intelligence that the talking points were changed to protect an ongoing FBI investigation. See, e.g., http://www.cbsnews.com/9301-250_162-57555984/who-changed-the-benghazi-talking-points/

[65] Email from Senior State Department Official to second Senior State Department Official explaining that the FBI "did not have major concerns" with the talking points and "offered only a couple minor suggestions." 8:59 p.m., September 14, 2012.

3. House Republican Conference (4/23/2013)

Key Quotes

"The White House and the State Department have made clear that the single adjustment that was made to those talking points by either of those two -- of these two institutions were changing the word 'consulate' to 'diplomatic facility,' because 'consulate' was inaccurate. Those talking points originated from the intelligence community. They reflect the IC's best assessments of what they thought had happened." – *White House Spokesman Jay Carney, White House Daily Press Briefing, November 28, 2012*

"Secondly, because the process was one of declassifying classified information, and in that process the talking points that were provided to Ambassador Rice to members of Congress and to others, including myself in the executive branch, were written in the way that was presented by Ambassador Rice." – *White House Spokesman Jay Carney, White House Daily Press Briefing, January 8, 2013*

Ambassador Rice received the approved talking points in advance of her appearances on Sunday, September 16, 2012 on various television programs.[66] **She was informed that the talking points were created for Congressional members, and modified to protect State Department equities and the FBI investigation.**[67] Ambassador Rice then appeared the next morning on five Sunday morning talk shows, during which she focused on the attacks being provoked by the Cairo events and the "hateful video."

The Administration made a conscious decision to focus on the deliberately misleading and incomplete narrative that demonstrations protesting a YouTube video evolved into attacks on the Benghazi Mission. This decision resulted in a senior Administration official appearing on major national news programs to discuss a terrorist attack against the United States without mentioning the known threat to the region by al Qa'ida affiliates, the likely participation by Ansar al-Sharia in the incident, and the previous attacks on Western interests in Benghazi.

---

[66] Email to Ambassador Rice, Saturday, September 15, 2012.
[67] *Id.*

IV.   **The Administration's investigations and reviews of the Benghazi attacks highlight its failed security policies leading to the attacks while undermining the ability of the United States government to bring the perpetrators to justice.**

A Compromised FBI Criminal Investigation

The Administration responded to the Benghazi attacks with an FBI investigation, as opposed to a more thorough military or intelligence response. Regrettably, the FBI simply did not have the ability to access the location of the attacks with sufficient speed to ensure that all evidence was accumulated as quickly as possible. Due to security concerns and bureaucratic entanglements among the Departments of Justice, State, and Defense,[68] the FBI team investigating the terrorist attacks did not access the crime scene until more than three weeks later, on October 4, 2012. During this time, the site was not secured, and curious locals and international media were able to pick through the burned-out remains of the U.S. facility. The FBI spent less than one day collecting evidence at the Benghazi Mission. FBI officials indicated that the security situation delayed and deterred a more thorough investigation of the site.

The FBI has interviewed all U.S. Government personnel on the ground during the attacks, but has encountered difficulty accessing other witnesses or suspects. For example, one suspect jailed in connection with the attacks, Ali Harzi, was released for lack of evidence on January 7, 2013, by Tunisian authorities. FBI agents questioned Mr. Harzi in December 2012, but the questioning did not result in sufficient information for the FBI to stop his release. Media reports also indicate that the FBI has recently been given access to question an individual of interest, Faraj al-Shibli, in Libya. The scope of that questioning is currently unconfirmed, and it remains unclear whether the access is sufficient enough to yield evidence that could be used to prosecute Shibli or other individuals.

FBI Director Robert Mueller testified before the Senate Select Committee on Intelligence (SSCI) that the investigation is complicated by the lack of security in eastern Libya.[69] Without significant progress in finding and questioning suspects, it appears that the decision to proceed with an FBI investigation – presumably with the intention of obtaining a criminal indictment in U.S. courts – was ill-advised. For instance, the United States responded to the attacks against U.S. embassies in Africa in the 1990s and against the U.S.S. Cole in 2000 with criminal investigations. On their own, those investigations failed to bring many of those responsible to justice and likely encouraged further terrorist activity. This approach is not the most effective method of responding to terrorist attacks against U.S. interests in foreign countries.

It was only after the September 11, 2001 attacks, when the United States responded to terrorism with military force, that the government successfully brought some of the perpetrators of those attacks and the previous attacks to justice. Terrorists who successfully attack U.S.

---

[68] The Department of Defense offered to provide a U.S. military security team to accompany the FBI team. This option was not pursued.
[69] Senate Select Committee on Intelligence, World Wide Threats Hearing, March 13, 2013.

interests are not deterred by criminal investigations. Because members of terrorist organizations that attack U.S. interests around the world are conducting more than a crime, they must be responded to accordingly to be thwarted.

The Administration's decision to respond to the terrorist attacks with an FBI criminal investigation did a public disservice in two ways. First, it prevented the American public from fully understanding the motivation of the terrorist attacks and the ongoing nature of the threat against U.S. interests in the region. Second, by using a compromised criminal investigation as a justification to initially withhold significant information, it skewed the public's perception and understanding of the events before, during, and after the terrorist attacks, thereby eroding public trust and confidence in the information the Administration did eventually share and release in the aftermath.

An Inadequate State Department Accountability Review Board Process

The State Department's Accountability Review Board (ARB) highlights the "systemic failures" of Washington, D.C.-based decision-makers that left the Benghazi Mission with significant security shortfalls. Yet, the Board also failed to conduct an appropriately thorough and independent review of which officials bear responsibility for those decisions.

After Secretary Clinton determined that the attacks that led to the deaths of Ambassador Stevens, Information Officer Sean Smith, and U.S. security personnel, and former U.S. Navy SEALs, Glen Doherty and Tyrone Woods on September 11, 2012, involved loss of life at or related to a U.S. mission abroad,[70] she convened an Accountability Review Board, headed by Thomas Pickering, a retired U.S. ambassador, to examine the facts and circumstances of the attacks and to report findings and recommendations.[71]

The ARB made several findings that are consistent with facts uncovered in the Committees' ongoing investigations:

1. there was no protest prior to the attack, which was "unanticipated" in "scale and intensity";
2. there was a "pervasive realization among personnel who served in Benghazi that the Special Mission was not a high priority for Washington when it came to security-related requests"; and
3. regarding the Special Mission's security posture, there was an inadequate number of DS staff in Benghazi on the day of the attack. [do we mean "was" or "was not?]

---

[70] "Convening of an Accountability Review Board To Examine the Circumstances Surrounding the Deaths of Personnel Assigned in Support of the U.S. Government Mission to Libya in Benghazi, Libya on September 11, 2012," Notice by the Department of State, Federal Register, October 4, 2012, available at https://www.federalregister.gov/articles/2012/10/04/2012-24504/convening-of-an-accountability-review-board-to-examine-the-circumstances-surrounding-the-deaths-of.
[71] *Id.*

A number of the ARB findings, however, are inconsistent with facts uncovered by the Committees and appear to incorrectly place or imply blame for the attacks:

- The Board determined "systemic failures" in Washington, D.C. led to decisions that left the Benghazi Mission with significant security shortfalls. Specifically, the Board found key leadership failures in the Diplomatic Security (DS) Bureau as well as in the Bureau of Near Eastern Affairs (NEA) which led to confusion over decision-making in relation to security and policy in Benghazi. These factors likely contributed to the insufficient priority given to the Benghazi Mission's security-related requests. The Board's finding regarding the security decisions in Benghazi, however, was limited to Diplomatic Security professionals and the Bureau of Near Eastern Affairs. **The Committees' review shows that the leadership failure in relation to security and policy in Benghazi extended to the highest levels of the State Department, including Secretary Clinton.**

- The Board attempted to shift blame to Congress, asserting Congress "must do its part ... and provide necessary resources to the State Department to address security risks and meet mission imperatives." This finding implies that a lack of appropriations from Congress led to the security decisions in Benghazi. **Under direct questioning from Members of Congress, State Department personnel have testified that funding was not a reason for the drawdown of security levels in Benghazi.**[72]

- The **Board determined there was no breach of duty by any single U.S. Government employee,** citing legal limits on the definition of breach of duty. The Committees find the Board's determination in the area of disciplinary action especially unsatisfactory, as the Board ascertained the gross mismanagement among senior leadership at the State Department contributed to the inadequate security for the Benghazi Mission.[73] **The House Foreign Affairs Committee expects to consider anticipated legislation to provide future Accountability Review Boards with the authority to recommend disciplinary action against a State Department employee when misconduct or unsatisfactory performance leads to a security incident.**

- The Board also determined the security systems and procedures in place were implemented properly. The Committees are deeply concerned with this determination as extensive oversight work uncovered repeated failures by senior State Department officials to support the U.S. Mission in Libya's security requests, even in the face of overwhelming evidence that such security was needed.

---

[72] Testimony of Deputy Assistant Secretary of State for Diplomatic Security Charlene Lamb before the House Committee on Oversight and Government Reform, October 10, 2012; email exchange between Assistant Secretary Eric Boswell and Diplomatic Security Chief Financial Officer Robert Baldre, September 28, 2012 ("I do not feel that we have ever been at a point where we sacrificed security due to a lack of funding...Typically Congress has provided sufficient funding.")

[73] Department of State, Accountability Review Board for Benghazi Attack of September 2012, Dec. 19, 2012, p. 4.

25

- The Board echoed other Administration attempts to lay blame for the Benghazi attacks at the feet of the Intelligence Community (IC) by highlighting that U.S. intelligence provided no immediate and specific warning of the attack. A Congressional review of the facts reveals that, while the IC had no awareness of an imminent attack on the TMF in Benghazi, the **IC provided State Department officials and others countless reports on the deteriorating security situation in Benghazi and the risks faced by U.S. diplomatic personnel**.

<u>**Analysis of the Accountability Review Board**</u>

While the work of the ARB provides some insight into the decisions leading up to the attacks, its report fundamentally fails to satisfy its legislative mandate to conduct a thorough review of accountability within the State Department.

While Secretary Hillary Clinton claimed she accepted "responsibility" for Benghazi, the Committees remain concerned that the ARB neglected to directly examine the role that she and her Deputy Secretaries played in overseeing the gross mismanagement or the "systemic failures" within the Department. The Committees note the Board has failed to provide a satisfactory explanation as to why it did not interview Secretary Clinton or her Deputies. In a similar vein, it is unclear why the ARB report made no reference to Under Secretary Patrick Kennedy's decision to withdraw a SST from Libya, despite multiple warnings from Ambassador Stevens of a deteriorating security environment. The ARB's complete omission of the roles played by these individuals undermines the credibility of its findings and recommendations.

The Committees have determined that this Accountability Review Board was staffed by current and former State Department employees. The Board's reluctance to undertake a more comprehensive investigation, and to make more forceful recommendations, may have stemmed from the fact that the State Department's decisions and actions were investigated internally, undermining public confidence that the review was objective and conducted by individuals free from institutional bias. The current "in-house orientation" of an ARB may have provided a built-in motivation or prejudice, even for the best-intentioned investigators, to deflect blame and to avoid holding specific individuals accountable, especially superiors. The House Foreign Affairs Committee will soon introduce legislation to increase the ARB's independence and objectivity. Although the report did provide some helpful recommendations regarding various State Department procedures, the Committees conclude it stopped well short of a full review of the policymakers, policies, and decisions that created the inadequate security situation that existed at the Benghazi Mission on September 11, 2012.

V.   **The Benghazi attacks revealed fundamental flaws in the Administration's approach to securing U.S. interests and personnel around the world.**

> *U.S. personnel on the ground in Benghazi on September 11, 2012 responded bravely and honorably, using all resources available to defend themselves and their colleagues against dozens of armed militants. The Committees' review of the attacks against U.S. interests revealed several policy failures that deserve attention and remediation if the United States hopes to avoid further catastrophes like that day.*

First, the attacks revealed the United States' poor defensive posture in North Africa and the Near East. The Committees are concerned that the Administration positioned the nation's military assets in the region and established force protection requirements for U.S. personnel in Libya based, in large part, on the absence of specific, tactical intelligence warnings of an imminent attack on U.S. facilities in Benghazi. This decision did not properly account for the generalized threat posed by al-Qa'ida-affiliated groups and other extremists, the many attacks that had already occurred in and around Benghazi, or the dynamic and evolving nature of these groups.

The attack also demonstrated the limitations of the U.S. military capability and capacity to respond to "Benghazi-style" attacks in the region. The strategic posture of U.S. AFRICOM requires continued focus and oversight. While the Defense Department contends that a dedicated AFRICOM special operations force could not have arrived in time to assist the efforts on the ground in Benghazi, the force's response time would have been dependent on the precise position of those assets and whether enablers were immediately available to such a force. There is a critical link between U.S. forward presence in Europe and the military's ability to respond to contingencies in Northern Africa in particular, and the broader Middle East, in general. Additional cuts to U.S. force posture within EUCOM will likely undermine AFRICOM's ability to conduct operations on the continent.[74]

Second, the Administration failed to acknowledge a deteriorating security environment and respond to the extensive body of intelligence reporting that did exist. The IC collected considerable information about the threats in the region, and disseminated regular assessments warning of the deteriorating security environment in Benghazi, evidenced by previous events targeting American interests, facilities, and personnel. Despite ample warning, the Administration simply failed to provide adequate security arrangements to reflect the level of known risk and threats faced by U.S. personnel in the region. Moreover, in response to the intelligence available and in anticipation that a terrorist attack could occur on the anniversary of the terrorist attacks of September 11, 2001, the military apparently raised its force protection levels at regional military installations. But the military did not increase its readiness or posture

---

[74] Testimony from EUCOM Commander, Admiral Stavridis, March 15, 2013, before the Armed Services Committee, "They [bases in Europe] are the forward operating bases for 21st century security. They allow us to support Carter Ham in Africa. They allow us to support Jim Mattis in the Levant, in the near Middle East, and indeed in Central Asia. So geography matters as well."

assets to respond to unforeseen events. The Administration's lack of sufficient consideration of the broader security and political context continues to lend doubt to the U.S. Government's ability to respond to, or prevent, the next attack on U.S. assets and interests in Libya and the region.

Third, the attacks highlight the failure of the Administration to properly plan for the post-Gadhafi environment. After the U.S.-backed Libyan revolution resulted in the end of the Gadhafi regime, the Administration failed to provide sufficient U.S. security elements to protect U.S. interests on the ground. Despite repeated requests for further security by U.S. officials working in the high-risk, high-threat environment, requests were denied by senior leadership at the State Department. Moreover, the Administration does not have a clear policy that defines U.S. interests or a strategy designed to comprehensively secure U.S. interests in the region and achieve U.S. policy goals. Thus, the Administration was willing to provide necessary force to expel Gadhafi in support of the Libyan opposition, yet it simply failed to provide sufficient protection for the U.S. personnel and interests that remained.

Fourth, the events after the attacks present similar concerns. The FBI was seriously hamstrung in its ability to quickly access the Benghazi site, and its investigation and interview of key witnesses were too slow. The Administration did not ensure adequate security for a swift, thorough, and accurate FBI investigation. It should have considered deploying other non-civilian agencies to perform the mission. A civilian investigative team is not the most effective resource to investigate a national security attack in an unstable region with inadequate security.

Fifth, the Administration perpetuated a deliberately misleading and incomplete narrative that the attacks evolved from a political demonstration by minimizing the role played by al-Qa'ida-affiliated entities and other groups. White House officials directed that talking points be changed to protect the reputation of the State Department, highlighting the overall desire to dismiss the continued threat posed by al-Qa'ida-affiliated and other extremist groups in the region. Specifically, the facts reveal that the talking points were modified to remove references to likely participation by Islamic extremists. They were also altered to remove references to the threat of extremists linked to al-Qa'ida in Benghazi and eastern Libya, including information about at least five other attacks against foreign interests in Benghazi by unidentified assailants, including a June 2012 attack against the British Ambassador's convoy. It is clear that the State Department expressed concerns – and was backed by the White House – that the information be removed to avoid criticism for ignoring the general threat environment in Benghazi.

In sum, the events in Benghazi thus reflect this Administration's lack of a comprehensive national security strategy or effective defense posture in the region. **This singular event will be repeated unless the United States recognizes and responds to the threats faced around the world, and properly positions resources and security assets to reflect those threats.** Until that time, the United States will remain in a reactionary mode and should expect many more

3. House Republican Conference (4/23/2013)

situations like Benghazi, where those on the ground act bravely, but the United States simply fails to provide the resources for an adequate response. Ultimately, those opposed to U.S. interests will continue to take advantage of perceived U.S. weakness, the United States will continue to lose credibility with our allies, and we will face the worst of all possible outcomes in strategically important locations around the world.

Congress must maintain pressure on the Administration to ensure that the United States takes all necessary steps to find the Benghazi attackers. Congress will also articulate to the American people the true nature of the threats faced around the world, and advocate for a more robust and proper defense posture for the United States. The Committees expect the Administration to fully comply with all current and future document requests about the attacks, and the Committees will continue reviewing several outstanding questions detailed below.

In light of the facts and unanswered questions documented in this progress report, the House Armed Services Committee will continue to review:

- The U.S. government's assumptions and risk analysis – as reflected in the U.S. military and State Department posture in Libya and the region – given the historic importance and activities of extremists and al-Qa'ida-associated groups in Libya;

- The precise nature of the intelligence, if any, that was lost by the failure of U.S. officials to gain quick access to the U.S. facilities in Benghazi after the attacks;

- U.S. policymakers' assumptions about al-Qa'ida, the global jihad, and the use of applying U.S. military resources to weak states, ungoverned spaces, and insecure contexts;

- The 1) operational capability, 2) resourcing, 3) readiness, and 4) intelligence collection and analysis of our forces in light of the Benghazi attacks;

- The implications of the events in Benghazi for conventional forces', the Fleet Anti-Terrorism Forces' (FAST), and special operations forces' training, readiness, resourcing, and posture;

- The U.S. Africa Command's Commander in-Extremis Force (CIF) for fully operational capability and posture; and

- The intelligence, surveillance, and reconnaissance (ISR) capability, capacity, and requirements analysis of our forces in light of the Benghazi attacks.

The House Foreign Affairs Committee will continue to review:

- The ARB process and the need to create a more independent review body with greater ability to make disciplinary recommendations;

- The responsibility of senior State Department officials for the failure to provide proper security prior to the Benghazi attacks;

- Needed improvements in embassy security; and

- The State Department's alertness to the overall political climate and resultant terrorist threats in high-risk environments.

The House Judiciary Committee will continue to review:

- The Administration's decision to respond to the attacks with an FBI investigation;

- The U.S. government's access to specific detainees and potential suspects; and

- The status of the FBI investigation.

The House Oversight and Government Reform Committee will continue to review:

- Interagency coordination, information sharing, and decision making leading up to, during, and after the attacks in Benghazi, particularly with a view toward both preventing and improving the response to similar attacks in the future;

- The Administration's lack of transparency and accountability, including providing misleading information to the public and Congress;

- The inadequacy of the Administration's investigation of the attacks, including the decision to treat the attacks as a law enforcement matter and the shortcomings of the Accountability Review Board;

- The Administration's treatment of personnel and whistleblowers following the attack on Benghazi; and

- Any new or outstanding issues raised by whistleblowers.

- The Committee will also amplify and support the efforts of other Committees, as requested.

The House Permanent Select Committee on Intelligence will continue to review:

- The IC's success at identifying and tracking the attackers;

- The IC's information sharing among agencies and the incorporation of on-the-ground information into formal intelligence channels to better allow analysts to review such information in a timely fashion; and

- The value of on-the-ground reporting versus other intelligence reporting in a crisis.

Appendix I: Oversight Activities by Committee

The Committees have thus far reviewed tens of thousands of documents, including agency and White House emails, intelligence reporting, summaries of FBI interviews, classified and unclassified cables, and the various versions of the talking points created for HPSCI and used by Ambassador Susan Rice. They have also spoken with dozens of government officials in both interviews and open testimony. As the Committees' reviews are ongoing, they expect full cooperation and compliance by the Administration with all past and future document and interview requests.

<u>House Armed Services Committee:</u>

- Systematic monitoring of intelligence traffic and multiple secure calls with DoD.

- HASC staff briefings and discussions with outside experts.

- HASC Chairman formal letters of inquiry to:

  - President Barack Obama
  - General Martin Dempsey, Chairman of the Joint Chiefs of Staff
  - Vice Admiral Kurt Tidd, Director of Operations, The Joint Staff
  - Lieutenant General Flynn, Director of the Defense Intelligence Agency
  - General Carter Ham, Commander of U.S. Africa Command (AFRICOM)
  - Admiral William McRaven, Commander of U.S. Special Operations Command (SOCOM)

- September 12, 2012: Staff classified briefing on Weapons of Mass Destruction (WMD) in Libya.

- September 19, 2012: Full Committee hearing on the attack in Benghazi.

- October 18, 2012: Staff classified briefing on intelligence and operations related to the attack in Benghazi.

- October 29, 2012: Chairman letter to the President.

- November 20, 2012: Staff classified briefing on intelligence and operations related to the attack in Benghazi.

- November 16, 2012: Staff participated in DoD briefing to House Members.

- November 29, 2012: Full Committee, Members only, briefing on the attack in Benghazi.

- February 6, 2013: Full Committee briefing on intelligence and operations related to North and East Africa.

- March 15, 2013: Full Committee hearing on the posture of U.S. EUCOM and U.S. AFRICOM.

House Foreign Affairs Committee:

- HFAC sent six letters – individually and collaboratively with sister Committees – requesting documents and information from the State Department. Obtained a public commitment by Secretary Kerry to reassess the restricted manner by which documents have been provided to the Committee.

- Reviewed thousands of pages of documents and information produced by the State Department pursuant to this investigation. It has interviewed State Department and DoD personnel.

- Approached a DS agent who was on the scene in a not-yet-successful effort to obtain additional information. This individual wishes to remain anonymous.

- Building on its Benghazi investigation, the Committee is taking a broader look at embassy security to determine whether the State Department is adequately protecting its personnel at other diplomatic facilities. Improving embassy security is a Committee legislative priority. The Committee is particularly concerned about, and is currently investigating, the security situation at the U.S. Embassy in Afghanistan.

- November 14, 2012: Classified briefing for Committee Members and cleared staff.

- November 15, 2012: Full Committee hearing with private experts entitled, "Benghazi and Beyond: What Went Wrong on September 11, 2012 and How to Prevent it from Happening at other Frontline Posts, Part I."

- December 19, 2012: Classified briefing for Committee Members and cleared staff with Ambassador Pickering and Admiral Mullen, Chair and Vice Chair of the Accountability Review Board.

- December 20, 2012: Full Committee hearing with State Department Deputy Secretaries Burns and Nides entitled, "Benghazi Attack, Part II: The Accountability Review Board Report."

- January 23, 2013: Full Committee hearing with Secretary of State Hillary Clinton entitled, "Terrorist Attack in Benghazi: The Secretary of State's View." (Committee Members submitted more than 100 Questions For the Record and have received responses to nearly all.)

3. House Republican Conference (4/23/2013)

<u>**House Judiciary Committee:**</u>

- Following the September 11, 2012, Benghazi, Libya terrorist attack, House Judiciary Committee staff and members received classified briefings from IC components, including the FBI.

<u>**House Committee on Government and Oversight Reform**</u>

- September 20, 2012: Letter from National Security Subcommittee Chairman Jason Chaffetz to Secretary of State Hillary Clinton requesting documents and information related to the Benghazi attacks and Libya-related security decisions.

- September 27, 2012: Staff interview of Lieutenant Colonel Andrew Wood, former commander of the Site Security Team at Embassy Tripoli.

- October 1, 2012: House Oversight and Government Reform Committee Chairman Darrell Issa and Chairman Chaffetz interview Eric Nordstrom, former Regional Security Officer at Embassy Tripoli.

- October 2, 2012: Letter from Chairmen Issa and Chaffetz to Secretary Clinton requesting information about the State Department's awareness of the deteriorating security environment in Libya.

- October 6, 2012: Chairman Chaffetz travels to Stuttgart, Germany to meet with General Carter Ham, Commanding Officer, U.S. Africa Command.

- October 7, 2012: Chairman Chaffetz travels to Tripoli, Libya to meet with Embassy leadership.

- October 9, 2012: Transcribed interview of David Oliveira, former Assistant Regional Security Officer at the Benghazi Special Mission Compound.

- October 9, 2012: Transcribed interview of Charlene Lamb, Deputy Assistant Secretary of State for International Programs, Bureau of Diplomatic Security.

- October 10, 2012: Full Committee hearing entitled "The Security Failures of Benghazi."

- October 19, 2012: Letter from Chairmen Issa and Chaffetz to President Obama requesting information about White House involvement in Libya-related security decisions.

- October 25, 2012: Transcribed interview of Erfana Dar, former Special Assistant to Under Secretary of State for Management Patrick Kennedy.

- October 29, 2012: Letter from Chairmen Issa and Chaffetz to Secretary Clinton requesting information about any investigations conducted by the Department or the Government of Libya in response to the April 6, 2012 and June 6, 2012 bombings of the Benghazi Special Mission Compound.

- November 1, 2012: Letter from Chairmen Issa and Chaffetz to Secretary Clinton requesting documents and information related to media reports about pre-attack surveillance of the Benghazi Special Mission Compound.

- November 16, 2012: Letter from Chairmen Issa and Chaffetz to Secretary Clinton reiterating the Committee's unfulfilled request for documents and information related to the Benghazi attacks.

- November 20, 2012: Letter from Chairmen Issa and Chaffetz to Acting CIA Director Michael Morrell requesting an official, unclassified timeline of CIA actions in response to the Benghazi attacks.

- November 26, 2012: Letter from Chairmen Issa and Chaffetz to Secretary of Defense Leon Panetta requesting information about the U.S. military response to the Benghazi attacks.

- December 13, 2012: Classified briefing by the Defense Department on actions taken in response to the Benghazi attacks.

- January 12, 2013: Chairman Issa travels to Rota, Spain to meet with military personnel sent to reinforce security at Embassy Tripoli immediately following the attacks in Benghazi.

- January 28, 2013: Joint letter from House Foreign Affairs Committee Chairman Ed Royce and Chairmen Issa and Chaffetz to Secretary Clinton requesting access to all documents reviewed by, and the names of all individuals interviewed by, the Accountability Review Board.

- March 15, 2013: Members of the Committee receive a classified briefing from General Ham.

- The Committee has reviewed over 25,000 pages of classified and unclassified documents made available by the State Department.

- The Committee has heard from, and continues to hear from, multiple individuals with direct and/or indirect information about events surrounding the attacks in Benghazi.

- Requested, received, and reviewed thousands of pages of documents, including emails, cables, and classified intelligence assessments. These documents contain various drafts of the talking points created for HPSCI and used by Ambassador Rice, and emails from Administration officials, including those from White House officials, related to the creation of those talking points. The Committee continues to submit questions for the record and receive documents from the IC on an ongoing basis.

- September 13, 2012: Full Committee classified roundtable discussion with NCTC Director Olsen.

- September 14, 2012: Full Committee classified roundtable discussion with Director of CIA, David H. Petraeus.

- November 15, 2012: Full Committee classified hearing on Benghazi attacks with officials from the Office of the Director of National Intelligence (ODNI), CIA, NCTC, DoD, FBI, and State.

- November 16, 2012: Full Committee classified hearing on Benghazi Attacks with former Director of CIA Petraeus.

- December 13, 2012: Full Committee classified hearing on efforts to find the Benghazi terrorists.

- March 19, 2013: Full Committee classified briefing led by ODNI General Counsel Bob Litt to discuss Benghazi talking points.

- The Committee staff conducted numerous staff meetings and maintains a running list of questions for the record.

- HPSCI Chairman Rogers sent a letter to Acting CIA Director Morell raising his concerns about information sharing and analytic issues uncovered to date.

Appendix II: Consolidated Timeline of Events

March-October 2011

The Libyan revolution was supported by the United States most directly in the form of NATO air operations, which lasted from March through October of 2011.

Tuesday, December 27, 2011

A State Department memorandum circulated at the end of 2011 recommended that U.S. personnel remain in Benghazi. It explained that many Libyans were "strongly" in favor of a U.S. outpost in Benghazi, in part because they believed a U.S. presence in eastern Libya would ensure that the new Tripoli-based government fairly considered eastern interests.

Wednesday, March 28, 2012

Ambassador Cretz sent a cable to Secretary Clinton requesting additional security assets. Specifically, he asked for the continued deployment of both Mobile Security Detachment (MSD) teams, or at least additional DS agents to replace them, as well as the full five DS agents which the December 2011 memorandum claimed would be stationed in Benghazi.

Friday, April 6, 2012

The Temporary Mission Facility (TMF) in Benghazi came under attack when disgruntled Libyan contract guards allegedly threw a small improvised explosive device (IED) over the perimeter wall. No casualties were reported.

Thursday, April 19, 2012

State responded to Ambassador Cretz's request for additional security assets. The cable response to Tripoli bears Secretary Clinton's signature, and specifically acknowledges Ambassador Cretz's March 28 request for additional security. Despite the Ambassador's March request, the April cable from Clinton stipulates that the plan to drawdown security assets will proceed as planned. The cable further recommends that State's Bureau of Diplomatic Security and the U.S Mission in Libya conduct a "joint re-assessment of the number of DS agents requested for Benghazi."

Wednesday, June 6, 2012

The TMF was attacked again by unknown assailants who used an IED powerful enough to blow a hole in the perimeter wall. Again, no casualties were reported.

Thursday, June 7, 2012

Ambassador Stevens made a personal plea for an increase in security. In a June 2012 email, he told a Department official that with national elections in July and August, the Mission "would feel much safer if we could keep two MSD teams with us through this period [to support] our staff and [personal detail] for me and the [Deputy Chief of Mission] and any VIP visitors." The

Department official replied that due to other commitments and limited resources, "unfortunately, MSD cannot support the request."

Monday, July 9, 2012
A July 2012 cable from Ambassador Stevens stressed that security conditions in Libya had not met the requisite benchmarks established by the Department and the U.S. Mission in Libya to initiate a security drawdown, and requested that security personnel, including the MSD teams, be permitted to stay. After being apprised of this pending request, Deputy Assistant Secretary Charlene Lamb exclaimed: "NO I do not [I repeat] not want them to ask for the MSD team to stay!" The MSD team was withdrawn, though it is unclear whether the Department ever formally rejected the Ambassador's July request.

Monday, June 11, 2012
Britain's ambassador to Libya was in a convoy of cars attacked in the eastern city of Benghazi. The convoy was hit by a rocket-propelled grenade (RPG). Two protection officers were injured.

Monday, August 27, 2012
U.S. officials were aware that Libya remained volatile. They were particularly concerned with the numerous armed militias that operated freely throughout the country. In August 2011, the State Department warned U.S. citizens against traveling to Libya, explaining that "inter-militia conflict can erupt at any time or any place."

- The security environment in Benghazi was similarly deteriorating throughout 2012. From June 2011 to July 2012, then-Regional Security Officer (RSO) for Libya Eric Nordstrom, the principal security adviser to the U.S. Ambassador to Libya, compiled a list of over 200 security incidents in Libya, 50 of which took place in Benghazi. These included violent acts directed against diplomats and diplomatic facilities, international organizations, and third-country nationals, as well as large-scale militia clashes.
- In spite of these mounting security concerns, for most of 2012 the Benghazi Mission was forced to rely on fewer than the approved number of DS agents. Specifically, while the State Department memorandum signed by Under Secretary Kennedy claimed that five agents would be provided, this was only the case for 23 days in 2012. Reports indicate the Benghazi Mission was typically staffed with only three agents, and sometimes as few as one or two.

Monday, September 10, 2012
Ambassador Stevens travelled to Benghazi on September 10, 2012, both to fill staffing gaps between principal officers in Benghazi, and to allow the Ambassador to reconnect with local contacts. There were also plans for him to attend the establishment of a new American Corner at a local Benghazi school.

<u>Tuesday, September 11, 2012</u>
All times are Eastern European Time (EET, Benghazi)

~9:42 p.m.   The attack begins at the TMF in Benghazi. Dozens of lightly armed men approached the TMF, quickly and deliberately breached the front gate, and set fire to the guard house and main diplomatic building. The attackers included members of Libya-based Ansar al-Sharia (AAS) and al-Qa'ida in the Lands of the Islamic Maghreb (AQIM), among other groups. A State Department officer in the TMF's Tactical Operations Center immediately put out calls for help to the TMF Annex -- another facility for U.S. officials -- the U.S. Embassy in Tripoli, and State Department Headquarters in Washington, DC. At the time of the attack, Ambassador Stevens, Sean Smith, the information management officer, and one of the five Diplomatic Security (DS) officers were located in Villa C, the main building of the TMF. (DoD timeline/pg. 11)

9:59 p.m.   An unarmed, unmanned, surveillance aircraft is directed to reposition overhead the Benghazi facility. (DoD timeline)

~10:02 p.m.   Within 20-minutes of the attack, Stevens, Smith, and the DS officer suffered effects from smoke inhalation inside the main diplomatic building and tried to escape by crawling along the floor towards a window. The DS officer unknowingly lost touch with Ambassador Stevens and Mr. Smith somewhere along the smoke-filled escape route. After crawling out of a window and realizing that Ambassador Stevens and Mr. Smith were not with him, the DS officer, under gunfire, repeatedly re-entered the burning building to search for them. The DS officer used his radio to call for help. Security officers from other parts of the TMF complex responded and supported the DS officer's search for the missing individuals. (pg. 11)

10:05 p.m.   In an "Ops Alert" issued shortly after the attack began, the State Department Operations Center notified senior Department Officials, the White House Situation Room, and others, that the Benghazi compound was under attack and that "approximately 20 armed people fired shots; explosions have been heard as well."

~10:07 p.m.   A U.S. security team departed the Annex for the TMF. The security team tried to secure heavy weapons from militia members encountered along the route, and

3. House Republican Conference (4/23/2013)

faced some resistance in getting to the TMF. Even in the face of those obstacles, the Annex security team arrived, under enemy fire, within 25 minutes of the beginning of the initial assault. Over the course of the following hour, the Annex security team joined the TMF security officers in searching for Ambassador Stevens and Mr. Smith. Together, they repelled sporadic gunfire and RPG fire and assembled all other U.S. personnel at the facility. Officers retrieved the body of Mr. Smith, but did not find Ambassador Stevens.

10:32 p.m. The National Military Command Center at the Pentagon, after receiving initial reports of the incident from the State Department, notifies the Office of the Secretary of Defense and the Joint Staff. The information is quickly passed to Secretary Panetta and General Dempsey. (DoD timeline)

11:00 p.m. Secretary Panetta and General Dempsey attend a previously scheduled meeting with the President at the White House. The leaders discuss potential responses to the emerging situation. (DoD timeline)

11:10 p.m. The diverted surveillance aircraft arrives on station over the Benghazi facility. (DoD timeline)

~11:15 p.m. After about 90 minutes of repeated attempts to go into the burning building to search for the Ambassador, the Annex security team assessed that the security situation was deteriorating and they could not continue their search. The Annex security team loaded all U.S. personnel into two vehicles and departed the TMF for the Annex. The exiting vehicles left under heavy gunfire and faced at least one roadblock in their route to the Annex. The first vehicle left around 11:15 p.m. and the second vehicle departed at about 11:30 p.m. <u>All surviving American personnel departed the facility by 11:30 p.m.</u>

Wednesday, September 12, 2012

12:06 p.m. In a second "Ops Alert" the State Department Operations Center reported that al-Qaeda linked Ansar al-Sharia claimed responsibility for the attack and had called for an attack on Embassy Tripoli

12:00-2:00 a.m. Secretary Panetta convenes a series of meetings in the Pentagon with senior officials including General Dempsey and General Ham. They discuss additional response options for Benghazi and for the potential outbreak of further violence throughout the region, particularly in Tunis, Tripoli, Cairo, and Sana'a. During these meetings, Secretary Panetta authorizes:

- A Fleet Antiterrorism Security Team (FAST) platoon, stationed in Rota, Spain, to prepare to deploy to Benghazi, and a second FAST platoon, also stationed in Rota, Spain, to prepare to deploy to the Embassy in Tripoli.
- A EUCOM special operations force, which is training in Central Europe, to prepare to deploy to an intermediate staging base in southern Europe.
- A special operations force based in the United States to prepare to deploy to an intermediate staging base in southern Europe.

During this period, actions are verbally conveyed from the Pentagon to the affected Combatant Commands in order to expedite movement of forces upon receipt of formal authorization.

12:30 a.m.   A seven-man security team from U.S. Embassy Tripoli, including two DoD personnel, departs for Benghazi.

~1:15 a.m.   The American security team from Tripoli lands in Benghazi. (DoD timeline)

2:30 a.m.   The National Military Command Center conducts a Benghazi Conference Call with representatives from AFRICOM, EUCOM, CENTCOM, TRANSCOM, SOCOM, and the four services.

2:39 a.m.   As ordered by Secretary Panetta, the National Military Command Center transmits formal authorization for the two FAST platoons, and associated equipment, to prepare to deploy and for the EUCOM special operations force, and associated equipment, to move to an intermediate staging base in southern Europe.

2:53 a.m.   As ordered by Secretary Panetta, the National Military Command Center transmits formal authorization to deploy a special operations force, and associated equipment, from the United States to an intermediate staging base in southern Europe.

5:00 a.m.   A second, unmanned, unarmed surveillance aircraft is directed to relieve the initial asset still over Benghazi.

5:15 a.m.   At around 5:15 a.m., within 15 minutes of the Tripoli team's arrival at the Annex from the airport, a short but deadly coordinated terrorist attack began at the Annex. The attack, which included small arms, rocket-propelled grenade (RPG), and well-aimed mortar fire, killed two American security officers, and severely wounded two others.

6:05 a.m.   AFRICOM orders a C-17 aircraft in Germany to prepare to deploy to Libya to evacuate Americans.

7:40 a.m.   The first wave of American personnel depart Benghazi for Tripoli via airplane. (DoD timeline)

10:00 a.m.   The second wave of Americans, including the fallen, depart Benghazi for Tripoli via airplane.

2:15 p.m.   The C-17 departs Germany en route to Tripoli to evacuate Americans.

7:17 p.m.   The C-17 departs Tripoli en route Ramstein, Germany with the American personnel and the remains of Mr. Sean Smith, Mr. Tyrone Woods, and Mr. Glen Doherty.

7:57 p.m.   The EUCOM special operations force, and associated equipment, arrives at an intermediate staging base in southern Europe.

8:56 p.m.   The FAST platoon, and associated equipment, arrives in Tripoli.

9:28 p.m.   The special operations force deployed from the United States, and associated equipment, arrives at an intermediate staging base in southern Europe.

10:19 p.m.   The C-17 arrives in Ramstein, Germany.

END OF SEPTEMBER 11 ATTACK TIMELINE

Wednesday, September 12, 2012
- FBI formally opens an investigation into the deaths of Ambassador Sevens and the three other Americans killed in the attack.
- Relying on analytical intuition with limited reporting on September 12, 2012, IC analysts correctly evaluated soon after the attacks that the event was a terrorist attack against a U.S. facility, likely conducted by Islamic extremists.

Thursday, September 13, 2012
Beginning on September 13, 2012, analysts began receiving and relying on a larger volume of diverse intelligence reporting that referenced protests and demonstrations in Benghazi. Analysts

revised their assessments again to determine finally that the attack was deliberate and that a protest was not occurring at the time of the attack. The IC's modification of its assessments reflects the reasonable evolution of tactical intelligence analysis.

Saturday, September 15, 2012
HPSCI staff received the IC talking points on the Benghazi attack.

Sunday, September 16, 2012
On Sunday, September 16, 2012, U.S. Ambassador to the United Nations Susan Rice appeared on five morning talk shows to discuss the Administration's account of the attack. In nearly identical statements, she stated that the attack was a spontaneous protest in response to a "hateful video."

Wednesday, September 19, 2012
The National Counterterrorism Center Director testified before the Senate Homeland Security and Government Affairs Committee that our diplomats died "in the course of a terrorist attack on our embassy." This testimony marked a significant shift in the Administration's rhetoric.

Thursday, September 20, 2012
After Director of NCTC's testimony, Administration officials began referring to the event as a terrorist attack. On September 20, 2012, Jay Carney stated that, "it is, I think, self-evident that what happened in Benghazi was a terrorist attack."

Friday, September 21, 2012
Secretary Clinton stated that, "What happened in Benghazi was a terrorist attack, and we will not rest until we have tracked down and brought to justice the terrorists who murdered four Americans."

Thursday, October 4, 2012
- Due to security concerns and bureaucratic entanglements among the Departments of Justice, State, and Defense, the FBI team investigating the terrorist attack did not access the crime scene until more than three weeks later, on October 4, 2012. The FBI spent less than one day collecting evidence at the TMF. FBI officials indicated that the security situation delayed and undermined a more thorough investigation of the site.
- Secretary Clinton convened an Accountability Review Board (ARB), headed by Thomas Pickering, a retired U.S. ambassador, to examine the facts and circumstances of the attacks and to report findings and recommendations.

3. House Republican Conference (4/23/2013)

<u>**Tuesday, October, 9, 2012**</u>
The State Department held a conference call briefing for reporters in which the Department publicly acknowledged that there had been no protest outside the Benghazi diplomatic facility prior to the assault. State Department officials would testify before the House Oversight and Government Reform Committee the next day.

<u>**Tuesday, November 27, 2012**</u>
Administration officials have blamed their initial statements on "evolving" intelligence reports. To that end, Ambassador Rice stated on November 27, 2012, that Acting CIA Director Michael Morell "explained that the talking points provided by the intelligence community, and the initial assessment upon which they were based, were incorrect in a key respect: there was no protest or demonstration in Benghazi."

Investigative Report on the Terrorist Attacks on U.S. Facilities in Benghazi, Libya, September 11-12, 2012

A report by Chairman Mike Rogers and Ranking Member C.A. Dutch Ruppersberger of the Permanent Select Committee on Intelligence

U.S. House of Representatives
113th Congress
November 21, 2014

4. House Permanent Select Committee on Intelligence (11/21/2014)

Executive Summary

The House Permanent Select Committee on Intelligence ("HPSCI" or "the Committee") conducted a comprehensive and exhaustive investigation into the tragic attacks against two U.S. facilities in Benghazi, Libya on September 11-12, 2012. The nearly two-year investigation focused on the activities of the Intelligence Community ("IC") before, during, and after the attacks. During the course of thousands of hours of detailed investigation, HPSCI reviewed thousands of pages of intelligence assessments, cables, notes, and emails; held 20 Committee events and hearings; and conducted detailed interviews with senior intelligence officials and eyewitnesses to the attacks, including eight security personnel on the ground in Benghazi that night.

This report details the findings and conclusions of HPSCI's investigation. In summary, the Committee first concludes that the CIA ensured sufficient security for CIA facilities in Benghazi and, without a requirement to do so, ably and bravely assisted the State Department on the night of the attacks. Their actions saved lives. Appropriate U.S. personnel made reasonable tactical decisions that night, and the Committee found no evidence that there was either a stand down order or a denial of available air support. The Committee, however, received evidence that the State Department security personnel, resources, and equipment were unable to counter the terrorist threat that day and required CIA assistance.

Second, the Committee finds that there was no intelligence failure prior to the attacks. In the months prior, the IC provided intelligence about previous attacks and the increased threat environment in Benghazi, but the IC did not have specific, tactical warning of the September 11 attacks.

Third, the Committee finds that a mixed group of individuals, including those affiliated with Al-Qa'ida, participated in the attacks on U.S. facilities in Benghazi, although the Committee finds that the intelligence was and remains conflicting about the identities, affiliations, and motivations of the attackers.

Fourth, the Committee concludes that after the attacks, the early intelligence assessments and the Administration's initial public narrative on the causes and motivations for the attacks were not fully accurate. There was a stream of contradictory and conflicting intelligence that came in after the attacks. The Committee found intelligence to support CIA's initial assessment that the attacks had evolved out of a protest in Benghazi; but it also found contrary intelligence, which ultimately proved to be the correct intelligence. There was no protest. The CIA only changed its initial assessment about a protest on September 24, 2012, when closed caption television footage became available on September 18, 2012 (two days after Ambassador Susan Rice spoke), and after the FBI began publishing its interviews with U.S. officials on the ground on September 22, 2012.

Fifth, the Committee finds that the process used to generate the talking points HPSCI asked for—and which were used for Ambassador Rice's public appearances—was flawed. HPSCI asked for the talking points solely to aid Members' ability to communicate publicly using the best available intelligence at the time, and mistakes were made in the process of how those talking points were developed.

Finally, the Committee found no evidence that any officer was intimidated, wrongly forced to sign a nondisclosure agreement or otherwise kept from speaking to Congress, or polygraphed because of their presence in Benghazi. The Committee also found no evidence that the CIA conducted unauthorized activities in Benghazi and no evidence that the IC shipped arms to Syria.

This report, and the nearly two years of intensive investigation it reflects, is meant to serve as the definitive House statement on the Intelligence Community's activities before, during, and after the tragic events that caused the deaths of four brave Americans. Despite the highly sensitive nature of these activities, the report has endeavored to make the facts and conclusions within this report widely and publicly available so that the American public can separate the actual facts from the swirl of rumors and unsupported allegations. Only with a full accounting of the facts can we ensure that tragedies like the one that took the lives of Ambassador Chris Stevens, Sean Smith, Tyrone Woods, and Glen Doherty never happen again.

4. House Permanent Select Committee on Intelligence (11/21/2014)

Introduction

On September 11, 2012, armed militias with ties to terrorist organizations, including al-Qa'ida, attacked the State Department Temporary Mission Facility (TMF) and the CIA's Annex in Benghazi, Libya. The attacks killed Ambassador Christopher Stevens and State Department Information Officer Sean Smith. Security personnel from CIA's Annex in Benghazi responded to the attacks, rescued the remaining State Department officers, and brought them back to the CIA Annex. The CIA also launched, in coordination with the U.S. military, a security team from Tripoli to aid in the security of the remaining facility in Benghazi and to rescue the then-missing Ambassador Stevens. Upon learning that Ambassador Stevens was dead, the Tripoli Team traveled to the Annex. Within minutes of their arrival, a well-coordinated and deadly mortar attack killed security officers Tyrone Woods and Glen Doherty, and severely wounded two others. Following the mortar attack, the CIA Chief of Benghazi Base, the lead officer on the ground, determined that the CIA Annex was no longer defensible, and all U.S. personnel evacuated to the Benghazi airport. After Ambassador Stevens' body was recovered, all U.S. personnel departed on two flights to Tripoli.

Immediately after being notified of the attacks, the House Permanent Select Committee on Intelligence launched an investigation to focus on the role of the Intelligence Community (IC) before, during, and after the attacks. The Committee conducted twenty full Committee events; interviewed nine eyewitnesses present in Benghazi during the attacks; reviewed thousands of pages of intelligence reports, cables, assessments, and emails; and received responses to dozens of questions for the record. The Committee continues to inquire about the IC's role in efforts to find those who conducted the attacks and bring those responsible to justice.

As the Committee focused its review on the U.S. Intelligence Community, this report does not assess State Department or Defense Department activities other than where those activities impact, or were impacted by, the work of the intelligence community.[1]

Finally, this report provides as much information as possible for public consideration. It includes descriptions of events based on firsthand accounts of the events that night, including the perspectives of the eight surviving U.S. personnel and the CIA's Chief of Benghazi Base, who were present during the attacks. The Committee also interviewed the CIA's Chief of Station in Tripoli. Most of these CIA personnel remain under cover. Their continued anonymity and the confidentiality of their specific tactics and security protocols are critical to their ability to continue to defend U.S. installations and personnel.[2] With this in mind, in the course of this investigation, and through the publication of this report, the Committee has sought to declassify as much information as possible while protecting names, sources, methods, and operational information that would damage national security if revealed. The unredacted version of this Report, and all supporting documentation, no matter the classification level, has been made available to all HPSCI Members.

---

[1] To the maximum degree possible, within the constraints of classification, the Committee has coordinated with other committees of jurisdiction.

[2] To protect their identities, this report refers to them either by their position or Officer #1-8.

SECRET

No classified information redacted or excluded in any way changes the key facts, findings or conclusions contained in this bipartisan report.

Timeline of Events on September 11 and 12, 2012[3]

Timeline (all times are local)[45678]

Before the attack	Libyan security officials are outside of the TMF.
09:42 PM	DS personnel alert the CIA Annex and U.S. Embassy in Tripoli of the attack. State Diplomatic Security (DS) personnel and local guard force run across the TMF compound. The Libyan security officials depart. Three DS officers are in the Threat Operations Center (TOC). Attackers appear at the front gate.
09:43PM	A small explosion, probably an RPG, is visible near main gate. Several attackers come through the gate and are on the TMF compound.
09:45 PM	Attackers with terrorist paraphernalia enter the compound. Several attackers are in front of the main gate.
09:46 PM	Some attackers leave the compound in a vehicle.
09:46 PM	Other attackers reenter the TMF front gate.
09:46 PM	CIA personnel at the Annex gather weapons and equipment.
09:57 PM	There is fire at the guard house.
10:01 PM	Villa C is engulfed in smoke.
10:03 PM	Annex security team departs for the TMF.
10:06 PM	Attackers loot a building on the compound.

---

[3] This timeline was developed from the totality of evidence compiled by HPSCI throughout the course of the investigation, including surveillance, and reconnaissance (ISR) video footage; FBI intelligence reports; CIA cables; and email traffic. The timeline is also largely corroborated by witnesses' personal recollections. Some of the details of the precise timing that night varied among eyewitnesses, which is expected when witnesses rely on their recollections of a chaotic event.

[4] Video Footage of CIA Annex and State Department TMF September 11-12, 2012.

[5] FBI Briefing on Benghazi Investigation January 13, 2013.

[6] Predator ISR video footage of Benghazi September 11-12, 2012.

[7] As described in this narrative, seven additional personnel arrived from Tripoli to assist the Temporary Mission Facility and the Annex, bringing the total to 35 U.S. personnel on the ground that night.

[8] DoD ISR was controlled by Joint Special Operations Command (JSOC) liaison in Stuttgart, Germany.

4. House Permanent Select Committee on Intelligence (11/21/2014)

10:18 PM	A State Department diplomatic security officer throws a smoke grenade to cover his movement across the compound.
10:32 PM	Fewer attackers present.
10:32 PM	DS agents enter Villa B.
10:35 PM	Three DS agents from Compound B take a vehicle from the area near the TOC to Compound C.
10:40 PM	DS agents encounter friendly locals.
10:43 PM	DS agents go to the TOC to get gas masks and then return to look for Ambassador Stevens and Sean Smith.
10:45 PM	First video evidence of CIA Annex Team at TMF.
10:50 PM	Several U.S. personnel and local friendly forces are near Compound C and look for Ambassador Stevens. Some Annex personnel and local guard forces try to set up a perimeter, while others search for Ambassador Stevens.
10:56 PM	Small arms fire increases.
11:10 PM	Another explosion on the TMF accompanied by additional small arms fire.
11:11 PM	An unarmed Predator arrives and provides intelligence, surveillance, and reconnaissance (ISR) of the compound for the first time.
11:16 PM	Additional small arms fired.
11:19 PM	DS agents evacuate compound in first vehicle. CIA security team and friendly local militia remain at the TMF.
11:21 PM	U.S. personnel are on a roof at the TMF.
11:21 PM	DS agents arrive at the Annex.
11:31 PM	Annex security team departs the TMF compound. Small arms fired on the TMF compound.
11:36 PM	Annex security team returns to the Annex.
11:45 PM -12:45 AM	Mass looting at TMF. Over 100 people on or outside the TMF compound.

4. House Permanent Select Committee on Intelligence (11/21/2014)

12:15 AM	Tripoli Team departs Tripoli airport en route to Benghazi airport.
12:30 AM -1:00 AM	Security team repels an attack on the Annex.
01:11 AM	More small arms fire is directed at an Annex flood light.
01:23 AM	Tripoli Team is on the Benghazi airport tarmac.
01:50 AM	Multiple men are on the street outside the Annex.
01:56 AM	Two suspicious men are observed walking in an area near the Annex.
02:00 -2:30AM	Security team repels another attack on the Annex.
02:30-5:14AM	No suspicious activity experienced at the Annex.
04:53 AM	Tripoli Team leaves Benghazi airport en route to the Annex.
05:04 AM	Tripoli Team and Libyan militia arrive at the Annex.
05:14 AM	RPG attack on the Annex.
05:15 AM	Mortar attacks on the Annex. Five mortars land within 1 minute and 9 seconds.
06:14 AM	Libya Shield militia vehicles return to evacuate the Annex.
06:33 AM	Libya Shield convoy departs the Annex with all personnel en route to the airport.
06:55 AM	Convoy arrives at the airport.

I. **CIA security personnel on the ground in Benghazi, Libya, during the attacks that began on September 11, 2012, exhibited bravery and tactical expertise, saving the lives of fellow Americans from the State Department under difficult conditions.**

On September 11, 2012, the United States maintained a total of 28 U.S. personnel in Benghazi, at both the CIA's Base (the Annex) and the State Department's mission facility, called the Temporary Mission Facility (TMF). Ambassador Stevens traveled to Benghazi from Tripoli on September 10, 2012, to be present at a September 11 ceremony establishing a new American Corner at a local Benghazi school with the Turkish chief of mission in Benghazi.[9] He had other meetings planned that week, during which CIA was to provide additional security.[10]

At appropriately 9:40 PM on September 11, 2012, dozens of armed men approached the State Department's Benghazi facility. As the men approached, three Libyan security officers in a car outside the TMF drove away without warning U.S. personnel.[11] The attackers quickly breached the front gate. Within 20 minutes, the attackers had subdued local guard forces and set fire, using gasoline, to the February 17th Brigade guard house and Villa C, the main building of the Benghazi Mission where Ambassador Stevens, Sean Smith, and the Diplomatic Security (DS) agent were located. The State Department had contracted with the February 17th Brigade and the Blue Mountain Group to provide local security for the TMF facility. All available information indicates that the February 17th Brigade guards were inside the walls of the compound and did not detect or report information about the attackers before the attackers breached the gate.[12]

The attackers included members of several Islamic extremist groups, including al-Qa'ida in the Lands of the Islamic Maghreb (AQIM), Libya-based Ansar al-Sharia (AAS) and the Muhammad Jamal Network (MJN).[13]

At 9:42 PM, a State DS officer in the TMF's Tactical Operations Center (TOC) called the Benghazi CIA security team leader on his cell phone to alert him that the TMF was under attack and to request assistance.[14] The CIA Annex was approximately 2.4 kilometers driving distance from the TMF.[15] Within 19 minutes of the attack, Ambassador Stevens, Mr. Smith, and the DS agent who attempted to remain secure in a safe room were forced to leave due to the smoke. They suffered

---

[9] American Corners are partnerships between the Public Affairs sections of United States Embassies and host institutions. They provide access to current and reliable information from and about the United States to the general public overseas via book collections, the Internet, and local programming.

[10] HPSCI Transcript "Subcommittee Interview with Officers 1 and 2," November 13, 2013 pg. 20.

[11] HPSCI Transcript, "Full Committee Hearing with DNI Clapper, ADCIA Morell, D/NCTC Olsen, and Under Secretary Kennedy, which included the NCTC Presentation on the Benghazi Attacks," November 15, 2012 pg. 18; FBI Briefing on Benghazi Investigation January 13, 2013; video footage; FBI interviews indicate that they left because they had only one gun and were frightened. HPSCI Transcript "Subcommittee Interview with Officers 1 and 2," November 13, 2013 pg. 8.

[12] HPSCI Transcript "Full Committee Hearing with DNI Clapper, ADCIA Morell, D/NCTC Olsen, and Under Secretary Kennedy, which included the NCTC Presentation on the Benghazi Attacks," November 15, 2012; video footage.

[13] NCTC "Libya: Terrorists and Extremists Reportedly Associated with the Benghazi Attacks" September 9, 2013 (Authored by CIA, NCTC, and FBI); CIA WIRe: "Terrorists and Extremists Reportedly Associated with the Benghazi Attacks," September 9, 2013.

[14] HPSCI Transcript "Subcommittee Interview with Officers 1 and 2," November 13, 2013 pgs. 7-8, 17.

[15] NCTC Presentation "The Benghazi Attacks," November, 15, 2012 slide 4.

debilitating effects from smoke inhalation as Villa C burned. All three tried to escape by crawling along the floor towards a window. Due to the thick smoke, the DS agent lost contact with Ambassador Stevens and Mr. Smith along the escape route. After crawling out of a window and realizing that the Ambassador and Mr. Smith were not with him, the DS agent, under gunfire, repeatedly re-entered the burning building to search for them, but was unsuccessful.[16]

Security officers from CIA's Benghazi Annex recalled hearing explosions from an unknown location around 9:40 PM.[17] After receiving a phone call from the TMF's area security officer that assistance was needed, the Benghazi CIA security team chief immediately assembled his five available team members to share what he knew and order them to prepare for a rescue mission.[18] He also alerted the CIA Deputy Chief of Base who notified the Benghazi Chief of Base.[19] Meanwhile, the security team members prepared their weapons, equipment, and vehicles to depart for the TMF in 5 to 6 minutes.[20]

After departing the Annex, the security team tried unsuccessfully to secure heavy weapons from militia members it encountered along the way. The security team also faced resistance, including gunfire, along the route.[21] Although it is not clear at what exact time the team arrived at the TMF, the Committee confirmed they were are on the TMF compound no more than 42 minutes after they departed the Annex.[22]

The State Department security officers who notified the CIA Annex in Benghazi also notified the State Department Regional Security Officer (RSO) in Tripoli. That officer subsequently notified the leader of CIA's security team in Tripoli. The leader of security in Tripoli then met with the CIA Chief of Station in Tripoli and U.S. military officers in Tripoli to discuss their options.[23] Throughout the night, the CIA security and U.S. military officers who made up the "Tripoli Team" acted in concert, operating under appropriate authorities. CIA's Tripoli security chief led the team and maintained operational control of its actions. He transferred tactical control to the U.S. military officers at appropriate times, depending on the specific action.[24]

The U.S. military personnel's first action was to proactively redirect an unarmed DoD Predator reconnaissance plane that was collecting intelligence over Darnah, Libya, to cover Benghazi.[25] The Tripoli Team also monitored the situation and immediately began planning a rescue operation. According to the CIA's Tripoli security team chief, they started getting reports from the field that Villa

---

[16] HPSCI Transcript, "Full Committee Hearing with DNI Clapper, ADCIA Morell, D/NCTC Olsen, and Under Secretary Kennedy, which included the NCTC Presentation on the Benghazi Attacks," November 15, 2012 pg. 20.
[17] HPSCI Transcript "Subcommittee Interview with Officers 1 and 2," November 13, 2013 pg. 8.
[18] HPSCI Transcript "Subcommittee Interview with Officers 1 and 2," November 13, 2013 pg. 20.
[19] HPSCI Transcript "Subcommittee Interview with Officers 1 and 2," November 13, 2013 pg.19-20.
[20] HPSCI Transcript "Subcommittee Interview with Officers 1 and 2," November 13, 2013 pg. 8; HPSCI Transcript "Subcommittee Interview with Officers 3, 4, and 5," November 14, 2013 pg. 15. The 21-minute period between the initial breach of the TMF and the departure of the CIA rescue team from the Annex is described later in this report.
[21] HPSCI Transcript "Full Committee Hearing with DNI Clapper, ADCIA Morell, D/NCTC Olsen, and Under Secretary Kennedy, which included the NCTC Presentation on the Benghazi Attacks," November 15, 2012.
[22] Video footage.
[23] HPSCI Transcript "Subcommittee Staff Interview with Officer 8," December 13, 2013 pgs. 2-4.
[24] HPSCI Transcript "Subcommittee Staff Interview with Officer 8," December 13, 2013 pgs. 9-10.
[25] HPSCI Transcript "Subcommittee Staff Interview with Officer 8," December 13, 2013 pgs. 3-4.

4. House Permanent Select Committee on Intelligence (11/21/2014)

C was on fire. Further, they were told that the Benghazi-based team had not yet located Ambassador Stevens, and had one individual killed and others wounded. At that time, the Chief of Station in Tripoli helped the Team secure transport, and within 45 minutes the Team was moving to the airfield.[26]

The Chief of Station in Tripoli and other Members of the Tripoli Team confirmed that the Team left Tripoli Station within 45 minutes of being notified.[27] Traffic delayed the Team's arrival at the Tripoli airport.[28] They departed the Tripoli airport on a 60-minute chartered flight for Benghazi at about 12:15 AM.[29]

While the Tripoli Team mobilized and moved to the Tripoli airport, the Annex security team joined State Department officers and helpful members of the February 17th Brigade in fighting the attackers at the TMF. The team repelled sporadic gunfire and RPG fire while assembling all remaining U.S. personnel at the TMF. The security officers were able to retrieve the body of Sean Smith, but they were unable to locate Ambassador Stevens. After 90 minutes of repeated attempts to enter the burning Villa C to search for the Ambassador, officers assessed that the security situation had deteriorated, and they were forced to abandon their search for the Ambassador in order to save the remaining U.S. personnel.[30] The Annex security team loaded all U.S. personnel into vehicles to return to the Annex, with the first vehicle departing at 11:19 PM and the second vehicle departing at 11:30 PM.[31] The unarmed DoD Predator arrived and began recording events on the ground at approximately 11:11 PM, eight minutes prior to the first vehicle's departure and after the first attack had ended.[32]

As the State Department officers exited the Benghazi TMF in the first vehicle heading east, they encountered heavy gunfire and a roadblock en route to the Annex.[33] The CIA officers who departed 11 minutes later headed west, avoided the roadblock, and returned to the Annex without incident.[34] All U.S. personnel from the Annex at the TMF, with the exception of Ambassador Stevens, were accounted for at the CIA Annex by 11:36 PM. At this point, there were 26 Americans at the Annex, 14 of whom were trained security personnel.[35]

Within approximately one hour, at about 12:30 AM, the attackers began one of several attempts

---

[26] HPSCI Transcript "Subcommittee Staff Interview with Officer 8," December 13, 2013 pgs. 4-5.

[27] HPSCI Transcript "Subcommittee Interview with the former Chief of Tripoli Station," April 1, 2014 pg. 7.

[28] HPSCI Transcript "Subcommittee Interview with Officers 6 and 7," December 3, 2013 pg. 4, 25-26.

[29] HPSCI Transcript "Full Committee Hearing with DNI Clapper, ADCIA Morell, D/NCTC Olsen, and Under Secretary Kennedy, which included the NCTC Presentation on the Benghazi Attacks," November 15, 2012 pg. 26.

[30] HPSCI Transcript "Subcommittee Interview with Officers 1 and 2," November 13, 2013 pg. 23.

[31] HPSCI Transcript "Full Committee Hearing with DNI Clapper, ADCIA Morell, D/NCTC Olsen, and Under Secretary Kennedy, which included the NCTC Presentation on the Benghazi Attacks," November 15, 2012; Video footage; HPSCI Transcript "Subcommittee Interview with Officers 1 and 2," November 13, 2013; HPSCI Transcript "Subcommittee Interview with Officers 3, 4, and 5," November 14, 2013.

[32] Predator ISR video footage of Benghazi September 11-12, 2012.

[33] HPSCI Transcript "Full Committee Hearing with DNI Clapper, ADCIA Morell, D/NCTC Olsen, and Under Secretary Kennedy, which included the NCTC Presentation on the Benghazi Attacks," November 15, 2012 pgs. 25-26 and 28.

[34] HPSCI Transcript "Full Committee Hearing with DNI Clapper, ADCIA Morell, D/NCTC Olsen, and Under Secretary Kennedy, which included the NCTC Presentation on the Benghazi Attacks," November 15, 2012 pgs. 25-26 and 28.

[35] HPSCI Transcript "Full Committee Hearing with DNI Clapper, ADCIA Morell, D/NCTC Olsen, and Under Secretary Kennedy, which included the NCTC Presentation on the Benghazi Attacks," November 15, 2012 pgs. 25-26 and 28.

to assault the Annex. Some of this attack was captured on video.[36] CIA personnel recounted that the attacks included RPGs, satchel charges, gelatin explosives, and small arms fire, with around five to ten people amassing in the adjacent field. These security personnel were able to repel the attackers. Around 2:00 to 2:30 AM, there was a second attempt on the compound that lasted about 5 to 10 minutes that was also repelled.[37] The personnel on the ground consistently described a second short attack at the Annex that occurred somewhere between 2:00 and 2:30 AM, followed by a lull of activity before the Tripoli Team arrived at the Annex at 4:53 AM.[38]

The Tripoli Team, composed of seven U.S. personnel (five CIA and two U.S. military), arrived at the Benghazi airport just before the Predator observed them on the tarmac at 1:23 AM.[39] The Team's mission at that point was to locate and rescue Ambassador Stevens.[40] The Tripoli Team later received reports from Tripoli Station that the Ambassador was at a local hospital.[41]

Prior to landing in Benghazi, the DoD members of the Tripoli Team made arrangements with General Hasani, the commander of Libya's then-fledgling special forces cadre in Benghazi, for a Hilux truck, weapons, and an escort. The Team believed that General Hasani would be the most reliable interlocutor in Benghazi, but no truck was available when the Tripoli Team landed. The U.S. military Team Leader tried to call General Hasani, but the General's phone was apparently turned off.[42]

While holding on the tarmac of the Benghazi airport without their pre-arranged transportation, the Team was approached by about 30 militiamen from different groups offering assistance. It was not entirely clear to the Team which groups were present, which were trustworthy, and which posed a threat. The Team had to vet militia members on the spot.[43]

The Tripoli Team intended to travel to the hospital because they had received reports that there was a wounded American alive at the hospital.[44] But their mission was further complicated on the tarmac because the local militia at the airport did not want to take them to the hospital.[45] It was not clear why those individuals did not want to travel to the hospital.[46] Additionally, the Team received some confusing (and ultimately inaccurate) intelligence reports; first that Ansar al-Sharia held the security

---

[36] Video footage.

[37] HPSCI Transcript "Subcommittee Interview with Officers 1 and 2," November 13, 2013 pgs. 37-38.

[38] HPSCI Transcript "Subcommittee Interview with Officers 1 and 2," November 13, 2013 pg. 38; HPSCI Transcript "Subcommittee Interview with Officers 3, 4, and 5," November 14, 2013 pg. 141.

[39] HPSCI Transcript, "Full Committee Hearing with DNI Clapper, ADCIA Morell, D/NCTC Olsen, and Under Secretary Kennedy, which included the NCTC Presentation on the Benghazi Attacks," November 15, 2012; Predator ISR video footage of Benghazi September 11-12, 2012.

[40] HPSCI Transcript "Subcommittee Staff Interview with Officer 8," December 13, 2013 pgs. 10-12.

[41] HPSCI Transcript, "Full Committee Hearing with DNI Clapper, ADCIA Morell, D/NCTC Olsen, and Under Secretary Kennedy, which included the NCTC Presentation on the Benghazi Attacks," November 15, 2012 pg. 29.

[42] HPSCI Transcript "Subcommittee Staff Interview with Officer 8," December 13, 2013 pgs. 10-12.

[43] HPSCI Transcript "Subcommittee Staff Interview with Officer 8," December 13, 2013 pgs. 10-12.

[44] HPSCI Transcript "Subcommittee Staff Interview with Officer 8," December 13, 2013 pg. 11.

[45] HPSCI Transcript "Subcommittee Staff Interview with Officer 8," December 13, 2013 pgs. 10-12.

[46] HPSCI Transcript "Subcommittee Staff Interview with Officer 8," December 13, 2013 pgs. 10-12.

contract for the hospital;[47] and second that the Ambassador's cell phone had been located nearby.[48]

The confusion at the airport lasted for about three and a half hours until the Tripoli Team received a report that a deceased Westerner had been identified at the hospital. The Chief of Station in Tripoli then ordered the team to return to its original mission, which was to move to the Benghazi Annex to collect non-security personnel and transport them to the airport for evacuation to Tripoli.[49]

Once the Tripoli Team announced its intention to go to the Annex, four Toyota Land Cruisers arrived. The Tripoli Team was hesitant to use the vehicles, but the Team had few options.[50] Thus, the Tripoli Team departed the airport for the Annex in the Libyan Shield militia vehicles at 4:53 AM, was held up briefly at a checkpoint, and arrived at the Annex at 5:04 AM. The Team invited into the Annex one militia member whose assistance would prove critically valuable to the evacuation of the Annex. The Libyan militia vehicles remain parked outside the Annex until the final attack began.[51]

After much review, HPSCI uncovered no evidence that the Libyan Shield militia played a role in the final attack or tipped off the attackers of the Tripoli Team's presence.

Once the Tripoli Team arrived at the Annex, the Tripoli security chief conferred with the Benghazi Chief of Base and organized an evacuation of non-essential personnel from the Annex.[52] Meanwhile, the other Tripoli Team officers spread out to assess the situation, locate all personnel, and fill any security gaps. Glen Doherty, who was a member of the Tripoli Team, climbed up to the roof of the main building to assist his friend and colleague Ty Woods with physical security.[53]

At 5:15 AM, about 11 minutes after the Tripoli Team's arrival at the Annex, terrorists conducted a short but deadly and coordinated attack against the Annex from multiple directions. Attackers launched a complex coordinated attack on the Annex that included a salvo of five mortar rounds, with an RPG and small arms fire.[54] The first mortar round hit the north wall. The second and third mortar rounds were direct hits on the roof of building #3. The fourth mortar landed just outside the Annex compound. The fifth mortar round was a direct hit on building #3. The three deadly mortars landed within a few meters of each other during a one minute and nine second period. The Tripoli security chief recalled that the mortar fire was far more accurate than anything he had seen during his tour in

---

[47] CIA's January 8, 2014 response to a Committee inquiry states that at the time of the attacks "Ansar al-Sharia was tasked with providing security for a different hospital in Benghazi—the al-Jala hospital—as part of the local government's effort to delegate security responsibility to militias to counter rising instability and to moderate the group's extremist agenda."[47]

[48] HPSCI Transcript "Subcommittee Staff Interview with Officer 8," December 13, 2013 pg. 13; HPSCI Staff MFR "FBI Update on Benghazi Investigation," February 7, 2014.

[49] HPSCI Transcript "Subcommittee Staff Interview with Officer 8," December 13, 2013 pgs. 12-13.

[50] HPSCI Transcript "Subcommittee Staff Interview with Officer 8," December 13, 2013 pgs. 13-16.

[51] Predator ISR video footage of Benghazi September 11-12, 2012; HPSCI Transcript "Full Committee Hearing with DNI Clapper, ADCIA Morell, D/NCTC Olsen, and Under Secretary Kennedy, which included the NCTC Presentation on the Benghazi Attacks," November 15, 2012 pgs. 29-31.

[52] HPSCI Transcript "Subcommittee Staff Interview with Officer 8," December 13, 2013 pg. 20.

[53] HPSCI Transcript "Subcommittee Staff Interview with Officer 8," December 13, 2013 pg. 20.

[54] HPSCI Transcript "Full Committee Hearing with DNI Clapper, ADCIA Morell, D/NCTC Olsen, and Under Secretary Kennedy, which included the NCTC "Presentation on the Benghazi Attacks," November 15, 2012 pgs. 30-31.

Afghanistan when the Taliban launched mortars three times a day against his base and were "lucky to put one inside the wire."[55]

The attack on the Annex mortally wounded Woods and Doherty and severely wounded another CIA security officer and one State Department DS Officer. Following the mortar fire, the remaining members of the security team rescued and began treating the wounded officers while repelling attackers, who continued to fire on the Annex for a short time. The Benghazi and Tripoli security team leaders discussed whether they should try to stay to protect the Annex. They decided that they could not secure the roofs of the Annex due to the indirect fire and their lack of appropriate weapons. Chief of Base in Benghazi concurred with their assessment and approved the evacuation.[56]

The Libyan Shield militia members who had remained in the vehicles departed the Annex compound as soon as the RPG round hit the north wall and were not available to facilitate an immediate evacuation. The Libyan Shield official who entered the Annex with the Tripoli Team remained sheltered with the U.S. personnel and he called the vehicles back. The Libyan Shield official arranged for vehicles to transport all remaining personnel from the Annex to the airport. The Libyan Shield vehicles returned at 6:14 AM. All remaining U.S. personnel loaded in the vehicles and departed the Annex at 6:33 AM for the airport. The convoy arrived at the airport at 6:55 AM.[57]

During this time, the Libyan government, in coordination with the U.S. State Department, arranged to have the body of Ambassador Stevens delivered to the airport. All U.S. personnel, including the bodies of the four dead Americans, departed Benghazi for Tripoli on two flights, one at about 7:30 AM and the other at about 10:00 AM. By 11:35 AM, all U.S. personnel had arrived in Tripoli.[58]

II. **In the months prior to the attacks, the IC provided intelligence about previous attacks and the increased threat in Benghazi, but it did not have specific, tactical warning of the September 11 attacks. The CIA was conducting no unauthorized activity in Benghazi and was not collecting and shipping arms to Syria. The CIA ensured sufficient security for CIA facilities in Benghazi and was able to assist the State Department in Benghazi.**

Finding #1: **There is no evidence of an intelligence failure. Prior to the Benghazi attacks, the CIA provided sufficient strategic warning of the deteriorating threat environment to U.S. decision-makers, including those at the State Department. The IC did not fail to provide specific, tactical warning of the attacks in Benghazi because it had no credible intelligence about the attacks before they began.**

---

[55] Video footage; HPSCI Transcript "Full Committee Hearing with DNI Clapper, ADCIA Morell, D/NCTC Olsen, and Under Secretary Kennedy, which included the NCTC "Presentation on the Benghazi Attacks," November 15, 2012 pgs. 30-31; HPSCI Transcript "Subcommittee Staff Interview with Officer 8," December 13, 2013 pg. 20.

[56] HPSCI Transcript "Subcommittee Staff Interview with Officer 8," December 13, 2013 pgs. 26-27.

[57] Video footage; Predator ISR video footage of Benghazi September 11-12, 2012; [57] HPSCI Transcript "Subcommittee Staff Interview with Officer 8," December 13, 2013 pgs. 27-28; HPSCI Transcript "Full Committee Hearing with DNI Clapper, ADCIA Morell, D/NCTC Olsen, and Under Secretary Kennedy, which included the NCTC Presentation on the Benghazi Attacks," November 15, 2012 pg. 31.

[58] HPSCI Transcript "Full Committee Hearing with DNI Clapper, ADCIA Morell, D/NCTC Olsen, and Under Secretary Kennedy, which included the NCTC Presentation on the Benghazi Attacks," November 15, 2012 pg. 33.

One of the first questions HPSCI pursued is whether the U.S. government had or should have had intelligence that could have prevented or disrupted the attacks, and thus whether there was an intelligence failure. Accordingly, soon after the attacks, HPSCI requested and reviewed the volume of the IC's reporting about Libya, and specifically material produced by the CIA in the months leading up to the attacks.[59]

HPSCI found no evidence of an intelligence failure, and an internal CIA analytic review provided to the Committee on January 4, 2013, corroborates the Committee's findings. Specifically, during the 12 months preceding the attacks, CIA published 54 pieces of finished intelligence analysis related to the security situation in eastern Libya, the groups operating there, and the capabilities of the Libyan security services.[60] In numerous analytical products, CIA specifically highlighted the threats to Western interests in eastern Libya.[61] For example, CIA published a WIRe article in June 2012 titled "Attack on British Diplomatic Convoy Underscores Risks to Western Interests", which included an accompanying chronology of attacks against Western interests since April 2012.[62] Throughout 2012, there were more than 20 attacks against Western and international interests in Benghazi.[63] The IC monitored these attacks and other extremist activities in North Africa, and it published hundreds of reports and assessments related to threats to Western interests in the region before the September 11 attacks.[64]

These reports and assessments, which were available to senior U.S. policymakers, including those at the State Department and the White House, made clear that there were serious and credible threats to American interests and facilities in the region and in Benghazi specifically. This information was also available to U.S. personnel in Libya. Indeed, CIA's Chief of Tripoli Station testified that he actually had a long conversation with Ambassador Stevens the Saturday before the Ambassador traveled to Benghazi and reviewed the security situation.[65]

Given the volume of threat information provided by the IC, the Committee concludes that any U.S. official responsible for facilities or personnel in Benghazi had sufficient warning of the deteriorating security situation in Benghazi and the demonstrated intent and capability of anti-U.S. extremists in the region to attack Western, and specifically, U.S. targets.

---

[59] HPSCI review of Benghazi Intelligence Review (October 2012 ODNI-provided package of 429 intelligence cables, reports, and assessments ranging from February to October 2012).

[60] CIA "Analytic Line Review on CIA's Assessments of the 11-12 September 2012 Attacks in Benghazi," January 4, 2013.

[61] CIA WIRe "Terrorism: AQIM Growing Diverse Network in Libya," August 27, 2012; CIA WIRe "Libya: Recent Attacks Highlight Persistent Threats in Eastern Libya," August 1, 2014; CIA WIRE "Libya: Al-Qa'ida Establishing Sanctuary," July 6, 2014; CIA WIRe "Libya: Recurring Internal Violence Highlights Security Challenges Facing Successor Government," June 26, 2012; CIA WIRe "Libya: Attack on British Diplomatic Convoy Underscores Risks to Western Interests," June 11, 2012.

[62] CIA "Analytic Line Review on CIA's Assessments of the 11-12 September 2012 Attacks in Benghazi," January 4, 2013.

[63] HPSCI Transcript "Full Committee Hearing with DNI Clapper, ADCIA Morell, D/NCTC Olsen, and Under Secretary Kennedy, which included the NCTC "Presentation on the Benghazi Attacks," November 15, 2012 pg. 11.

[64] HPSCI review of Benghazi Intelligence Review (October 2012 ODNI-provided package of 429 intelligence cables, reports, and assessments ranging from February to October 2012).

[65] HPSCI Transcript "Subcommittee Interview with the former Chief of Tripoli Station," April 1, 2014 pg. 13.

4. House Permanent Select Committee on Intelligence (11/21/2014)

HPSCI also reviewed why the IC did not provide an immediate and specific tactical warning of the attacks in Benghazi. Relevant documents confirm that the IC did not possess intelligence indicating planning or intentions for attacks on the Benghazi facility on or about September 11, 2012.[66] And thus the IC did not fail to provide such warning. Furthermore, the Committee did not find evidence to suggest the IC could have collected intelligence to warn of the attacks.

After the attacks, CIA reported on September 15, 2012, that ████████, a former Transitional National Council security official in Benghazi, said he received, very shortly before the attack, information of a possible imminent attack against the TMF and tried to notify the Libyan Intelligence Service the day of the attacks. However, he was unable to make contact and relay the information.[67] CIA's Chief of Tripoli Station sent this information to senior CIA officers on September 16, 2012, including then-Deputy Director Michael Morell. Mr. Morell directed that analysts review the information to determine if there was anything there that would change their assessments of what happened.[68]

This specific report by ████ to the Libyans—if it even occurred—remains uncorroborated.

Finding #2: CIA provided sufficient security personnel, resources, and equipment to defend against the known terrorist threat and to enable CIA operations in Benghazi. There is no evidence that the CIA turned down requests for additional security resources at the Annex.

An adequate number of highly trained security personnel defended the Annex, which also contained physical security features to enable secure CIA operations despite the increased threat in the region. Indeed, CIA security officers demonstrated that capability during the attacks. Security personnel used their vehicles and weapons to simultaneously mount a rescue operation at the TMF while also defending the CIA Annex.[69] Concurrent with both of those operations, CIA deployed a separate team from Tripoli with additional security officers to rescue Ambassador Stevens and further bolster CIA's defensive capabilities in Benghazi.[70] Even after the deadly mortar strikes at the Annex, some remaining CIA officers at the Annex believed they could continue to defend the Annex without additional support.[71]

According to the first of two site vulnerability assessments conducted by the CIA prior to the attacks, the Annex's physical security features included numerous advantages over those of the TMF.[72] The TMF's lone advantage was that it was larger and was less vulnerable from the street. The TMF's distance from the street allowed for added protection from a bomb blast at or near the walls of one of the facilities, and would provide additional time for security officers to respond before attackers could reach

---

[66] HPSCI review of Benghazi Intelligence Review (October 2012 ODNI-provided package of 429 intelligence cables, reports, and assessments ranging from February to October 2012).
[67] CIA Email: "Fw: Per your request – more explanation on Tripoli Station assessment on attacks".
[68] CIA Email to SSCI Staff, "Answers to SSCI Benghazi Questions from August 2013," September 6, 2013.
[69] HPSCI Transcript "Subcommittee Interview with Officers 3, 4, and 5," November 14, 2013 pg. 11.
[70] HPSCI Transcript, "Full Committee Hearing with CIA's former Chief of Benghazi Base," May 22, 2013, pg. 13.
[71] HPSCI Transcript "Subcommittee Staff Interview with Officer 8," December 13, 2013 pg. 26.
[72] Benghazi Base, Libya Comparative Analysis: Site Vulnerability, ████████.

the operational buildings.[73] According to CIA officers' testimony and documentation, CIA continued to add physical security features to the Annex and upgraded their operational posture after both reviews and prior to the attacks.[74] The Committee found no evidence that the CIA turned down requests for additional resources at the Annex. Further, CIA's low profile in Benghazi generally provided it an additional layer of security.[75] Finally, in response to the continued growing threat against Western personnel and interests in Benghazi, CIA implemented additional security measures, including:

Shortly after the Chief of Station in Tripoli arrived in country, he consulted with the Chief of Benghazi Base, personally assessed the security situation, and took actions that were intended to improve logistics, security, and communication that ultimately proved critical in enabling the Tripoli Team to quickly travel to Benghazi that night.[77]

Finding #3: **State Department security personnel, resources, and equipment were unable to counter the terrorist threat that day, and they required CIA assistance.**

Although HPSCI generally does not review State Department security capabilities, and this review did not set out to review those capabilities, evidence the Committee received related to the level of the State Department's security capabilities in Benghazi.

CIA security personnel testified that State Department DS agents repeatedly stated they felt ill-equipped and ill-trained to contend with the threat environment in Benghazi. According to eyewitnesses testifying before HPSCI, the DS agents knew well before the attacks that they could not defend the TMF against an armed assault. The DS agents also told CIA about their requests for additional resources that

---

[73] Benghazi Base, Libya Comparative Analysis: Site Vulnerability, ▮▮▮▮▮▮▮▮.
[74] HPSCI Transcript "Subcommittee Interview with the former Chief of Tripoli Station," April 1, 2014 pg. 13; HPSCI Transcript "Subcommittee Staff Interview with Officer 8," December 13, 2013 pg. 41.
[75] HPSCI Transcript "Subcommittee Interview with Officers 3, 4, and 5," November 14, 2013 pg. 6.
[76] CIA Cable Benghazi 14986 "Security Recommendations for Benghazi Base Following the Recent Attacks Against Western Targets," ▮▮▮▮▮▮; CIA-provided Summary of Post-Review Actions in Response to Security Recommendations.
[77] HPSCI Transcript "Subcommittee Interview with the former Chief of Tripoli Station," April 1, 2014 pgs. 3-4.

were pending with the U.S. Embassy in Tripoli.[78] The CIA security contractors noted the security flaws of the TMF. In their view, it was a very large compound with too few guards and large spaces for attackers, such as snipers, to hide.[79]

Upon arriving at the TMF the night of the attacks, the CIA security team observed that some, perhaps all, of the DS agents were unarmed and one of them was not wearing shoes.[80] At the Annex, only one DS agent participated in the defense of the Annex, but he was in a defensive position on the roof of Annex building #3 when it was hit with the mortar rounds and was severely injured. The other DS agents remained in a secure area with the CIA case officers and support staff.

Finding #4: The CIA was not collecting and shipping arms from Libya to Syria.

Multiple media outlets have reported allegations about CIA collecting weapons in Benghazi and facilitating weapons from Libya to Syria.[81] The eyewitness testimony and thousands of pages of CIA cables and emails that the Committee reviewed provide no support for this allegation.

Committee Members and staff asked all witnesses what they observed at the Benghazi Annex and whether they had any information to support allegations about weapons being collected and transported to Syria. Each witness reported seeing only standard CIA security weapons at the base. No witness testified that non-CIA weapons were brought to the Annex. Security personnel and officers testified that they had complete access to the Annex and would have observed any weapons, such as MANPADs, stored at the facility. Security personnel and officers also testified that nobody told them to hide or withhold any information from the Committee. This record is consistent throughout the Committee interviews by Members and staff.[82]

According to testimony from CIA Deputy Director Morell and confirmed by other witnesses, the CIA's mission in Benghazi was to collect foreign intelligence. From the Annex in Benghazi, the CIA was collecting intelligence about foreign entities that were themselves collecting weapons in Libya and facilitating their passage to Syria. The Benghazi Annex was not itself collecting weapons. The Committee has not seen any credible information to dispute these facts.[83]

---

[78] HPSCI Transcript "Subcommittee Interview with Officers 3, 4, and 5," November 14, 2013 pg. 38.

[79] HPSCI Transcript "Subcommittee Interview with Officers 3, 4, and 5," November 14, 2013 pg. 37.

[80] HPSCI Transcript "Subcommittee Interview with Officers 3, 4, and 5," November 14, 2013 pgs. 115-116.

[81] Fox News "Was Syrian weapons shipment factor in ambassador's Benghazi visit?," October 25, 2012.

[82] HPSCI Transcript "Subcommittee Interview with Officers 1 and 2," November 13, 2013; HPSCI Transcript "Subcommittee Interview with Officers 3, 4, and 5," November 14, 2013; HPSCI Transcript "Subcommittee Interview with Officers 6 and 7," December 3, 2013; HPSCI Transcript "Subcommittee Staff Interview with Officer 8," December 13, 2013; HPSCI Transcript "Full Committee Hearing with CIA's former Chief of Benghazi Base," May 22, 2013, pg. 34; HPSCI Transcript "Subcommittee Interview with Officers 1 and 2," November 13, 2013 pg. 11; HPSCI Transcript "Subcommittee Interview with Officers 3, 4, and 5," November 14, 2013 pg. 7; HPSCI Transcript "Subcommittee Interview with Officers 6 and 7," December 3, 2013 pg. 74; HPSCI Transcript "Subcommittee Interview with the former Chief of Tripoli Station," April 1, 2014 pgs. 67-68.

[83] HPSCI Transcript "Full Committee Hearing with Deputy CIA Director Michael Morell," May 22, 2013 pgs. 62-64; HPSCI Transcript "Subcommittee Interview with the former Chief of Tripoli Station," April 1, 2014 pgs. 67-68.

III. Al-Qa'ida-affiliated groups participated in the attacks on U.S. facilities in Benghazi, and the appropriate U.S. personnel made reasonable tactical decisions about how to respond to the attacks and rescue fellow Americans. There was neither a stand down order nor a denial of available air support, and no American was left behind.

Finding #5: A mixed group, including members of al-Qa'ida in the lands of the Islamic Maghreb (AQIM), al-Qa'ida in the Arabian Peninsula (AQAP), al-Qa'ida in Iraq (AQI), the Muhammad Jamal Network (MJN), Ansar al-Sharia (AAS), and Abu Abaydah Ibn Jarah Battalion (UJB) participated in the attacks, along with Qadafi loyalists.

In addition to individual assessments immediately following the attacks, the IC has produced a series of six assessments intended to comprehensively identify terrorists and extremists associated with the Benghazi attacks. According to those assessments, AAS, AQIM, and MJN were involved in the attacks while members of AQAP, AQI, and UJB also participated. Additionally, reports stated that Qadafi loyalists likely joined in the attacks.[84] In the most recent of those six assessments, the IC identified 85 individuals who had some level of participation in the attacks and an additional four known extremists who are affiliated with the suspected attackers. That assessment relies on 146 citations that include reports from CIA, NSA, FBI, DoD, the State Department, and the Open Source Center.[85] The FBI continues to pursue a subset of individuals who they believe participated in the attacks. The IC continues to collect intelligence on these individuals as well as search for others that may have not yet been identified.

The discussion below highlights the intelligence on some of the key attackers and, in some cases, their affiliation with al-Qa'ida. The lack of a coherent structure among Libyan militias and terrorists groups, with often overlapping allegiances, is a challenge to identifying those involved.[86]

AAS posted a video on YouTube on September 12, 2012, claiming participation in the attacks, but it took down the posting shortly thereafter.[87] In September 2013, AAS reportedly pledged its support to AQIM.[88] Abu Khattalah, an AAS leader, was probably one of the ringleaders of the attacks and was at the TMF that night.[89] Media outlets reported in August 2013 that federal authorities filed criminal charges on several Benghazi suspects, including Abu Khattalah, and he was subsequently

---

[84] "[The deputy Libyan interior minister] said the Libyan government suspected the gunmen were loyal to former leader Moammar Gaddafi." Washington Post, "Chaos at U.S. Consulate in Libya," September, 12, 2012.

[85] CIA WIRe "Libya: Terrorists and Extremists Reportedly Associated with the Benghazi Attacks," January 28, 2013; CIA WIRe "Libya: Terrorists and Extremists Reportedly Associated with the Benghazi Attacks," February 26, 2013; CIA WIRe "Libya: Terrorists and Extremists Reportedly Associated with the Benghazi Attacks," August 12, 2013; CIA WIRe "Libya: Terrorists and Extremists Reportedly Associated with the Benghazi Attacks," September 9, 2013; CIA WIRe "Libya: Terrorists and Extremists Reportedly Associated with the Benghazi Attacks," March 24, 2014; CIA WIRe "Libya: Terrorists and Extremists Reportedly Associated with the Benghazi Attacks," July 24, 2014.

[86] NCTC Current: "Libya: Update on Benghazi Suspects," September 11, 2013.

[87] HPSCI Transcript, "Full Committee Hearing with DNI Clapper, ADCIA Morell, D/NCTC Olsen, and Under Secretary Kennedy, which included the NCTC Presentation on the Benghazi Attacks," November 15, 2012 pg 46.

[88] CIA Extremist Profile – ██████████████ August 28, 2013.

[89] HPSCI Transcript, "Full Committee Hearing with DNI Clapper, ADCIA Morell, D/NCTC Olsen, and Under Secretary Kennedy, which included the NCTC Presentation on the Benghazi Attacks," November 15, 2012 pg. 65.

4. House Permanent Select Committee on Intelligence (11/21/2014)

detained and transported to the United States for trial.[90] Sufyan bin Qumu, the spiritual leader of AAS-Darnah, a former Guantanamo Bay detainee, and a trainee at an al-Qa'ida terrorist training camp in Afghanistan in 1993, probably played some role in the attacks,[91] even though reliable intelligence indicates that Qumu was not in Benghazi on the night of the attacks.[92] Qumu and Khattalah were both AAS leaders at the time, knew each other, and ran in the same circles, but the nature of their relationship is still not fully clear.

Ample intelligence reporting from multiple sources indicates Khattalah's role in the attacks. For example, CIA's then-Chief of Base in Benghazi told Committee staff that available sources suggest that Abu Khattalah and his group were responsible for the attacks.[93] ████████████████████████████████ [94] ██. In an August 2013 CNN interview, Khattalah acknowledged that he was at the TMF after the attacks but denied he was involved in the violence.[95] On June 17, 2014, the White House announced, and it was widely reported, that the U.S. successfully conducted a unilateral operation in Benghazi, Libya to capture Khattalah.[96] He is now in U.S. federal custody.

According to a February 7, 2014, FBI briefing to Committee staff, ████████████████████ indicates that ██ and ordered them to attack the TMF on September 11—in response to both the anti-Islamic video and Ayman al-Zawahiri's fatwa to avenge the death of al-Qa'ida deputy Abu Yaha al-Libi. According to these reports, ████████████████████████████████ If true, this evidence would corroborate an earlier ████ report ████████████ that indicated ████████ ordered the attacks in revenge for the death of al-Libi and other intelligence ████████████████████████████████████ that other extremists were involved.[97]

Another suspect, Faraj al Chalabi, was an al-Qa'ida terrorist linked to the 1994 terrorist murder of two German tourists.[98] In February 2014, CIA assessed that he was the amir of a group that claimed responsibility for recent attacks against U.S. facilities and citizens in Libya and pledged to conduct more

---

[90] New York Times "U.S. Charges Libyan Milita Leader in Benghazi Attack," August 6, 2013; Indictment, United States v. Khatallah, No. 1:14-cr-00141 (D.D.C. June 26, 2014).

[91] Department of Defense Joint Task Force Guantanamo Bay, Cuba "Update Recommendation to Transfer to the Control of Another Country for Continued Detention (TRCD) for Guantanamo Detainee, ISN: USLY-000557DP (S).

[92] FBI Briefing to HPSCI Staff "FBI Update on Benghazi Investigation," February 7, 2014.

[93] HPSCI Staff MFR "Meeting with the former Chief of Benghazi Base," December 14, 2012.

[94] CIA WIRe "Libya: Terrorists and Extremists Reportedly Associated with the Benghazi Attacks," March 24, 2014.

[95] NCTC "Libya: Terrorists and Extremists Reportedly Associated with the Benghazi Attacks," September 9, 2013 (Authored by CIA, NCTC, and FBI); CNN "First Criminal Charges Filed in Benghazi Attack Probe," August 7, 2013 www.cnn.com/2013/08/06/politics/benghazi-charges/

[96] Statement by the President on the Apprehension of Ahmed Abu Khattalah, June, 17, 2014 www.whitehouse.gov

[97] CIA WIRe "Libya: Terrorists and Extremists Reportedly Associated with the Benghazi Attacks" March 24, 2014.

[98] NCTC "Libya: Terrorists and Extremists Reportedly Associated with the Benghazi Attacks," September 9, 2013 (Authored by CIA, NCTC, and FBI).

attacks, most likely against U.S. interests in Libya.[99] He was detained in Pakistan shortly after the Benghazi attacks and was later sent to Libya, where he was eventually released in June 2013.[100] NCTC assessed in June 2013 that he almost certainly would reengage in plotting against U.S. and Western interests.[101] On July 15, 2014, press reported that Chalabi's body was recovered the previous day. Chalabi was reportedly seen two days prior, in the custody of a local militia in Marj, Libya.[102]

The IC began to receive intelligence on the attackers and their affiliations immediately following the attacks. In January 2013, CIA conducted a review of the analytic products between September 12, 2012, and October 11, 2012, that addressed the attacks. The review found that CIA accurately assessed on September 12 and 13, 2012, that members of AAS and of various al-Qa'ida affiliates perpetrated the attacks. As new reporting provided greater information and detail, CIA gained corroborating reporting to support their previous assessments. This line of analysis remained consistent through the timeframe of the line analytic review and continues to be supported today.[103]

<u>Finding #6</u>: Appropriate personnel on the ground in Benghazi made the decision to send CIA officers to rescue the State Department officers at the TMF.

Eyewitness testimony and video footage confirm the initial testimony to the Committee by NCTC Director Olsen that the CIA deployed an Annex security team to the TMF soon after the attacks began. Specifically, upon receiving the first call of an attack from an assistant Regional Security Officer at 9:42PM, the Annex security team leader gathered the five other available security officers that were at the Annex, and he told them what he knew. They immediately began putting on their gear and preparing vehicles for a rescue operation.[104]

The Annex security team leader then informed the Deputy Chief of Base in Benghazi, who informed his supervisor about the incident at the TMF. As the security officers were putting on their gear, the Benghazi Chief of Base, his deputy, and the Annex security team leader discussed the rescue operation. They discussed the security team's lack of information about exactly what the situation was and their lack of heavy weaponry. The Chief of Base in Benghazi began calling local militias to try to get additional security assistance. He was especially interested in locating pick-up trucks with large caliber machine guns. The Chief of Base made several phone calls, but his initial efforts were unsuccessful.[105] According to the team members, it took about five minutes to prepare their weapons, ammunition, gear, equipment, and vehicles.[106] After that, they prepared to depart for the TMF. After 21

---

[99] CIA WIRe "Libya: Benghazi Attacks Suspect Probably Targeting U.S. Interests," February 11, 2014.

[100] Fox News "Libyans Release Suspect Linked to Benghazi Attack," June 27, 2013.

[101] NCTC "Snapshot of the Worldwide Terrorist Threat to U.S. Interests," June 26, 2013.

[102] CNN "Where are the Benghazi Suspects," July 15, 2014.

[103] CIA WIRe "Libya: Benghazi Attacks Suspect Probably Targeting U.S. Interests," February 11, 2014.

[104] Video footage; HPSCI Transcript, "Full Committee Hearing with DNI Clapper, ADCIA Morell, D/NCTC Olsen, and Under Secretary Kennedy, which included the NCTC Presentation on the Benghazi Attacks," November 15, 2012 pg 20; HPSCI Transcript "Subcommittee Interview with Officers 1 and 2," November 13, 2013 pgs. 18-20; and HPSCI Transcript "Subcommittee Interview with Officers 3, 4, and 5," November 14, 2013 pgs. 16-17.

[105] HPSCI Transcript "Subcommittee Interview with Officers 1 and 2," November 13, 2013 pgs. 18-22, 45, 50, 61, 67-68; HPSCI Transcript "Full Committee Hearing with the former CIA Chief of Benghazi Base," May 22, 2013 pgs. 23-24.

[106] HPSCI Transcript "Subcommittee Interview with Officers 3, 4, and 5," November 14, 2013 pg. 15.

minutes, before receiving arrangements for support from local militias, the team departed in two vehicles for the TMF.[107][108][109]

The Committee found no evidence that any individual from the Annex called CIA Headquarters or CIA officers in Tripoli to seek approval to launch the rescue mission. The CIA security team chief in Benghazi, in consultation with the Chief of Base, made the decision to organize the rescue mission and to commence the operation. The Benghazi security team did not receive any orders from CIA Headquarters or Tripoli with regard to the rescue operation.

Finding #7: **Prior to the CIA security team departing for the TMF, the Annex leadership deliberated thoughtfully, reasonably, and quickly about whether further security could be provided to the team. Although some security officers voiced a greater urgency to depart for the TMF, no officer at CIA was ever told to stand down.**

The evidence from eyewitness testimony, ISR video footage, closed-circuit television recordings, and other sources provides no support for the allegation that there was any stand-down order. Rather, there were mere tactical disagreements about the speed with which the team should depart prior to securing additional security assets.[110]

The 21-minute period between the time the Annex personnel first learned of the attack and when they departed reflects the time the Team needed to put on gear and the time during which the Chief of Base in Benghazi tried to secure local militias to assist in the mission. Annex leadership also considered the impact of the departure of the security officers on the security of the Annex. The Annex had minimal security forces available for the 93 minutes that the team was gone, and there was neither a requirement nor an expectation for the CIA security personnel to defend the State Department's facility in Benghazi. Nonetheless, some Annex team members wanted urgently to depart the Annex for the TMF to save their State Department colleagues. The Chief of Base in Benghazi, however, ordered the team to wait so that the seniors on the ground could ascertain the situation at the TMF and whether they could secure heavy weaponry support from local militias.[111]

---

[107] Video footage.

[108] HPSCI Transcript, "Full Committee Hearing with DNI Clapper, ADCIA Morell, D/NCTC Olsen, and Under Secretary Kennedy, which included the NCTC Presentation on the Benghazi Attacks," November 15, 2012 pg. 20.

[109] The 21 minutes is discussed extensively in the next section of this report.

[110] HPSCI Transcript "Subcommittee Interview with Officers 3, 4, and 5," November 14, 2013 pgs. 17-19, 27-28,44, 50, 80, 83, 88-89; HPSCI Transcript "Subcommittee Interview with Officers 1 and 2," November 13, 2013 pgs. 18-22, 45, 50, 61, 67-68; HPSCI Transcript "Full Committee Hearing with the former CIA Chief of Benghazi Base," May 22, 2013 pgs. 23-24.

[111] One officer felt that the 21 minute delay was too long. His testimony on the timeline is, however, internally inconsistent. His testimony is also inconsistent with other officers on the ground and with then-Deputy Director of the CIA Michael Morell. Given this officer's inconsistent testimony, HPSCI used all other eyewitnesses' accounts to confirm the timeline. HPSCI Transcript "Full Committee Hearing with the former CIA Chief of Benghazi Base," May 22, 2013 pgs. 23-24; HPSCI Transcript "Subcommittee Interview with Officers 1 and 2," November 13, 2013 pgs. 18-22, 45, 50, 61, 67-68; HPSCI Transcript "Subcommittee Interview with Officers 3, 4, and 5," November 14, 2013 pg. 17-19, 27-28,44, 50, 80, 83, 88-89; HPSCI Transcript "Full Committee Hearing with Deputy CIA Director Michael Morell," May 22, 2013 pgs. 35-36.

Based on all of the available evidence, the Committee concludes that the Annex team left in a timely and appropriate manner. None of the officials who testified believed that the 21-minute delay was due to a stand down order from CIA headquarters or from Tripoli Station. Indeed, Deputy Director Morell also testified that the decision to seek militia support was a "very prudent decision and I believe that that was the Benghazi senior intelligence official's decision to make, and I have not questioned that decision and I don't believe any of my senior officers have questioned that decision." He also said: "It has occurred to me that had the Benghazi senior intelligence official sent them the moment they were ready at that 15 minute mark and they had gotten to the TMF and they had all been killed, what I would be explaining to you now is why the Benghazi senior intelligence official was not more careful and did not try to get some help."[112]

Testimony from an active, senior CIA official who has personal experience in crisis situations and who testified at a hearing with Mr. Morell, provided a detailed validation of Morell's assessment. He said:

> A lot of folks that have not been in the situation where they are in charge in an emergency that is in a military situation or a situation involving violence, sometimes they think the decision that that person in charge, that commander is making is just do you go right now or do you not go, when the reality is there [are] a lot of choices that you can make in that situation, there is a lot of nuance, and the choice you make can have grave implications for a lot of people.

> I have been involved. I have had to roll out as part of a response force and I have been part of the decision-making process on rolling out as part of a response force, and I have been the person in charge. And I wish I could tell you I have done it perfect every time, but I haven't. I have been involved in some hasty roll outs, I have directed some hasty roll outs, and it is very fortunate that I didn't contribute to making the situation worse.

> But I think our chief in Benghazi did the right thing. The situation of violence, you know, partway across town, not a lot of information, knowing that it could be very bad and choosing to develop the situation, try to get a little bit more information and try to get some tactical assistance before having people launch in the direction of the TMF. I have looked at it a bunch of ways. I think he made the right call.

> I have seen situations where people rolled out right away and they ended up having to be rescued. I have seen situations where people rolled out right away and they got ambushed on the way because it was part of an enemy plan. I have seen situations where people got lost, vehicles rolled over, and so forth, and instead of coming to the assistance of somebody, you actually detracted from the assistance that they were going to get.

> So I think he made a good call trying to develop a little bit more information and a little bit more tactical support before rolling out. It is possible to wait too long in those situations, you know. It is a call the person is making at the moment based on a lot of inputs and a lack of information

---

[112] HPSCI Transcript "Full Committee Hearing with Deputy CIA Director Michael Morell," May 22, 2013 pgs. 35-36.

and some bogus information. But I think the Chief made the right call, tried hard to gain some advantages so the response team would have better odds of success and better command of the information situation. That wasn't coming and then they rolled out.[113]

Finding #8: The decision to send CIA officers from Tripoli to Benghazi to rescue the Ambassador and bolster security of the U.S. personnel in Benghazi was a tactical decision appropriately made by the senior officers on the ground.

After hearing of the attacks in Benghazi, the CIA security team in Tripoli responded immediately and without hesitation, even without a command order. There was an inherent assumption that a security team would depart as soon as possible. The Tripoli Team departed within 45 minutes of receiving their first phone call about the attacks. Indeed, when receiving the first reports from the Annex team at the TMF that Villa C was on fire, the Chief of Station in Tripoli quickly assisted the security team in gathering necessary assets, including a chartered plane that landed in Benghazi by 1:00 AM.[114]

Finding #9: The Tripoli Team's decision not to move to the hospital to retrieve Ambassador Stevens was based on the best intelligence at the time.

The Tripoli Team initially departed as a CIA quick reaction force to support CIA officers. Once they were on the ground in Benghazi and received reports that Ambassador Stevens was missing and perhaps at the hospital, tactical control of the team was handed to the U.S. military personnel who were part of the Tripoli Team. Together with the lead U.S. military officer, the CIA Tripoli Team lead had decided that the Annex team was successfully defending the U.S. personnel at the Annex and that the Tripoli Team should move to the hospital to rescue the Ambassador.

While planning the movement and trying to arrange secure transportation, the Chief of Station in Tripoli called to inform the officers in Benghazi that Ansar al-Sharia had the security contract for that hospital. Ansar al-Sharia had already posted online that the group was involved in the attack on the TMF.[115] Testimony revealed that the militia at the airport would not offer the Tripoli Team assistance in getting to the hospital.[116] Once it was confirmed that the Ambassador had been killed, the mission changed back from a rescue operation to its original mission—to secure and evacuate all the non-essential personnel from the Annex.[117]

Information available after the attacks confirms that the reports the Team received at the time were not accurate. The CIA has no information that Ansar al-Sharia provided security for the Benghazi Medical Center prior to or during the attacks on the U.S. facilities in Benghazi. Instead, at the time of the attacks, Ansar al-Sharia was tasked with providing security for a different hospital in Benghazi—the al-Jala hospital—as part of the local government's effort to delegate security responsibility to militias to counter rising instability and to moderate the group's extremist agenda, according to clandestine

---

[113] HPSCI Transcript "Full Committee Hearing with Deputy CIA Director Michael Morell," May 22, 2013 pgs. 36-37.

[114] HPSCI Transcript "Subcommittee Staff Interview with Officer 8," December 13, 2013 pgs. 5-8.

[115] HPSCI Transcript "Subcommittee Staff Interview with Officer 8," December 13, 2013 pgs. 12-13.

[116] HPSCI Transcript "Subcommittee Staff Interview with Officer 8," December 13, 2013 pgs. 12-13.

[117] HPSCI Transcript "Subcommittee Staff Interview with Officer 8," December 13, 2013 pgs. 12-13.

reporting.[118]

Finding #10: **The CIA received all military support that was available. Neither the CIA nor DOD denied requests for air support. One CIA security officer requested a Spectre gunship that he believed was available, but his commanding officer did not relay the request because he correctly knew the gunship was not available.**

This review did not set out to assess the Defense Department's activities during the attacks. The House Armed Services Committee report, however, thoroughly addresses the military response to the Benghazi attacks. That report demonstrates that senior-level officials at DoD made decisions in a timely manner and did not delay in ordering forces to respond. The report also said there was no stand down order issued and that the DoD response was limited by DoD's force posture leading up to the attacks. The HASC report concluded that the U.S. military's response to the Benghazi attack was severely degraded because of the location and readiness posture of the U.S forces, and because of lack of clarity about how the terrorist action was unfolding.[119]

When the Benghazi security team was ready to depart for the TMF, one officer twice suggested that it might be a good idea if there were a Spectre gunship and a surveillance flight in the air.[120] Surveillance support had already been directed to Benghazi prior to that request. Specifically, after hearing of the attacks and conferring in Tripoli, officers in Tripoli conferred with military operators in Tripoli and learned there was an unarmed Predator available over Darnah, Libya, which was collecting on other matters. Security personnel consulted with the Tripoli operations center, passed the TMF coordinates to the military operators, and they directed, through an AFRICOM liaison officer in Stuttgart, Germany, the Predator UAV to fly over Benghazi.[121] After this first aircraft began running low on fuel, it was replaced by a separate unarmed Predator UAV.

A member of the security team who served in Tripoli four months earlier had inquired about the availability of air assets and believed a Spectre gunship was based and available in Sigonella, Italy. He assumed that it was still available that night, though he admitted that it was not his job to know whether it was available.[122] Those officers who had attended emergency action committee meetings had discussed intimately what, if any, U.S. military resources were in the area. Those officers knew exactly what was and was not in the area, and they understood that there was no air support or any other assets in the general area. Once the aircraft carrier pulled out at the end of Operation Freedom Falcon, the officers knew air support was not in the area.[123]

The lack of local air support was well-known. Indeed, an ████████ cable from CIA headquarters to personnel in Libya that predated the attacks explained that "the primary course of action

---

[118] CIA Email to HPSCI Staff, January 8, 2014.
[119] House Armed Services Committee "Majority Interim Report: Benghazi Investigation Update," pgs. 13-22.
[120] HPSCI Transcript "Subcommittee Interview with Officers 3, 4, and 5," November 14, 2013 pg. 17.
[121] HPSCI Transcript "Subcommittee Staff Interview with Officer 8," December 13, 2013 pgs. 8-17, 25, 37-38.
[122] HPSCI Transcript "Subcommittee Interview with Officers 3, 4, and 5," November 14, 2013 pgs. 17-20, 27, 38, 50-53, 61, 100-108, 157-158.
[123] HPSCI Transcript "Subcommittee Interview with Officers 1 and 2," November 13, 2013 pgs. 41-43.

for officers operating in Libya during a personnel recovery scenario should be to move away from enemy activity as there is no mechanism/authorities in place for the field to leverage Emergency Close Air Support. The Base should be prepared to recover its officer(s) with local resources within its capabilities and limitations."[124]

IV.	**After the attacks, the early intelligence assessments and the Administration's initial public narrative on the causes and motivations for the attacks were not fully accurate. HPSCI asked for the talking points, which Ambassador Rice ended up using for her talk show appearances on September 16, solely to aid the Members' ability to communicate publicly using the best available intelligence at the time. The process and edits made to these talking points was flawed.**

Finding #11: Ambassador Rice's September 16 public statements about the existence of a protest, as well as some of the underlying intelligence reports, proved to be inaccurate.

After reviewing hundreds of pages of raw intelligence, as well as open source information, it was clear that between the time when the attacks occurred and when the Administration, through Ambassador Susan Rice, appeared on the Sunday talk shows, intelligence analysts and policymakers received a stream of piecemeal intelligence regarding the identities/affiliations and motivations of the attackers, as well as the level of planning and/or coordination. Much of the early intelligence was conflicting, and two years later, intelligence gaps remain.

Various witnesses and senior military officials serving in the Obama Administration testified to this Committee, the House Armed Services Committee, and the Senate Armed Services Committee that they knew from the moment the attacks began that the attacks were deliberate terrorist acts against U.S. interests.[125] No witness has reported believing at any point that the attacks were anything but terrorist acts.

Along those lines, in the Rose Garden on September 12, 2012, President Obama said that four "extraordinary Americans were killed in an attack on our diplomatic post in Benghazi," and said that: "[n]o acts of terror will ever shake the resolve of this great nation, alter that character, or eclipse the light of the values that we stand for."

However, it was not clear whether the terrorist attacks were committed by al-Qa'ida or by various groups of other bad actors, some of who may have been affiliated with al-Qa'ida. Early CIA, NCTC, DIA, and CJCS intelligence assessments on September 12th and 13th stated that members of AAS and various al-Qa'ida affiliates "likely," "probably," or "possibl[y]" participated in the attacks.[126]

---

[124] CIA Cable "DIRECTOR ▮▮▮▮▮▮" ▮▮▮▮▮▮▮▮

[125] HASC Briefing Transcript "DOD's Preparation for the Terrorist Attacks in Benghazi (Part II, AFRICOM)," June 26, 2013; FOX News The Benghazi Transcripts: Top Defense officials briefed Obama on 'attack' not video or protest, January 13, 2013 http://foxnews.com/politics/2014/01/14/benghazi-transcripts-top-defense-officials-briefed-obama-on-attack-not-video-or/

[126] CIA "Executive Update," September 12, 2012; CIA "Libya Spot Commentary," September 12, 2012 1200EDT; NCTC Libya Crisis Update "Ansar al-Shari'a Likely Conducted Benghazi Attack," September 12, 2012 1200 EDT; DIA "Libya: Terrorists Likely Involved in Attack on U.S. Consulate in Benghazi," September 12, 2012; NCTC Libya Spot Report.

For example, on September 12, NCTC reported: "Ansar al Shar'ia, with support from other Islamic extremists in the area, probably perpetrated yesterday's attack on the U.S. Consulate in Benghazi."[127] None of the reports made a definitive assessment of attribution or affiliation that first week after the attacks. A September 12 DIA report, for example, spoke of "unidentified terrorists,"[128] and an NCTC assessment reported that the "Benghazi populace" heard about a security breach at the U.S. Embassy in Cairo and they decided to storm the facility in Benghazi.[129] Libyan government officials told the media that the perpetrators of the attacks were loyalists of ousted and deceased Libyan leader Muammar Qadhafi.[130]

On September 14, CIA Director Petraeus spoke extensively to the Committee about AAS and AQIM's participation in the attacks. However, he did not say that they conducted or orchestrated the attacks. In November 2012, he testified that the CIA still "cannot yet establish responsibility, but there are several data points we are continuing to follow."[131]

Weeks after the attacks, intelligence reports similarly remarked on the "fragmentary and contradictory reporting about who organized the attack," and that it is "unclear if any group or person exercised overall command and control and if the extremist group leaders directed their members to participate in the attacks or the attackers did so on their own."[132] To this day, significant intelligence gaps regarding the identities, affiliations and motivations of the attackers remain.[133]

As for motivation, while Reuters published a series of news articles right after the attacks that included interviews of individuals who claimed they were eyewitnesses to protests at the compound,[134] there were also early reports that the attacks were not spurred by a protest in Benghazi.[135] The first CIA assessment about the attacks, a September 12th Executive Update, said "the presence of armed assailants from the incident's outset suggests this was an intentional assault and not the escalation of a peaceful protest."[136] On September 15, the CIA assessed that the attacks were inspired by the September 11 storming of the U.S. Embassy in Cairo.[137] On September 12, the DIA reported that there were no indications of preoperational planning, but that a mix of terrorists attackers "likely leveraged a target of

---

"Elements of Ansar al-Sharia Probably Conducted Benghazi Attack," September 13, 2012 0600 EDT; CJCS "Terrorism: Threats Emanating from North Africa Grow...," September 13, 2013; DIA "Possible Terrorist Involvement and Motivations Behind the U.S. Consulate Attack in Benghazi," September 13, 2012.

[127] NCTC, "Libya Crisis Update," September 12, 2012 (1200).

[128] DIA, "Libya: Terrorists Likely Involved in Attack on U.S. Consulate in Benghazi," September 12, 2012.

[129] NCTC, "Libya Crisis Update," September 12, 2012 (1200).

[130] Washington Post, "Chaos at U.S. Consulate in Libya," September, 12, 2012.

[131] David Petraeus, "Full Committee Hearing on Benghazi," November 16, 2012 pg. 10.

[132] CIA/NCTC, "Response to Questions on the People Involved in the Benghazi Attacks," September 23, 2012.

[133] CIA, "Libya: Terrorists and Extremists Reportedly Associated with the Benghazi Attacks," March 24, 2014.

[134] Reuters, "Obama Vows to Track Down Ambassador's Killers," September 12, 2012.

[135] One CIA assessment about the attacks, a September 12th Executive Update, said that "the presence of armed assailants from the incident's outset suggests this was an intentional assault and not the escalation of a peaceful protest." CIA, "Libya: Executive Update," September 12, 2012.

[136] CIA "Executive Update," September 12, 2012

[137] CIA, "Libya: Variety of Extremists Participated in Benghazi Attacks," September 15, 2012.

opportunity amidst security vulnerabilities created by protest activity."[138] Weeks afterwards, CIA and NCTC reported that "the attack probably was not specifically planned for 11 September."[139] In total, analysts received 21 reports that a protest occurred in Benghazi—fourteen from the Open Source Center; one from CIA, two from DoD, and four from NSA.[140]

Mr. Morell testified that the "first indication that there may not have been a protest arrived on 14 September in the form of an intelligence report from Tripoli Station," which he did not recall reading. He also indicated he got an email from the Chief of Station in Tripoli (who was not in Benghazi for the attacks) on the morning of Saturday, September 15, which he read as part of his morning reading that day.[141] That email stated that Tripoli Station "assesses the 11-12 September attacks in Benghazi were not spurred by local protests." Chief of Station continued: "We lack any ground-truth information that protest actually occurred, specifically in the vicinity of the consulate and leading up to the attack. We therefore judge events unfolded in a much different manner than in Tunis, Cairo, Khartoum, and Sanaa, which appear to be the result of escalating mob violence."[142]

Mr. Morell testified that this assessment "jumped out" at him immediately because it contradicted the analyst views. He therefore asked his Executive Assistant to request that the Chief of Station provide supporting information. Mr. Morell also testified that CIA Chiefs of Station "do not/not make analytic calls for the Agency." Rather, their job is to "collect information, not to do the analysis." Nonetheless, he testified, their "views are taken very seriously by both senior CIA officers and by CIA analysts, but the analytic side of the Agency, which has access to all the relevant information, makes the official CIA call on any analytic issue."[143]

On Sunday, September 16, 2012, Ambassador Rice stated:

But our current best assessment, based on the information that we have at present, is that, in fact, what this began as, it was a spontaneous—not a premeditated—response to what transpired in Cairo. In Cairo, as you know, a few hours earlier, there was a violent protest that was undertaken in reaction to this very offensive video that was disseminated. We believe that folks in Benghazi, a small number of people came to the Embassy to—or to the consulate, rather, to replicate the sort of challenge that was posed in Cairo. And then as that unfolded, it seems to have been hijacked, let us say, by some individual clusters of extremists who came with heavier weapons, weapons that as you know—in the wake of the revolution in Libya are—are quite common and accessible. And it then evolved from there.[144]

---

[138] DIA, "Libya: Terrorists Likely Involved in Attack on U.S. Consulate in Benghazi," September 12, 2012.

[139] CIA/NCTC, "Response to Questions on the People Involved in the Benghazi Attacks," September 23, 2012.

[140] CIA provided a binder of intelligence reporting that supported and refuted the idea that a protest occurred.

[141] Michael Morell, "Statement for the Record," April 2, 2014, page 17.

[142] CIA "Line Analytic Review of Benghazi Analysis" January 4, 2013; CIA Email Chief of Tripoli Station to Senior CIA Officers September 16, 2012 6:29 A.M.

[143] Michael Morell, "Statement for the Record," April 2, 2014, page 18.

[144] Susan Rice, Interview with Jake Tapper, *This Week*, September 16, 2012.

She referred to what happened in Cairo and Benghazi as a "direct result of a heinous and offensive video that was widely disseminated."[145]

On Saturday September 14, 2012, Deputy National Security Advisor, Ben Rhodes, wrote in an email titled "PREP CALL with Susan: Saturday at 4:00 ET" that one of the goals of Administration public statements should be "To underscore that these protests are rooted in an Internet video, and not a broader failure of policy."[146]

Whatever the larger policy issues, the conclusion that the "protests" were fully "rooted in a video" was incorrect, as were the underlying, early intelligence estimates concerning the video. Once the video footage became available on September 18, 2012, two days after Ambassador Rice spoke, and FBI reporting from interviews with U.S. officials on the ground began to be published on September 22, 2012, CIA changed its judgment and made it clear in a WIRe that ran on September 24th that CIA now assessed that no protest had occurred outside the TMF.[147] The FBI reports were the first formally reported indications that a protest did not occur in Benghazi.

Accordingly, Ambassador Rice's November 27, 2012, comments following her meeting with Acting CIA Director Morell, Senator McCain, Senator Graham, and Senator Ayotte acknowledged that the conclusion was incorrect. Following that meeting, she told reporters:

> In the course of the meeting, we explained that the talking points provided by the intelligence community, and the initial assessment upon which they were based were incorrect in a key respect: there was no protest or demonstration in Benghazi.

She continued:

> While, we certainly wish that we had perfect information just days after the terrorist attack, as is often the case, the intelligence assessment has evolved. We stressed that neither I nor anyone else in the Administration intended to mislead the American people at any stage in this process, and the Administration updated Congress and the American people as our assessments evolved.[148]

In fact, the intelligence assessments continue to evolve to this day, and the investigations into the motivations of the individual attackers are still ongoing. Part of the difficulty in making definitive assessments could in part be due to the fact that the two attacks can be distinguished by their apparent level of sophistication. For example, against the TMF, the attackers ignited diesel fuel, while against the Annex, the attackers used sophisticated mortar firing techniques. Secondly, Libya was, and remains, a chaotic place replete with skilled, armed fighters. As former CIA Director General David Petraeus explained, these groups retained their weapons and therefore did not need a lot of lead time to prepare

---

[145] Susan Rice, Interview with Jake Tapper, *This Week*, September 16, 2012.

[146] Email from Benjamin Rhodes, Deputy National Security Advisor, to senior Administration officials "RE: Prep Call with Susan: Saturday at 4:00 pm ET," September 14, 2012 8:09 PM.

[147] CIA WIRe "Libya: Updated Assessment of Benghazi Attacks," September 24, 2012.

[148] Washington Post "Susan Rice, CIA Director Meet with GOP Critics on Libya," November 27, 2012.

attacks.[149] The sophistication of the attacks does not necessarily imply lengthy pre-planning. Finally, Libya does not have a fully functioning government that can assist while providing the requisite security.

<u>Finding #12</u>: Deputy CIA Director Michael Morell made significant changes to the talking points.

For her public comments, Ambassador Rice used talking points developed at the request of HPSCI.[150]

At the end of the September 14 briefing with Director Petraeus, HPSCI Ranking Member Dutch Ruppersberger requested unclassified talking points to ensure members could speak about the events without compromising classified information.[151] He did not ask for more than what was known and could be discussed publicly.

Michael Morell testified at length about his role in the talking points, the coordination process within CIA, his interactions with the State Department and the White House, and why he believed the interagency process produced such a poor product.[152] He was aware of the State Department's interest and comments on the talking points, yet neither he, Director Petraeus, nor any other authority at CIA appears to have had any idea that Ambassador Rice or other Administration officials would use these talking points to explain the attacks to the American people.

Mr. Morell explained that he had initial concerns about an earlier draft of the talking points because he did not want the CIA to appear "self-serving and defensive" by creating the impression that the CIA had warned the State Department, "implying that if other parts of the government had been responsive the attacks may not have occurred and lives may not have been lost."[153]

Mr. Morell then made a large number of edits after a September 15 White House Deputies Committee meeting, which occurred via secure teleconference (not in person). The meeting addressed threats to facilities in North Africa, the Middle East, and South Asia. The Benghazi talking points were not on the meeting agenda and came up only when Mr. Morell raised them at the end of the meeting. Mr. Morell testified that at the end of the meeting, he raised the issue of the talking points. He said, "I was aware that there were some concerns in the interagency over the talking points, that I had concerns of my own, and that I would work on the talking points and circulate them to deputies for final coordination." According to Mr. Morell, there was no other discussion about the talking points at the Deputies Committee meeting or anywhere else until he sent out his next draft for final coordination. Mr. Morell testified that he checked with his executive assistant and a number of other meeting participants and confirmed that his recollection was accurate.

---

[149] David Petraeus, "Hearing on Benghazi," November 16, 2012, pp. 55-56.

[150] NBC "Meet the Press" Transcript February 23, 2014.

[151] David Petraeus, "Hearing on Benghazi," November 16, 2012, pg. 19.

[152] Michael Morell, "Hearing on Benghazi and the Obama Administration," April 2, 2014, CQ Congressional Transcripts. The specific changes to the talking points have been released to the public and declassified testimony from Michael Morell is attached to this report.

[153] Michael Morell, "Statement for the Record," April 2, 2014, pgs. 12-13.

After the Deputies Committee meeting, Mr. Morell removed the warning language and removed the word "Islamic" from the sentence: "There are indications that Islamic extremists participated in the attacks."[154] He testified that he did so "because I did not think it wise to say something publicly—in particular a religious reference—that might add even more volatility to an already agitated situation in the Middle East and North Africa."[155]

He also testified that he was not aware of previous edits, to include the removal of "al-Qa'ida" from an earlier draft. Additionally, Mr. Morell stated:

> The fact that they [the talking points] were not more robust, however, was in no way due to White House political influence, State Department concerns about how the Department might be portrayed publicly, or any interagency bureaucratic battles. The fact that they were not more robust was a reflection of how little we knew at the time, a reflection of what officers inside and outside CIA thought needed to be protected, and a reflection of what I thought would be fair to say about what CIA had or had not previously warned.[156]

He testified that he made this judgment based on his 30 years as an analyst.

Finding #13: **CIA's Office of Public Affairs also made substantive changes to the talking points by removing the reference to "ties to al-Qa'ida" in the second bullet of the original draft.**

As the declassified talking points emails reveal, CIA's Office of Public Affairs made three critical changes to the talking points. The office deleted the phrase "with ties to al Qa'ida" in the second bullet of the original draft; changed the word "attacks" in the first bullet of the talking points to "demonstrations;" and changed the assertion that Islamic extremists "participated in the attacks" to "participated in violent demonstrations." According to Mr. Morell, the emails indicate that OPA was itself "ensuring that the talking points contained no information that could compromise sources and methods, that nothing was said that could compromise the FBI investigation by prematurely attributing responsibility for the attacks on any one person or group, and finally, that the information pointing to any particular group was limited, and therefore we needed to be careful in talking in any certain terms about who was responsible."[157] As it relates to the last change, Mr. Morell testified that:

> [T]his change, which I admit was not elegant, was in response to a concern expressed by an NCS officer, and shared by [the Director of the Office of Terrorism Analysis], that the original phrasing could be interpreted to suggest that we had direct evidence that it was the extremists who were definitely responsible for the deaths of the Americans. And at that point in time, we did not have such evidence.[158]

---

[154] Michael Morell, "Statement for the Record," April 2, 2014, pg. 15.

[155] Michael Morell, "Statement for the Record," April 2, 2014, page 15.

[156] HPSCI Transcript "Full Committee Hearing with Deputy CIA Director Michael Morell" May 22, 2013.

[157] HPSCI Transcript "Full Committee Hearing with Deputy CIA Director Michael Morell" May 22, 2013 pg.13.

[158] HPSCI Transcript "Full Committee Hearing with Deputy CIA Director Michael Morell" May 22, 2013 pg. 14.

4. House Permanent Select Committee on Intelligence (11/21/2014)

Mr. Morell reported to the Committee that a clear lesson from CIA's review of the talking points is not to have the Office of Public Affairs at the center of the coordination process. [159] Substantive changes to analytic assessments, even those designed for public consumption, must be managed by the substantive experts to ensure accuracy.

Finding #14: Overall, the CIA could have placed more weight on eyewitness sources on the ground and should have challenged its initial assessments about the existence of a protest earlier.

CIA's initial September 12th Executive Update stated that "the presence of armed assailants from the incident's outset suggests this was an intentional assault and not the escalation of a peaceful protest."[160] This assessment lacked source information or any formal intelligence reporting to support it. For those reasons, it was not included in any subsequent products. But it proved to be accurate. The eyewitnesses from Benghazi were in Tripoli and Germany in the days after the attacks and could have provided information that supported this assessment sooner. However, their accounts of the events were not provided to analysts until the FBI published intelligence reports from their interviews. The FBI published the first of those reports on September 22, 2014.[161]

Further, as the CIA concedes, once that initial assessment about a protest was made, CIA compounded its error by not sufficiently challenging the assessment and by using imprecise language. The CIA Line Analytic Review of the Benghazi Attacks concluded in part:

> The view that the attack grew out of a protest at the TMF shaped subsequent IC analysis and affected the phrasing of the judgments in the analytic products. CIA initially did not closely question if a protest had occurred in Benghazi or demonstrate the sequence of events by which it ostensibly led to the attack, because analysts did not view the notion of a protest leading to an attack as implausible before the dissemination of credible reporting that there was no protest. As a result, however, CIA highlighted only some of the supporting intelligence of a protest and compounded the error by using imprecise language suggesting the attacks evolved out of protests, leaving the impression that random demonstrators may have perpetrated the attacks and clouding our assessment that individuals with links to al-Qa'ida and Islamic extremist militia groups were involved in the assault.[162]

The review added that the word "spontaneously," which was used in the 13 September WIRe article to describe how the attacks in Benghazi began, implied that those who attacked the TMF reacted without forethought to events they did not anticipate or control. However, because CIA already assessed that the perpetrators of the attacks in Benghazi acted purposefully in response to events in Cairo, a more accurate word would have been "opportunistically."[163]

---

[159] HPSCI Transcript "Full Committee Hearing with Deputy CIA Director Michael Morell" May 22, 2013 pg. 39.
[160] CIA "Executive Update" September 12, 2012.
[161] FBI "Attack on the Temporary Mission Facility in Benghazi Libya (Redacted FBI Intelligence Reports)," March 6, 2013.
[162] CIA "Analytic Line Review on CIA's Assessments of the 11-12 September 2012 Attacks in Benghazi," January 4, 2013.
[163] CIA "Analytic Line Review on CIA's Assessments of the 11-12 September 2012 Attacks in Benghazi," January 4, 2013.

4. House Permanent Select Committee on Intelligence (11/21/2014)

Furthermore, as mentioned previously in this report, on September 16, the CIA's Chief of Station in Tripoli sent to the then-Deputy Director of CIA and others at the CIA an email stating the Station's view that they lacked any "ground truth reporting" that a protest occurred and that the attacks did not appear to be the "result of escalating mob violence."[164]

Additionally, the Chief of Tripoli Station testified that he coordinated on analytic products following the crisis and removed references to the attacks being "hastily planned." He also highlighted why, based on his conversations with the security personnel who had been on the ground, the analysts should not rely on the ███ intelligence indicating that a protest occurred.[165]

On September 16, 2012, the Directorate of Intelligence agreed with the Chief of Tripoli Station's assessment that a "well-coordinated extremist force conducted the attack on the US Consulate and Base in Benghazi," and that clandestine reporting and signals intelligence "to date suggests the attackers opportunistically seized on earlier protests in Cairo—and possibly planned protests in Benghazi—to execute a deliberate attack on US interests." But it also stated that they continued to have "contradictory reporting about whether nonviolent demonstrations occurred prior to the directed attack on the US Consulate." It concluded by saying that the Station's assessment is the "most definitive account to date indicating that there were no peaceful protests on the day of the attack."[166]

Despite this assessment, the CIA continued to assess that a protest occurred until video footage became available on September 18, 2012, and FBI reporting from interviews with U.S. officials on the ground began to be published on September 22, 2012.[167] The FBI reports were the first formally reported indications that a protest did not occur in Benghazi.

V. **In the course of HPSCI's investigation, while some agencies were slow to respond to Committee inquiries, after an extensive and comprehensive search, there is no evidence that any officer was intimidated, forced to sign NDAs, or otherwise kept from speaking to Congress, or polygraphed because of their presence in Benghazi.**

Finding #15: **CIA did not intimidate or prevent any officer from speaking to Congress or otherwise telling his story.**

According to eyewitness testimony and documentation provided in the appendices to this report, CIA's Office of Security requested that the six CIA independent contractors who were present in Benghazi sign contract addendums and new non-disclosure agreements in a conference room just prior to the May 20, 2013, CIA Memorial Ceremony that honored Glen Doherty and Tyrone Woods, among others.

---

[164] CIA "Line Analytic Review of Benghazi Analysis," January 4, 2013; CIA Email Chief of Tripoli Station to Senior CIA Officers, September 16, 2012 6:29 A.M.

[165] HPSCI Transcript "Subcommittee Interview with the former Chief of Tripoli Station," April 1, 2014 pg. 18.

[166] CIA Memorandum For Director David Petraeus and Deputy Director Michael Morell "In response to a question about recent attacks on U.S. diplomatic facilities in Benghazi," September 16, 2012.

[167] CIA WIRe "Libya: Updated Assessment of Benghazi Attacks," September 24, 2012.

All CIA personnel interviewed by the Committee testified that they did not feel intimidated, dissuaded, or otherwise prevented from telling their story.[168] Further, the non-disclosure agreements they signed included a clause that: "I understand that nothing contained in this agreement prohibits me from reporting intelligence activities that I consider to be unlawful or improper directly to the Intelligence Oversight Board established by the President, or to any successor body that the President may establish, or to the Select Committee on Intelligence of the House of Representatives or the Senate. I recognize that there are established procedures for bringing such matters to the attention of the Agency's Inspector General or to the Director, Central Intelligence...."[169]

Three of the contractors testified that they signed contract addendums because their contracts lacked an "administrative services" section, which would have provided a contractual mechanism for CIA to reimburse them for their travel expenses to attend the ceremony. Those three stated that signing a new NDA along with a contract addendum was standard operating procedure and is something they have done many times. These three officers also testified that a CIA staff officer read them a draft letter from DCIA Brennan at the meeting.[170] This draft letter was signed on May 30, addressed to the witnesses, and informed them that HPSCI and SSCI requested to hear their first hand accounts. The letter also provides information on how to arrange meetings with the Committees.[171]

The testimony of these three contract security personnel corroborates CIA's explanation of the circumstances surrounding the secrecy agreements. CIA briefed the Committee and provided documentation asserting that CIA requested the contract security officers to sign new non-disclosure agreements so CIA could pay them for administrative services (e.g. travel to CIA to be notified of Congress's request to meet with them), rather than mission activities that were outlined in their contracts. CIA has provided evidence to the Committee that confirms that other contract security personnel signed contract addendums and updated non-disclosure agreements (not just the Benghazi security personnel). CIA's written explanation to the Committee follows:

> Congress mandated that the agencies notify every individual on the ground in Benghazi on 11 September, 2012 that the Congress was interested in speaking with them. CIA required a secure means to provide such notice. CIA therefore determined to provide the notice by directing the GRS ICs (independent contractors) to travel to CIA Headquarters so notice could be provided securely. CIA cannot require the IC's to travel except for government business purposes. Given these ICs had been in Benghazi on 11 September 2012 because they were performing under their contracts, their travel to receive notice qualified as an official government business purpose—an administrative purpose rather than a mission purpose—for which the CIA could require their travel, provided CIA paid their expenses. CIA therefore determined to schedule the travel so

---

[168] HPSCI Transcript "Full Committee Hearing with CIA's former Chief of Benghazi Base," May 22, 2013; HPSCI Transcript "Subcommittee Interview with Officers 1 and 2," November 13, 2013. pg. 48; HPSCI Transcript "Subcommittee Interview with Officers 3, 4, and 5," November 14, 2013 pgs. 24-36, 30-32, 34-36, 39-40, 64-73, 83-87, 97-99, 103, 124-127, 151-153; HPSCI Transcript "Subcommittee Interview with Officers 6 and 7," December 3, 2013 pgs. 36-38, 47-48; HPSCI Transcript "Subcommittee Staff Interview with Officer 8," December 13, 2013 pg. 43.

[169] Signed Non-Disclosure Agreement by CIA officer in Benghazi May 20, 2013.

[170] HPSCI Transcript "Subcommittee Interview with Officers 1 and 2," November 13, 2013; HPSCI Transcript "Subcommittee Interview with Officers 6 and 7," December 3, 2013.

[171] CIA Director Brennan letter to CIA officers in Benghazi May 30, 2013.

CIA could provide the mandated notice during the same period of time as the CIA's Annual Memorial Day Ceremony as this would provide the ICs the choice of attending the ceremony if they so desired. The GRS ICs traveled to CIA Headquarters as directed, and CIA officers read them my letter notifying them of Congress's interest in hearing their first-hand accounts of what occurred on the ground in Benghazi. In order to make clear that all GRS ICs could be required to come to CIA Headquarters for administrative purposes related to OCONUS incidence, including to speak to Congress if Congress requested, unbeknown to CIA senior leadership, CIA decided to modify the Statements of Work in all GRS IC contracts, including the two specifically brought back in order to receive the mandated notice. These modifications to the Statements of Work required all ICs who signed the contract modifications to execute new CIA secrecy agreements...[172]

The other three of the six contractors who signed new NDAs testified that they believed CIA's request for the new NDAs appeared odd. However, similar to the other three contractors, one of those contractors conceded that he had to sign a contract addendum on May 20 because he had already resigned from the Agency and the Agency needed to amend the contract to administratively justify reimbursing him for his travel expenses. Another contractor stated that he had to sign a contract addendum on May 20 because he was taking on different job responsibilities at CIA. Finally, the third contractor stated that he did not sign a contract addendum that day at all, which turned out to be innaccurate.[173] The CIA submitted evidence to the Committee proving all three officers signed contract amendments on May 20, 2013.[174]

These three security personnel are no longer contracted with the CIA and co-authored a book about their experiences in Benghazi—further showing that they are not being dissuaded or intimidated from telling their story.[175] The NDAs they signed also outline their agreement to submit any intelligence related manuscripts to CIA's Publication Review Board. They stated that they have already contacted CIA and intend to fully comply with pre-publication review requirements.

While the CIA's decision to request that the six independent security contractors sign new NDAs at the CIA Memorial Service may have been ill-timed considering the gravity of the Memorial Service, it was not improper.

Additionally, Director Brennan's negative response to HPSCI Chairman Rogers, August 2, 2013, letter asking whether any officer, either staff or contractor, had "been required to sign any non-disclosure agreement because of their presence at Benghazi or their participation in any activity related to the Benghazi attacks,"[176] was factually accurate. But, it should have taken into account the perception and public allegations that CIA personnel had been forced to sign Benghazi-related NDAs. The Chief of

---

[172] CIA Response to SSCI RFI "Circumstances of GRS IC Signing Secrecy Agreements," December 12, 2013.
[173] HPSCI Transcript "Subcommittee Interview with Officers 3, 4, and 5," November 14, 2013 pgs. 24-36, 30-32, 34-36, 39-40, 64-73, 83-87, 97-99, 103, 124-127, 151-153.
[174] Non Disclosure Agreements of CIA Benghazi contract officers signed May 20, 2013; Contract Addendums of CIA Benghazi contract officers Signed May 20, 2013.
[175] The Washington Times "Benghazi Security Squat Nabs Book Deal for $3M," June 28, 2013 http://www.washingtontimes.com
[176] Chairman Rogers Letter to DCIA Brennan August 2, 2013.

Contracts in the CIA's Office of Security informed the Committee in writing:

> "The signing of the NDA was solely in conjunction with the modifications to the SOW (statement of work) and the contracts. There was no direction or other pressure placed upon me to specifically have the Benghazi survivors sign the NDAs."[177]

As described above, the NDAs do not mention Benghazi. However, three of the personnel asked to sign them testified that they felt it was at least odd, and they perceived that the NDAs could have been related to Benghazi.

Finding #16: There is no evidence that the CIA conducted any unusual polygraph exams related to Benghazi.

CIA witnesses consistently testified that they had not undergone a polygraph examination following the Benghazi attacks. CIA confirmed that it had not conducted a polygraph examination of any officer following their assignments in Benghazi.[178]

Finding #17: While at times the agencies were slow to respond, ultimately the CIA, NCTC, FBI, and other Executive Branch agencies fully cooperated with the Committee's investigation.

Executive Branch agencies have testified at 20 events and provided thousands of pages of emails, documents, and evidence. DCIA Brennan wrote a letter to Benghazi eyewitnesses informing them of our interest in speaking with them and advising them of different methods they could use to speak to the Committee.[179] He also wrote a letter to Chairman Rogers affirming CIA leadership has consistently made clear to staff and contractors that they may communicate about the Benghazi attacks with the Committee. Director Brennan made all CIA personnel available in a timely fashion. The course of gathering and reviewing the large volume of information, investigating the issue in a deliberate manner, and minor logistical issues are largely responsible for the fact that most of the interviews did not take place until November 2013. All witnesses questioned expressed that nobody had attempted to intimidate them from or prevent them from testifying to the Committee. Many told Committee Members and Staff that they had no interest in talking with Congress and were hoping to continue their careers without having to revisit this issue again.

CIA responses to questions for the record and requests for information were fulsome (although it often took months and multiple requests for the CIA to provide responsive information). NCTC quickly compiled all available intelligence and evidentiary information to compile the November 15, 2012 presentation to the Committee that was eventually shared with the full House of Representatives. The presentation, which proved to be accurate, was exemplary.

ODNI's submission of all IC intelligence reporting and analysis leading up to and in response to

---

[177] CIA Email to HPSCI Staff December 16, 2013.
[178] HPSCI Transcript "Subcommittee Interview with Officers 1 and 2," November 13, 2013 pgs. 43-44; HPSCI Transcript "Subcommittee Interview with Officers 3, 4, and 5," November 14, 2013 pg. 73-74.
[179] CIA Director Brennan letter to CIA officers in Benghazi, May 30, 2013.

the Benghazi attacks was initially incomplete and hastily organized. The package was described to the Committee as comprehensive but critical documents were missing and the package was far from thorough. The White House initially allowed ODNI to only make available the various versions of the talking points on a limited, a read-only basis. After repeated Member inquiries and senior level engagements, the ODNI eventually released the documents.

The FBI, which is also investigating the attacks, has actively participated in Committee hearings and has provided verbal updates to staff, consistent with its need to protect ongoing investigations and prosecutions. The Committee understands and appreciates FBI's need to protect investigations and prosecutions, but it did find the FBI to have over-relied on this justification at times, without actually determining whether classified, closed-door testimony would have had a negative impact. Nonetheless, the Committee finds that the FBI ultimately was sufficiently forthcoming.

Conclusion

This report is the result of nearly two years of intensive investigation. The House Permanent Select Committee on Intelligence reviewed thousands of pages of intelligence assessments, cables, notes, and emails; held 20 Committee events and hearings; and conducted detailed interviews with senior intelligence officials and eyewitnesses to the attacks, including eight security personnel on the ground in Benghazi that night. Members and Staff spent thousands of hours intensively looking at every aspect of the tragedy. The report is therefore meant to serve as the definitive House statement on the Intelligence Community's activities before, during and after the tragic events that caused the deaths of four brave Americans. Despite the highly sensitive nature of these activities, the report has endeavored to make the facts and conclusions within this report widely and publicly available so that the American public can separate actual fact from rumor and unsupported innuendo. Only with a full accounting of the facts can we ensure that tragedies like this one never happen again.

Appendices

1. Additional Views
2. Minority Views
3. November 15, 2012 NCTC Presentation Slides
4. HPSCI Full Committee Hearing Transcript: November 15, 2012 NCTC Presentation
5. HPSCI Full Committee Hearing Transcript: May 22, 2013 DDCIA Morell Testimony
6. Copy of one of the Benghazi Contractor NDAs

113th Congress 2d Session	SENATE	S. Report 113–134

REPORT

of the

U.S. SENATE SELECT COMMITTEE ON INTELLIGENCE

REVIEW

of the

TERRORIST ATTACKS ON U.S. FACILITIES IN BENGHAZI, LIBYA, SEPTEMBER 11-12, 2012

together with

ADDITIONAL VIEWS

―――

January 15, 2014.—Ordered to be printed

―――

―――

U.S. GOVERNMENT PRINTING OFFICE

WASHINGTON : 2014

DIANNE FEINSTEIN, CALIFORNIA, CHAIRMAN
SAXBY CHAMBLISS, GEORGIA, VICE CHAIRMAN

JOHN D. ROCKEFELLER IV, WEST VIRGINIA   RICHARD BURR, NORTH CAROLINA
RON WYDEN, OREGON   JAMES E. RISCH, IDAHO
BARBARA A. MIKULSKI, MARYLAND   DANIEL COATS, INDIANA
MARK UDALL, COLORADO   MARCO RUBIO, FLORIDA
MARK WARNER, VIRGINIA   SUSAN COLLINS, MAINE
MARTIN HEINRICH, NEW MEXICO   TOM COBURN, OKLAHOMA
ANGUS KING, MAINE

HARRY REID, NEVADA, EX OFFICIO
MITCH McCONNELL, KENTUCKY, EX OFFICIO
CARL LEVIN, MICHIGAN, EX OFFICIO
JAMES INHOFE, OKLAHOMA, EX OFFICIO

DAVID GRANNIS, STAFF DIRECTOR
MARTHA SCOTT POINDEXTER, MINORITY STAFF DIRECTOR
DESIREE THOMPSON SAYLE, CHIEF CLERK

United States Senate

SELECT COMMITTEE ON INTELLIGENCE

WASHINGTON, DC 20510–6475

January 15, 2014

The Honorable Patrick Leahy
President Pro Tempore
437 Russell Senate Bldg.
United States Senate
Washington, DC 20510

Dear Mr. President:

On behalf of all members of the Select Committee on Intelligence, we are filing the enclosed Committee report titled, "SSCI Review of Terrorist Attacks on U.S. Facilities in Benghazi, Libya, September 11-12, 2012." The report was approved by voice vote of the Committee at a meeting held on December 12, 2013.

Senate Resolution 400 of the 94th Congress (1976) charges the Committee with the duty to oversee and make continuing studies of the intelligence activities and programs of the United States Government, and to report to the Senate concerning those activities and programs. Pursuant to its responsibilities under Senate Resolution 400, the Committee undertook an in-depth examination of the matters described in the report.

The report we are submitting for printing is the declassified version and unclassified Additional Views. (Officials of the Executive Branch have already had an opportunity to review the report for classification purposes.) The classified report is available for Members to read in the Committee's secure spaces.

Sincerely,

Dianne Feinstein
Chairman

Saxby Chambliss
Vice Chairman

Enclosure

<table>
<tr><td>113th Congress
2d Session</td><td>SENATE</td><td>S. Report
113–134</td></tr>
</table>

Mrs. Feinstein, from the Select Committee on Intelligence,
submitted the following

REPORT

of the

U.S. SENATE SELECT COMMITTEE ON INTELLIGENCE

REVIEW

of the

TERRORIST ATTACKS ON U.S. FACILITIES IN BENGHAZI, LIBYA, SEPTEMBER 11-12, 2012

together with

ADDITIONAL VIEWS

January 15, 2014.—Ordered to be printed

SENATE SELECT COMMITTEE ON INTELLIGENCE

United States Senate

113th Congress

DIANNE FEINSTEIN, CALIFORNIA, CHAIRMAN
SAXBY CHAMBLISS, GEORGIA, VICE CHAIRMAN

JOHN D. ROCKEFELLER IV, WEST VIRGINIA	RICHARD BURR, NORTH CAROLINA
RON WYDEN, OREGON	JAMES RISCH, IDAHO
BARBARA A. MIKULSKI, MARYLAND	DANIEL COATS, INDIANA
MARK UDALL, COLORADO	MARCO RUBIO, FLORIDA
MARK WARNER, VIRGINIA	SUSAN COLLINS, MAINE
MARTIN HEINRICH, NEW MEXICO	TOM COBURN, OKLAHOMA
ANGUS KING, MAINE	

HARRY REID, NEVADA, EX OFFICIO MEMBER
MITCH MCCONNELL, KENTUCKY, EX OFFICIO MEMBER
CARL LEVIN, MICHIGAN, EX OFFICIO MEMBER
JAMES INHOFE, OKLAHOMA, EX OFFICIO

David Grannis, Staff Director
Martha Scott Poindexter, Minority Staff Director
Desiree Thompson Sayle, Chief Clerk

SSCI Review of the Terrorist Attacks on U.S. Facilities in Benghazi, Libya, September 11-12, 2012

I. PURPOSE OF THIS REPORT

The purpose of this report is to review the September 11-12, 2012, terrorist attacks against two U.S. facilities in Benghazi, Libya. This review by the Senate Select Committee on Intelligence (hereinafter "SSCI" or "the Committee") focuses primarily on the analysis by and actions of the Intelligence Community (IC) leading up to, during, and immediately following the attacks. The report also addresses, as appropriate, other issues about the attacks as they relate to the Department of Defense (DoD) and Department of State (State or State Department).

It is important to acknowledge at the outset that diplomacy and intelligence collection are inherently risky, and that all risk cannot be eliminated. Diplomatic and intelligence personnel work in high-risk locations all over the world to collect information necessary to prevent future attacks against the United States and our allies. Between 1998 (the year of the terrorist attacks against the U.S. Embassies in Kenya and Tanzania) and 2012, 273 significant attacks were carried out against U.S. diplomatic facilities and personnel.[1] The need to place personnel in high-risk locations carries significant vulnerabilities for the United States. The Committee intends for this report to help increase security and reduce the risks to our personnel serving overseas and to better explain what happened before, during, and after the attacks.

II. THE COMMITTEE'S REVIEW[2]

Hearings, Briefings, and Meetings: The Committee began its initial review of the September 11, 2012, terrorist attacks against the U.S facilities in Benghazi, Libya, on September 13, 2012, which transitioned into a formal review a few

---

[1] U.S. Department of State, Bureau of Diplomatic Security, *Significant Attacks Against U.S. Diplomatic Facilities and Personnel, 1998-2012*, revised July 2013. This report also states on page i: "This information is not an all-inclusive compilation; rather, it is a reasonably comprehensive listing of significant attacks."

[2] The Committee notes that the IC, State, and DoD provided the Committee with hundreds of key documents throughout this review, although sometimes with a significant amount of resistance, especially from State. This lack of cooperation unnecessarily hampered the Committee's review.

1

weeks later. This report and our findings and recommendations are based upon the extensive work conducted by Committee Members and staff during this review, including the following hearings, briefings, and meetings (which included interviews of U.S. personnel on the ground during the attacks):

- Three Committee oversight hearings with witnesses from the Office of the Director of National Intelligence (ODNI), National Counterterrorism Center (NCTC), Central Intelligence Agency (CIA), Federal Bureau of Investigation (FBI), State, and DoD;

- Two Committee briefings with David Petraeus—one while he was CIA Director and one after his resignation;

- Three Committee briefings with Robert Litt, ODNI General Counsel, regarding the issue of the CIA Talking Points;

- Four on-the record Member and staff meetings with:

  1. Gregory Hicks, Deputy Chief of Mission (DCM) in Tripoli during the attacks;[3]

  2. Mark Thompson, Acting Deputy Assistant Secretary for Counterterrorism at the State Department;

  3. Eric Nordstrom, former Regional Security Officer (RSO) in Libya; and

  4. the former CIA Chief of Base in Benghazi who was at the Annex on the night of the attacks; and

- At least 17 other staff briefings and meetings, including interviews of U.S. Government security personnel on the ground in Benghazi the night of the attacks.

---

[3] Mr. Hicks met with Committee staff, without Senators, in a follow-up session. *See* SSCI Transcript, *Staff Interview of Gregory Hicks*, June 19, 2003.

  <u>Documents and Video Reviewed</u>: The Committee reviewed: (1) thousands of intelligence reports and internal documents (including e-mails, cables, etc.) which were provided by the IC, the State Department, and DoD; (2) written responses to Committee questions for the record; (3) numerous open-source materials; and (4) surveillance videos related to the attacks.

III. DESCRIPTION OF THE SEPTEMBER 11-12, 2012, ATTACKS

  The sequence of events in Benghazi on the night of September 11, 2012, and the morning of September 12, 2012, have been widely described in media and other reports. There were effectively at least three different attacks against U.S. facilities in fewer than eight hours. Understanding the evolution and the sequence of attacks is important to provide the context in which Americans in Benghazi and Tripoli and U.S. officials in Washington, D.C., evaluated events as they unfolded and formulated operational and policy responses. Below are the key details about the three attacks.

1. <u>Attack on the U.S. Temporary Mission Facility at Approximately 9:40 p.m.</u>

  At approximately 9:40 p.m. Benghazi time, on September 11, 2012, dozens of attackers easily gained access to the U.S. Temporary Mission Facility (hereinafter "the TMF," "the Mission facility," or "the Mission compound") by scaling and then opening the front vehicle gate.[4] Over the course of the entire attack on the TMF, at least 60 different attackers entered the U.S. compound and can be seen on the surveillance video recovered from the Mission facility.[5] The attackers moved unimpeded throughout the compound, entering and exiting buildings at will.

  After entering the Mission facility, the attackers used diesel fuel to set fire to the barracks/guard house of the Libyan 17th February Brigade militia, which served as a security force provided by the host nation for the Mission compound, and then proceeded towards the main buildings of the compound.[6] A Diplomatic Security (DS) agent working in the Tactical Operations Center (TOC) of the Mission

---

[4] SSCI Transcript, *Hearing on the Attacks in Benghazi*, November 15, 2012, p. 24.

[5] James R. Clapper, Director of National Intelligence, *Joint Statement for the Record, SSCI Hearing on the Attacks in Benghazi*, November 15, 2012, p. 3.

[6] Ibid.

facility immediately activated the Imminent Danger Notification System.[7] He also alerted the CIA personnel stationed at the nearby CIA Annex (hereinafter "the Annex"), the Libyan 17th February Brigade, the U.S. Embassy in Tripoli, and the Diplomatic Security Command Center (DSCC) in Washington, D.C.[8]

There were five DS agents at the Mission compound that night. Two had traveled from Tripoli with U.S. Ambassador to Libya Christopher Stevens (who was staying at the Mission compound in Benghazi), and three others were assigned to the Mission facility. In addition to the five DS agents on duty, there were three armed members of the Libyan 17th February Brigade militia, three Libyan National Police officers, and five unarmed members of a local security team contracted through a British company, Blue Mountain Group, who were guarding the Mission facility that night. In addition, six armed CIA security personnel (plus an interpreter) operating out of the nearby Annex were able to respond quickly after receiving word of the attack.

After the DS agent in the Tactical Operations Center at the Temporary Mission Facility alerted the Annex security team that the TMF was under attack at approximately 9:40 p.m., the Chief of Base called the ███████████████ ███████████, "who advised that he would immediately deploy a ███ ████ force to provide assistance," according to a September 19, 2012, cable that provided the joint CIA Station/Base report on the events surrounding the September 11-12 attacks.[9]

Two armored vehicles were prepared so the security team could respond from the Annex. Approximately 20-25 minutes after the first call came into the Annex that the Temporary Mission Facility was under attack, a security team left the Annex for the Mission compound. In footage taken from the Annex's security cameras, the security team can be observed departing the CIA Annex at 10:03 p.m. Benghazi time. During the period between approximately 9:40 p.m. and 10:03 p.m. Benghazi time, the Chief of Base and security team members attempted to secure assistance and heavy weapons (such as .50 caliber truck-mounted machine guns) from the 17th February Brigade and other militias that had been assisting the United States.[10] Then, the team drove to the Mission facility and made their way

---

[7] NCTC and FBI, *The 11-12 September Attacks on US Facilities in Benghazi*, November 13, 2012, p. 3.
[8] Ibid.
[9] E-mail from ██████████ to ██████████, "Fw: Subject: Eyes Only – Tripoli Station and Benghazi Base Report on Events of 11-12 September," containing CIA TRIPOLI 27900, September 19, 2012, p. 2.
[10] Classified Report of the Department of State Accountability Review Board (ARB), December 18, 2012, p. 27.

4

onto the Mission compound in the face of enemy fire, arriving in the vicinity of the compound at approximately 10:10 p.m. Benghazi time.[11] The Committee explored claims that there was a "stand down" order given to the security team at the Annex. Although some members of the security team expressed frustration that they were unable to respond more quickly to the Mission compound,[12] the Committee found no evidence of intentional delay or obstruction by the Chief of Base or any other party.[13]

Meanwhile, a DS agent secured Ambassador Stevens and State Department Information Management Officer Sean Smith in the "safe area" of the main building of the Mission facility (Building C). The attackers used diesel fuel to set the main building ablaze and thick smoke rapidly filled the entire structure. According to testimony of the Director of the NCTC, the DS agent began leading the Ambassador and Mr. Smith toward the emergency escape window to escape the smoke.[14] Nearing unconsciousness himself, the agent opened the emergency escape window and crawled out. He then realized he had become separated from the Ambassador and Sean Smith in the smoke, so he reentered and searched the building multiple times.[15] The DS agent, suffering from severe smoke inhalation, climbed a ladder to the roof where he radioed the other DS agents for assistance and attempted unsuccessfully to ventilate the building by breaking a skylight.[16]

Other DS agents went to retrieve their M-4 carbine assault rifles from Building B when the attack began. When they attempted to return to the main building (Building C) to help protect the Ambassador, they encountered armed attackers and decided to return to Building B to take cover rather than open fire. They eventually regrouped, made their way to a nearby armored vehicle, and then drove over to assist the agent on the roof of Building C searching for the

---

[11] NCTC and FBI, *The 11-12 September Attacks on US Facilities in Benghazi*, November 13, 2012, p. 4; E-mail from CIA Office of Congressional Affairs (OCA) staff to Staff Director, House Permanent Select Committee on Intelligence (HPSCI), et al., "Background Points used on 1 Nov," November 2, 2012, p. 1.

[12] SSCI Memorandum for the Record, "Staff Briefing and Secure Video Teleconference (SVTC) with CIA Benghazi Survivors," June 27, 2013.

[13] According to informal notes obtained from the CIA, the security team left for the Annex without the formal approval of the Chief of Base, *see* attachments to e-mail from CIA staff ███████████ to CIA staff ████ ███████, September 23, 2012. However, a Memorandum for the Record prepared by the Deputy Chief of Base specifically states that the Chief "authorized the move" and the Chief told the Committee: "We launched our QRF [Quick Reaction Force] as soon as possible down to the State [Department] compound." ███████, Memorandum for the Record, "Events of 11-12 SEP 2012 at Benghazi Base, Libya," September 19, 2012, p. 1; and SSCI Transcript, *Member and Staff Interview of former Chief of Base*, December 20, 2012, p. 3.

[14] SSCI Transcript, *Hearing on the Attacks in Benghazi*, November 15, 2012, pp. 27-29.

[15] NCTC and FBI, *The 11-12 September Attacks on US Facilities in Benghazi*, November 13, 2012, p. 4.

[16] Unclassified Report of the ARB, December 18, 2012, p. 22.

Ambassador and Mr. Smith. After numerous attempts, they found Mr. Smith, who was deceased.[17] The DS agents did not fire a single shot that night during the attack on the Temporary Mission Facility, according to testimony before the Committee.[18]

Outside the compound, the security team asked 17th February Brigade members to "provide cover" for them to advance to the gate of the Temporary Mission Facility with gun trucks. The 17th February Brigade members refused, saying they preferred to negotiate with the attackers instead. Eventually, the security team initiated their plan of assault on the Mission compound. Some members of the 17th February Brigade "jump[ed] into the vehicle" and "a few 17 Feb members follow[ed] behind on foot to support the team," according to the informal CIA notes provided to the Committee.[19]

When the security team from the Annex arrived on the grounds of the Mission facility, "the officers exchanged fire with the attackers."[20] The CIA security team carried ██ .[21] After pushing back the attackers, the security team joined in the search for the Ambassador.

At approximately 11:10 p.m. Benghazi time, an unarmed, unmanned DoD Predator surveillance aircraft, which had been diverted approximately one hour earlier by U.S. Africa Command (AFRICOM) from another intelligence collection mission in eastern Libya, arrived over the Mission compound and soon after

---

[17] Charlene Lamb, Deputy Assistant Secretary of State for International Programs, Bureau of Diplomatic Security, U.S. Department of State, *Statement for the Record,* House Committee on Oversight and Government Reform (HOGR), *Hearing on the Security Failures of Benghazi,* October 10, 2012, p. 6.

[18] SSCI Transcript, *Hearing on Security Issues at Benghazi and Threats to U.S. Intelligence and Diplomatic Personnel and Facilities Worldwide Since the Attacks,* December 4, 2012, p. 67. However, on page 47 of its classified report, the ARB concluded: "While none of the five DS agents discharged their weapons, the Board concluded that this was a sound tactical decision, given the overwhelming degree to which they were outgunned and outnumbered. A decision to discharge their weapons may well have resulted in more American deaths that night, without saving lives. The multiple trips that DS agents and Annex security team members made into a burning, smoke-filled building showed readiness to risk life and limb to save others."

[19] *See* attachments to e-mail from CIA staff ████████████ to CIA staff ████████████, September 23, 2012.

[20] CIA TRIPOLI 27900, September 19, 2012, p. 3.

[21] SSCI Transcript, *Benghazi Follow Up with Staff,* May 22, 2013, p. 72.

detected a roadblock several blocks east of the Mission facility.[22] During this time, State and CIA personnel re-entered the burning compound numerous times in an attempt to locate Ambassador Stevens, but to no avail. Under the impression that the Ambassador "had already been taken from that compound and that he'd been kidnapped," the leader of the Annex security team decided that U.S. personnel needed to evacuate to the Annex for their safety.[23] DS special agents agreed with the decision to evacuate.

Together, CIA and DS security personnel made a final search for the Ambassador before leaving for the Annex in two separate armored vehicles.[24] One vehicle encountered heavy fire as it ran a roadblock several blocks east of the Mission compound.[25] Both vehicles were eventually able to make their way to the Annex, which was approximately two kilometers away. By approximately 11:30 p.m. Benghazi time, all U.S. personnel, except for the missing Ambassador, had departed the Mission compound.[26] Mr. Smith's remains were also taken to the Annex.

2. <u>Attack on the CIA Annex from Approximately 11:56 p.m. until 1:00 a.m.</u>

The U.S. personnel evacuating the Mission facility were followed by some of the attackers to the CIA Annex nearby.[27] Although officially under cover, the Annex was known by some in Benghazi as an American facility. At approximately 11:56 p.m. Benghazi time, sporadic arms fire and rocket-propelled grenades (RPGs) were fired at the Annex.[28] Over the next hour, the Annex took sporadic small arms fire and RPG rounds, the security team returned fire, and the attackers dispersed.[29] It is likely U.S. personnel injured or possibly killed some of the attackers during the exchange of fire. "[T]hey probably took casualties. I'm quite sure they took casualties," according to the Chief of Base.[30]

---

[22] DoD, *Timeline of Department of Defense Actions on September 11-12, 2012,* April 1, 2013, p. 1.

[23] SSCI Transcript, *Member and Staff Interview of former Chief of Base,* December 20, 2012, p. 5; SSCI Transcript, *Hearing on the Attacks in Benghazi,* November 15, 2012, p. 35.

[24] HOGR Transcript, *Hearing on the Security Failures of Benghazi,* October 10, 2012, p. 32; NCTC and FBI, *The 11-12 September Attacks on U.S. Facilities in Benghazi,* November 13, 2012, pp. 4-5.

[25] SSCI Transcript, *Hearing on the Attacks in Benghazi,* November 15, 2012, p. 35.

[26] NCTC and FBI, *The 11-12 September Attacks on US Facilities in Benghazi,* November 13, 2012, p. 5.

[27] SSCI Transcript, *Member and Staff Interview of former Chief of Base,* December 20, 2012, p. 60.

[28] NCTC and FBI, *The 11-12 September Attacks on US Facilities in Benghazi,* November 13, 2012, p. 5.

[29] E-mail from CIA OCA staff to Staff Director, HPSCI, et al., "Background Points used on 1 Nov." November 2, 2012, p. 1.

[30] SSCI Transcript, *Member and Staff Interview of former Chief of Base,* December 20, 2012, p. 61.

At approximately 1:15 a.m. Benghazi time, a seven-man reinforcement team of additional U.S. security personnel from Tripoli landed at the Benghazi airport and began to negotiate with the local Libyan militias for transportation and a security convoy.[31] Upon learning Ambassador Stevens was still missing and that the situation at the Annex had calmed, the team focused on locating the Ambassador and trying to obtain information on the security situation at the Benghazi Medical Center where he was said to be.[32] An individual at the hospital made calls from the Ambassador's cell phone to numbers stored in the phone, including to some numbers in Tripoli and to one of the RSOs. After an exchange of calls between the individual in possession of Stevens's phone and some of the Americans, the Americans became concerned that the caller could be luring U.S. personnel into an ambush at the hospital and concluded it was too risky to go to the hospital.

After more than three hours of negotiations and communications with Libyan officials who expressed concern about the security situation at the hospital, the Libyan government arranged for the Libyan Shield Militia to provide transportation and an armed escort from the airport.[33] After learning that Ambassador Stevens was almost certainly dead and that the security situation at the hospital was uncertain, the team opted to go to the Annex to support the other U.S. personnel.[34] The security team from Tripoli departed the airport for the Annex at approximately 4:30 a.m. Benghazi time.[35]

3. <u>Attack on the CIA Annex at Approximately 5:15 a.m.</u>

At approximately 5:00 a.m. Benghazi time, the security team from Tripoli arrived at the Annex just moments before the third attack that night. At approximately 5:15 a.m. Benghazi time, mortar rounds began to hit the Annex. Two security officers, Tyrone Woods and Glen Doherty, were killed when they took direct mortar fire as they engaged the enemy from the roof of the Annex.[36] The mortar fire also seriously injured one other security officer and one DS special

---

[31] NCTC and FBI, *The 11-12 September Attacks on US Facilities in Benghazi*, November 13, 2012, p. 6.

[32] E-mail from CIA OCA staff to Staff Director, HPSCI, et al., "Background Points used on 1 Nov," November 2, 2012, p. 1.

[33] SSCI Transcript, *Benghazi Follow Up with Staff*, May 22, 2013, p. 34.

[34] E-mail from CIA OCA staff to Staff Director, HPSCI, et al., "Background Points used on 1 Nov," November 2, 2012, p. 1.

[35] SSCI Transcript, *Benghazi Follow Up with Staff*, May 22, 2013, p. 34.

[36] NCTC and FBI, *The 11-12 September Attacks on US Facilities in Benghazi*, November 13, 2012, p. 6.

agent, necessitating the evacuation of the Annex.[37] That attack lasted only 11 minutes, then dissipated.[38] The mortar fire was particularly accurate, demonstrating a lethal capability and sophistication that changed the dynamic on the ground that night. According to testimony by the Chief of Base, it was only after this third wave of attacks, when the mortars hit, that he decided it was necessary to evacuate the personnel from the Annex.[39]

Less than an hour later, a heavily-armed Libyan militia unit arrived to help evacuate the Annex of all U.S. personnel to the airport. The Ambassador's body, which had been secured by a local Libyan coordinating with the State Department, was also transported from the Benghazi Medical Center to the airport. By approximately 10:00 a.m. Benghazi time, all U.S. personnel and the bodies of the four dead Americans departed from Benghazi to Tripoli.[40]

IV. FINDINGS AND RECOMMENDATIONS

Warnings Before the Attacks and Failures to Provide Security

FINDING #1: In the months before the attacks on September 11, 2012, the IC provided ample strategic warning that the security situation in eastern Libya was deteriorating and that U.S. facilities and personnel were at risk in Benghazi.

The IC produced hundreds of analytic reports in the months preceding the September 11-12, 2012, attacks, providing strategic warning that militias and terrorist and affiliated groups had the capability and intent to strike U.S. and Western facilities and personnel in Libya. For example:

- On June 12, 2012, the Defense Intelligence Agency (DIA) produced a report entitled, "Libya: Terrorists Now Targeting U.S. and Western Interests." The report noted recent attacks against the U.S. Mission compound in Benghazi,

---

[37] SSCI Transcript, *Member and Staff Interview of former Chief of Base*, December 20, 2012, p. 42.

[38] E-mail from CIA OCA staff to Staff Director, HPSCI, et al., "Background Points used on 1 Nov," November 2, 2012, p. 1.

[39] SSCI Transcript, *Member and Staff Interview of former Chief of Base*, December 20, 2012, p. 42, in which the Chief of Base said: "Until the mortar attack, we were pretty comfortable that we could stave off any type of ground assault on the Annex."

[40] NCTC and FBI, *The 11-12 September Attacks on US Facilities in Benghazi,* November 13, 2012, p. 7.

the growing ties between al-Qa'ida (AQ) regional nodes and Libya-based terrorists, and stated: "We expect more anti-U.S. terrorist attacks in eastern Libya ███████████████, due to the terrorists' greater presence there….This will include terrorists conducting more ambush and IED [improvised explosive device] attacks as well as more threats against ███████████████████████."[41]

- On June 18, 2012, the Pentagon's Joint Staff produced a slide in its daily intelligence report entitled, "(U) Terrorism: Conditions Ripe for More Attacks, Terrorist Safe Haven in Libya." In the slide, the Joint Staff assessed: "███████████ support will increase Libyan terrorist capability in the permissive post-revolution security environment. Attacks will also increase in number and lethality as terrorists connect with AQ associates in Libya. Areas of eastern Libya will likely become a safe haven by the end of 2012 ████████████████████████████."[42]

- On July 2, 2012, DIA produced a report that discussed the founding of Ansar al-Sharia (AAS) entitled, ████████████████████████ ████████████████ The report stated: ████████████ ██████████████████████████████[43] ████████████████████████████████████ ████████████████████████████████████ ████████████████████"[44]

- On July 6, 2012, CIA produced a report entitled, "Libya: Al-Qa'ida Establishing Sanctuary." In the report, CIA stated: "Al-Qa'ida-affiliated groups and associates are exploiting the permissive security environment in Libya to enhance their capabilities and expand their operational reach. This year, Muhammad Jamal's Egypt-based network, al-Qa'ida in the Arabian Peninsula (AQAP), and al-Qa'ida in the Lands of the Islamic Maghreb (AQIM) have conducted training, built communication networks, and

---

[41] DIA, "Libya: Terrorists Now Targeting U.S. and Western Interests," Defense Intelligence Report, June 12, 2012.
[42] Joint Staff, "Terrorism: Conditions Ripe for More Attacks, Terrorist Safe Haven in Libya," J-2 Intelligence Update, June 18, 2012.
[43] Qumu was released from Guantanamo Bay in 2007.
[44] DIA, "██," Defense Intelligence Digest, July 2, 2012.

facilitated extremist travel across North Africa from their safe haven in parts of eastern Libya."[45]

- On August 19, 2012, the Pentagon's Joint Staff produced a slide in its daily intelligence report entitled, "(U) Libya: Terrorists to Increase Strength During Next Six Months." In the slide, the Joint Staff stated: "There are no near-term prospects for a reversal in the trend towards a terrorist safe haven in Libya, and areas of eastern Libya will likely become a broader safe haven by the end of 2012. The conditions in Libya will allow terrorists to increase attacks against Western and Libyan interests in the country, as well as attempt attacks in the region and possibly Europe in the next six months."[46]

- On September 5, 2012, AFRICOM produced a Theater Analysis Report entitled, "(U) Libya: Extremism in Libya Past, Present, and Future." The report contained a map showing how "█████████████████ are actively exploiting the open operating environment in Libya." (The map is located in Appendix IV of this report). The report also noted: "Disarray in Libya's security services, and a likely focus by authorities on pursuit of Qadhafi loyalists is likely allowing jihadists in Libya freedom to recruit, train, and facilitate the movement of fighters and weapons. The threat to Western and U.S. interests and individuals remains high, particularly in northeast-Libya."[47]

- On September 7, 2012, DIA produced a report entitled, "███████████████████████ ████████" that stated: "███"[48]

---

[45] CIA, "Libya: Al-Qa'ida Establishing Sanctuary," WIRe, July 6, 2012.
[46] Joint Staff, "Libya: Terrorists to Increase Strength During Next Six Months," J-2 Intelligence Update, August 19, 2012.
[47] United States Africa Command, "Libya: Extremism in Libya Past, Present, and Future," United States Africa Command Theater Analysis Report, September 5, 2012.
[48] DIA, "█████████████████████████████," Defense Intelligence Digest, September 7, 2012.

5. Senate Select Committee on Intelligence (1/14/2014)

State Department officials, including Ambassador Stevens, were aware of, and had regular access to, threat reporting on Libya. According to DCM Greg Hicks, he and Ambassador Stevens regularly read the intelligence coming out of the CIA and communicated with the ██████████████████████, and other intelligence officials on a daily basis.[49] As part of this regular interaction, the Ambassador was provided with an intelligence "read book," which would include information on the security situation and terrorism issues. The read book was also supplied to the Embassy's RSO.[50]

As the Accountability Review Board found, there were at least 20 security incidents involving the Temporary Mission Facility, international organizations, non-governmental organizations, and third-country nationals and diplomats in the Benghazi area in the months leading up to the September 11, 2012, attacks.[51] The

---

[49] SSCI Transcript, *Member and Staff Interview of Gregory Hicks and Mark Thompson*, June 12, 2013, p. 39.

[50] SSCI Transcript, *Benghazi Follow Up with Staff*, May 22, 2013, p. 36.

[51] The 20 security incidents detailed in the unclassified report of the ARB on pages 15-16 are as follows:

- March 18, 2012—Armed robbery occurs at the British School in Benghazi.
- March 22, 2012—Members of a militia searching for a suspect fire their weapons near the U.S. Mission and attempt to enter.
- April 2, 2012—A British armored diplomatic vehicle is attacked after driving into a local protest; the vehicle was damaged but occupants uninjured.
- April 6, 2012—A gelatina bomb or "fish bomb" (traditional homemade explosive device used for fishing) is thrown over the Temporary Mission Facility's north wall.
- April 10, 2012—An IED (gelatina or dynamite stick) is thrown at the motorcade of the United Nations (UN) Special Envoy to Libya in Benghazi.
- April 26, 2012—The principal officer of the U.S. Mission is evacuated from the International Medical University (IMU) after a fistfight escalated to gunfire between Tripoli-based trade delegation security personnel and IMU security.
- April 27, 2012—Two South African nationals in Libya as part of a U.S.-funded weapons abatement, unexploded ordnance removal, and demining project are detained at gunpoint by militia, questioned, and released.
- May 22, 2012—Benghazi-based International Committee of the Red Cross (ICRC) building is struck by RPGs.
- May 28, 2012—A previously unknown organization, Omar Abdurrahman group, claims responsibility for the ICRC attack and issues a threat against the United States on social media sites.
- June 6, 2012—IED attack on the Temporary Mission Facility; the IED detonates with no injuries but blows a large hole in the compound's exterior wall. Omar Abdurrahman group makes an unsubstantiated claim of responsibility.
- June 8, 2012—Two hand grenades target a parked United Kingdom (UK) diplomatic vehicle in Sabha (800 km south of Benghazi).
- June 11, 2012—While in Benghazi, the British Ambassador's convoy is attacked with an RPG and possible AK-47s; two UK security officers are injured. The UK closes its mission in Benghazi the following day.

Intelligence Community reported on several of these incidents in finished intelligence products prior to the September 11, 2012, attacks, including:[52,53,54,55]

- April 6, 2012—A small IED was thrown over the wall of the Temporary Mission Facility.

- April 10, 2012—An explosive device was thrown at a convoy in Benghazi carrying the head of the UN mission to Libya.

- May 22, 2012—The ICRC building in Benghazi was attacked with RPGs. The Omar Abdul Rahman Brigade[56] claimed responsibility for the attack, according to press, social media, and other intelligence.

- June 6, 2012—An IED exploded near the main gate of the Mission facility in Benghazi, creating a 9x12 foot hole in the exterior wall. The Omar Abdul Rahman Brigade claimed responsibility for the attack, according to press reporting and a web forum.

- June 8, 2012—Two hand grenades were placed under two parked UK diplomatic vehicles in Sabha (800 km south of Benghazi).

- June 11, 2012—Unknown assailants using two RPGs and small-arms attacked a three-vehicle convoy in Benghazi carrying the British Ambassador.

- June 12, 2012—An RPG attack occurs on the ICRC compound in Misrata (400 km west of Benghazi).
- June 18, 2012—Protestors storm the Tunisian consulate in Benghazi.
- July 29, 2012—An IED is found on grounds of the Tibesti Hotel in Benghazi.
- July 30, 2012—A Sudanese consul in Benghazi is carjacked and his driver is beaten.
- July 31, 2012—Seven Iranian-citizen ICRC workers are abducted in Benghazi.
- August 5, 2012—ICRC Misrata office is attacked with RPGs; ICRC withdraws its representatives from Misrata and Benghazi.
- August 9, 2012—A Spanish-American dual national NGO worker is abducted from the Islamic Cultural Center in Benghazi and released the same day.
- August 20, 2012—A small bomb is thrown at an Egyptian diplomat's vehicle parked outside of the Egyptian consulate in Benghazi.

[52] CIA, "Libya: Struggling To Create Effective Domestic Security System," WIRe, August 29, 2012.
[53] CIA, "Libya: Attack on British Diplomatic Convoy Underscores Risks To Western Interests," WIRe, June 11, 2012.
[54] CIA, "Libya: Recent Attacks Highlight Persistent Threats in Eastern Libya," WIRe, August 1, 2012.
[55] DIA, "Libya: Terrorists Now Targeting U.S. and Western Interests," Defense Intelligence Report, June 12, 2012.
[56] An unknown group fighting under the name of Omar Abdul Rahman, who is commonly referred to as the "Blind Sheikh." The Omar Abdul Rahman Brigade is also referred to as the Omar Abdurrahman group in this report.

- June 12, 2012—The ICRC building in Misratah[57] was attacked by either an RPG or bomb.

- July 17, 2012—Unknown assailants attacked with small arms a three-vehicle, armored UN convoy as it left Darnah (250 km east of Benghazi).

- July 29, 2012—A number of IEDs are found and defused at the Tibesti Hotel in Benghazi. The Tibesti Hotel is frequented by foreign diplomats and businessmen and was previously used by Ambassador Stevens as a base of operations.

- August 1, 2012—The former regime military intelligence building in Benghazi was bombed.

- August 5, 2012—Unknown assailants attacked the ICRC building in Misratah. ICRC facilities in Misratah and Benghazi were attacked four times between May and August, usually with RPGs.[58]

- August 6, 2012—Two U.S. military personnel in diplomatic vehicles were forced off the road and attacked near Tripoli.

In the months prior to the attack, Ambassador Stevens and other State Department officials in Libya outlined concerns via cables to State Department headquarters about the security of the Mission compound in Benghazi and made several requests for additional security resources. For example:

- On June 6, 2012, Stevens recommended the creation of ████████ ██████ teams, made up of locally hired personnel, in Benghazi and Tripoli.[59] The State Department attempted to create a team in Tripoli, but was unable to do so because it was difficult to find and clear appropriate personnel. A ██████████████ team was never created in Benghazi, despite the Ambassador's recommendation.[60]

---

[57] The IC spells the city "Misratah," but the ARB's report spells it "Misrata."
[58] The IC has since updated this information and now assesses that the ICRC facilities in Misratah and Benghazi were attacked five times between May and August, and on two occasions, the perpetrators used RPGs.
[59] State 12 TRIPOLI 37, June 6, 2012.
[60] SSCI Memorandum for the Record, "Staff Briefing with Under Secretary of State for Management Patrick Kennedy and Assistant Secretary of State for Diplomatic Security Eric Boswell," December 3, 2012.

████████████████

- On July 9, 2012, Stevens sent a cable to State Department headquarters requesting a minimum of 13 "Temporary Duty" (TDY) U.S. security personnel for Libya, which he said could be made up of DS agents, DoD Site Security Team (SST) personnel, or some combination of the two.[61] These TDY security personnel were needed to meet the requested security posture in Tripoli and Benghazi. The State Department never fulfilled this request and, according to Eric Nordstrom, State Department headquarters never responded to the request with a cable.[62]

- In an August 16, 2012, cable to State headquarters, Stevens raised additional concerns about the deteriorating security situation in Benghazi following an Emergency Action Committee (EAC) meeting held on August 15, 2012, in Benghazi. The EAC is an interagency group convened periodically in U.S. embassies and other facilities in response to emergencies or security matters. In this case, the head State Department officer in Benghazi, called the Principal Officer, convened the meeting "to evaluate Post's tripwires in light of the deteriorating security situation in Benghazi."[63] The cable summarizing this EAC included the following points:

  (1) The Principal Officer "remarked that the security situation in Benghazi was 'trending negatively'" and "that this daily pattern of violence would be the 'new normal' for the foreseeable future, particularly given the minimal capabilities of organizations such as the Supreme Security Council and local police."

  (2) A CIA officer "briefed the EAC on the location of approximately ten Islamist militias and AQ training camps within Benghazi."

  (3) The Principal Officer and a CIA officer "expressed concerns with the lack of host nation security to support the U.S. Mission [facility]."

---

[61] State 12 TRIPOLI 690, July 9, 2012.
[62] SSCI Transcript, *Member and Staff Interview of Eric Nordstrom*, June 27, 2013, pp. 32 and 60.
[63] State 12 TRIPOLI 55, August 16, 2012.

(4) A CIA officer "expressed concerns with Post's relationship with the [redacted] [local militia], particularly in light of some of the actions taken by the brigade's subsidiary members."

(5) The Regional Security Officer "expressed concerns with the ability to defend Post in the event of a coordinated attack due to limited manpower, security measures, weapons capabilities, host nation support, and the overall size of the compound."

Despite the clearly deteriorating security situation in Benghazi and requests for additional security resources, few significant improvements were made by the State Department to the security posture of the Temporary Mission Facility. Although the Mission facility met the minimum personnel requirements for Diplomatic Security agents as accepted by the U.S. Embassy in Tripoli at the time of the August 15 EAC meeting (specifically, the three Diplomatic Security agents were assigned to guard the Mission compound), the Committee found no evidence that significant actions were taken by the State Department between August 15, 2012, and September 11, 2012, to increase security at the Mission facility in response to the concerns raised in that meeting.[65]

According to the report of the ARB, "there appeared to be very real confusion over who, ultimately, was responsible and empowered to make decisions based on both policy and security concerns" at the State Department's Bureau of Diplomatic Security, Bureau of Near Eastern Affairs, the U.S. Embassy in Tripoli, and the Mission facility in Benghazi.[66] The Independent Panel on Best Practices, which the ARB recommended State establish to identify best practices from other

---

[64] State 12 TRIPOLI 55, August 16, 2012.
[65] The Committee recognizes that there were communications between State Department employees in Libya regarding security during this time period, including an August 22, 2012, document entitled, "Security Requests for U.S. Mission Benghazi" that was sent from DS agents in Benghazi to the RSO in Tripoli that included specific requests for (1) physical security, (2) equipment, and (3) manpower. There is no indication those requests were passed on to State Department Headquarters in the form of a cable.
[66] Unclassified Report of the ARB, December 18, 2012, p. 30.

agencies and countries, found that a "potential root cause for the confusion, lack of clear lines of authority, and communication at the headquarters level" was that "some senior Foreign Service officers and DS agents who met with the Panel identified the Under Secretary for Management (M) as the senior security official in the Department responsible for final decision making regarding critical security requirements," even though this role was "not identified by Congress in the Diplomatic Security Act of 1986."[67]

Additionally, the uncertain future of the Mission facility, due to its one-year expiration in December 2012, contributed to a lack of continuity for security staff and constrained decision-makers in Washington regarding the allocation of security enhancements to that facility.[68] The Temporary Mission Facility continued to be understaffed and under-resourced, a situation best summarized in a June 2012 document from the Principal Officer in Benghazi, commenting that "[i]f there is a real mission, fund us and find the staff."[69] The State Department did implement some physical security improvements in 2012, such as heightening the perimeter wall, installing concrete Jersey barriers, mounting safety grills on the safe area windows, and other minor improvements. However, as the classified version of the ARB report found, the Mission compound "included a weak and very extended perimeter, an incomplete interior fence, no mantraps and unhardened entry gates and doors. Benghazi was also severely under-resourced with regard to weapons, ammunition, [non-lethal deterrents] and fire safety equipment, including escape masks."[70]

In contrast, the CIA, in response to the same deteriorating security situation and IC threat reporting, consistently upgraded its security posture over the same time period. Specifically, the attack on the British Ambassador's convoy by a rocket-propelled grenade on June 11, 2012, led to a CIA security audit of the Annex. As a result, CIA quickly implemented additional security measures due to the threat of continued attacks against Western personnel in Benghazi. These security upgrades included the following:

---

[67] U.S. Department of State, *Report of the Independent Panel on Best Practices*, August 29, 2013, p. 3.

[68] An August 28, 2012, memo entitled, "Regional Security Officer Turnover" from the outgoing RSO stated: "U.S. Mission Benghazi has an uncertain future; Post is scheduled to close December 31, 2012. Various alternatives are being proposed, including colocating with the Annex. The RSO should be aware that requests for expensive security upgrades may be difficult to obtain as headquarters is hesitant to allocate money to a post that may be closing in a few months." Classified Report of the ARB, December 18, 2012, Appendix 6, p. 1.

[69] Email from ████████, "Response from Charlene," February 13, 2012, p. 3 (the document attached to this email is a series of bullet points).

[70] Classified Report of the ARB, December 18, 2012, p. 6.

5. Senate Select Committee on Intelligence (1/14/2014)

In addition to these improvements, the physical security of the Annex was much more robust than that of the Mission facility,

---

[71] CIA BENGHAZI 14986, June 12, 2012, pp. 3 and 5.

▮▮▮▮▮▮▮▮▮▮▮▮[72] By comparison, as the ARB
found, the Mission facility had received additional surveillance cameras, but they
remained uninstalled because the State Department had not yet sent out the
technical team necessary to install them. In addition, according to the ARB, the
camera monitor in the local guard force booth next to the main gate was inoperable
on the day of the attacks due to a needed repair by a technical team.[73]

There was also a significant difference in security staffing between the two
facilities. In September 2012, there were three Diplomatic Security agents
assigned to the Temporary Mission Facility, while there were nine security officers
out of a total of ▮ individuals at the CIA Annex.[74] On the night of the attack,
there were five DS agents present at the Mission compound, two of whom came
from Tripoli with the Ambassador.[75] In sum, the Mission facility had a much
weaker security posture than the Annex, with a significant disparity in the quality
and quantity of equipment and security upgrades.

The lack of security enhancements contributed to the security breakdown at
the Temporary Mission Facility the night of the attacks. Although the cable
following the August 15 Emergency Action Committee stated that requests "for
additional physical security upgrades and staffing needs" would be submitted
separately to the Embassy in Tripoli,[76] the Committee has not seen any evidence
that those requests were passed on by the Embassy, including by the Ambassador,
to State Department headquarters before the September 11 attacks in Benghazi.

---

[72] SSCI Transcript, *Member and Staff Interview of former Chief of Base*, December 20, 2012, p. 47.
[73] Unclassified Report of the ARB, December 18, 2012, p. 35.
[74] The ▮ CIA personnel in Benghazi included ▮▮▮▮▮▮

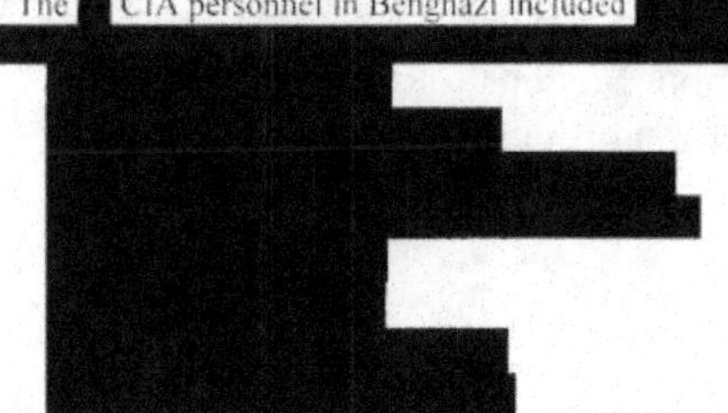

[75] SSCI Transcript, *Staff Briefing From the Intelligence Community on Benghazi*, November 1, 2012, pp. 7-8.
[76] State 12 TRIPOLI 55, August 16, 2012.

5. Senate Select Committee on Intelligence (1/14/2014)

There has been considerable public discussion about the DoD's Site Security
Team in Tripoli. The SST, which was provided by the DoD at no expense to the
Department of State, consisted of 16 special operations personnel detailed to the
Chief of Mission in Libya, although its numbers fluctuated slightly due to
rotations. SST personnel were based in and spent most of their time in Tripoli, but
traveled to Benghazi two or three times in order to: augment the lack of DS agents
there, do a security assessment of the Mission Facility in Benghazi, train local
guard forces, deliver excess defense equipment, and improve the security of the
Temporary Mission Facility.[77] According to testimony to the Committee, SST
personnel carried out a variety of duties including: (1) providing security; (2)
clearing unexploded ordnance from the site of the U.S. Embassy compound; (3)
establishing secure communications; and (4) carrying out medical duties.[78] The
SST provided the Ambassador with various security capabilities and, although not
located in Benghazi, provided a greater pool of security resources in Libya from
which the State Department could draw.

State Department headquarters made the decision not to request an extension
of the SST's mission in August 2012, approximately one month prior to the
attacks, because State believed that many of the duties of the SST could be
accomplished by local security forces, DS agents, or other State Department
capabilities.[79] As a result, DoD changed the mission of its DoD personnel in Libya
from protection of the U.S. Embassy to ▮▮▮▮▮▮▮▮▮ training with the Libyan
security forces.[80] ▮▮▮
▮▮▮▮▮▮▮▮▮▮▮▮▮▮▮▮▮▮[81] "DOD wanted to change the nature of the SST team as
much as State wanted it changed," according to former DCM Hicks.[82]

DoD confirmed to the Committee that Ambassador Stevens declined two
specific offers from General Carter Ham, then the head of AFRICOM, to sustain
the SST in the weeks before the terrorist attacks. After reading the August 16,
2012, EAC cable, General Ham called Ambassador Stevens and asked if the
Embassy needed the SST from the U.S. military, but Stevens told Ham it did not.
Shortly thereafter, Stevens traveled to Germany for a previously scheduled meeting

<hr>

[77] SSCI Transcript, *Benghazi Follow Up with Staff*, May 22, 2013, p. 51.

[78] Ibid., pp. 40-41 and 43-44.

[79] SSCI Transcript, *Hearing on the Attacks in Benghazi*, November 15, 2012, p. 145.

[80] SSCI Transcript, *Member and Staff Interview of Gregory Hicks and Mark Thompson*, June 12, 2013, p. 5.

[81] SSCI Transcript, *Benghazi Follow Up with Staff*, May 22, 2013, p. 42.

[82] SSCI Transcript, *Member and Staff Interview of Gregory Hicks and Mark Thompson*, June 12, 2013, p. 49.

with Ham at AFRICOM headquarters. Ham again offered to sustain the SST at the
meeting, and Stevens again declined.[83]

> **RECOMMENDATION:** The State Department must ensure that security
> threats are quickly assessed and security upgrades are put into place with
> minimal bureaucratic delay. The State Department has made changes since
> September 11, 2012, including the creation of a new position of Deputy
> Assistant Secretary for High-Threat Posts. Although this new position will
> help the State Department focus on high-threat posts, the State Department
> must make the institutional changes necessary to quickly and efficiently
> respond to emerging security threats—especially those threats that have been
> identified numerous times by the U.S. Intelligence Community. The
> Committee urges the State Department to consider the recommendation of its
> Independent Panel on Best Practices to, "as a matter of urgency, establish an
> Under Secretary for Diplomatic Security" to "bring security governance into
> the 21st Century and align security management with the realities of a post
> 9/11 threat environment."[84] As noted by the Chairman of the Independent
> Panel on Best Practices in his written testimony to a House Committee, this
> structural recommendation is not new and was suggested in a report written
> 14 years ago, following the 1998 East Africa Embassy bombings.[85]

> **RECOMMENDATION:** Only in rare instances—and only after a formal risk
> management plan[86] has been put into place—should State Department
> facilities that fall short of current security standards[87] be allowed to operate.
> Facilities that do not meet these standards should be prioritized for additional

---

[83] SSCI Transcript, *Benghazi Follow Up with Staff*, May 22, 2013, p. 47.

[84] U.S. Department of State, *Report of the Independent Panel on Best Practices*, August 29, 2013, pp. 5-6.

[85] Mark Sullivan, Chairman of the Independent Panel on Best Practices, *Testimony Before the House Committee on
Oversight and Government Reform*, September 19, 2013, p. 4; *See also* Booz-Allen & Hamilton, *Security and
Intelligence Management Study*, October 1999.

[86] As described by the Independent Panel on Best Practices, risk management is balancing the "criticality of the
program against the risk to the organization should it implement the program" and understanding, however, there
may be "a requirement to conduct critical programs in an environment where the residual risk is so severe that there
is a high likelihood its implementation will result in death or serious injury," U.S. Department of State, *Report of the
Independent Panel on Best Practices*, August 29, 2013, p. 10.

[87] The "security standards" are required by the Overseas Security Policy Board (OSPB) and the Secure Embassy
Construction and Counterterrorism Act of 1999 (SECCA).

security measures.[88] In these cases, temporary facilities should have the physical security, personnel, weapons, ammunition, and fire safety equipment needed to adequately address the threat. The Committee understands the need for State to have the flexibility to operate, on a temporary basis, out of facilities that fall short of these standards; however, these operations are extremely vulnerable, as seen in Benghazi.[89]

> **RECOMMENDATION**: As appropriate, the Deputy Assistant Secretary for High-Threat Posts should also find consistent ways to coordinate with the CIA to exchange best practices for high-threat posts and to discuss common security concerns.

> **RECOMMENDATION**: The IC and State Department should ensure all surveillance cameras at high-risk, high-threat facilities have sufficient resolution, nighttime visibility, remote monitoring capabilities, and redundancy to provide warning and situational awareness in the event of an attack. The Committee notes that the Independent Panel on Best Practices has recommended that the State Department establish a new office "for field expedient deployment of hardware, cutting-edge protective technology and procedures."[90]

> **FINDING #3**: There was no singular "tactical warning" in the intelligence reporting leading up to the events on September 11, 2012, predicting an attack on U.S. facilities in Benghazi on the 9/11 anniversary, although State and the

---

[88] The State Department's Office of Inspector General has recommended that components within the Department "develop minimum security standards that must be met prior to occupying facilities located in the Department of State-designated high-risk, high-threat environments and include new minimum security standards of occupancy in the *Foreign Affairs Handbook* as appropriate." U.S. Department of State, Office of Inspector General (IG), *Special Review of the Accountability Review Board Process*, September 2013, p. 29.

[89] The Independent Panel on Best Practices said: "Waivers for not meeting security standards have become common place in the [State] Department; however, without a risk management process to identify and implement alternate mitigating measures after a waiver has been given, Department employees, particularly those in high threat areas, could be exposed to an unacceptable level of risk." U.S. Department of State, *Report of the Independent Panel on Best Practices*, August 29, 2013, p. 8. A recent State IG report also found: "The Department of State has neither a conceptual framework nor a process for risk management. There is no one person or office specifically tasked to oversee the assessment of risks in critical, high-threat locales and weigh those risks against the U.S. Government's policy priorities to determine if the strategic value of the program outweighs the associated risk." U.S. Department of State, Office of the Inspector General, *Special Review of the Accountability Review Board Process*, September 2013, p. 1.

[90] U.S. Department of State, *Report of the Independent Panel on Best Practices*, August 29, 2013, p. 23.

To date, the Committee has not identified any intelligence or other information received prior to September 11, 2012, by the IC or State Department indicating specific terrorist planning to attack the U.S. facilities in Benghazi on September 11, 2012.

Although it did not reach the U.S. Intelligence Community until after the attacks, it is important to note that a former Transitional National Council (TNC) security official in Benghazi, █████████, had received information of a possible imminent attack against the Mission facility in advance. The official said that approximately four hours prior to the attack, he attempted to notify the Libyan Intelligence Service (LIS) that an attack was expected, but he was unable to reach two contacts he had in the LIS as they were out of the country.[91] The CIA has been unable to corroborate the official's claim that he attempted to provide the LIS with advance warning about the attack.

[91] NCTC and FBI, *The 11-12 September Attacks on US Facilities in Benghazi*, November 13, 2012, p. 3.
[92] Email from CIA Office of Congressional Affairs staff to SSCI Staff, "Answers to SSCI Benghazi Questions from August 2013," September 6, 2013.

5. Senate Select Committee on Intelligence (1/14/2014)

[REDACTED]

[REDACTED][94]

[REDACTED][95]

According to a January 4, 2013, letter from the Acting Director of the CIA, Michael Morell, "[t]he nature of the attacks suggested they did not involve significant pre-planning."[96] Although it may never be known with complete certainty, it is possible that the individuals and groups involved in the attacks had not planned on conducting those attacks until that day, meaning that specific tactical warning would have been highly unlikely. However, intelligence reports made clear that extremist groups in eastern Libya, including Ansar al-Sharia, were not only running training camps there, but also plotting and carrying out attacks against U.S. and Western interests in the months prior to the attacks in Benghazi.

---

[93] SSCI Transcript, *Briefing from the Intelligence Community on Benghazi*, November 1, 2012, p. 59-62; SSCI Transcript, *Benghazi Follow Up with Staff*, May 22, 2013, pp. 67-69.

[94] Email from NSA staff [REDACTED] to [REDACTED], et al, September 12, 2012, 05:37 a.m.

[95] Email from CIA staff [REDACTED] to "[REDACTED]" (staff of the CIA Directorate of Intelligence), September 16, 2012, 08:44 a.m.

[96] Letter from Acting CIA Director Michael Morell to SSCI Chairman Dianne Feinstein, January 4, 2013.

."[97] However, the collective assessment of the IC remains that the attacks "were deliberate and organized, but that their lethality and efficacy did not necessarily indicate extensive planning."[98]

> **RECOMMENDATION:** The IC must place a greater emphasis on collecting intelligence and open-source information, including extremist-affiliated social media, to improve its ability to provide tactical warnings, especially in North Africa, the Middle East, and other areas where the U.S. has facilities under high threat. Given the current resource-constrained budget environment, the Committee is working with the IC to identify resource gaps and realign assets to focus on those gaps, especially in North Africa.

> **FINDING #4:** Although the IC relied heavily on open source press reports in the immediate aftermath of the attacks, the IC conducted little analysis of open source extremist-affiliated social media prior to and immediately after the attacks.

Although it is impossible to draw definitive conclusions, there were fragmentary reports from the IC indicating that more in-depth intelligence exploitation of social media in the Benghazi area, including web postings by Libyan nationals employed at the Temporary Mission Facility, could have flagged potential security threats to the Mission facility or important information about the employees prior to the September 11, 2012, attacks.

> **RECOMMENDATION:** The IC should expand its capabilities to conduct analysis of open source information including extremist-affiliated social media particularly in areas where it is hard to develop human intelligence or there has been recent political upheaval. Analysis of extremist-affiliated social media should be more clearly integrated into analytic products, when appropriate.

---

[97] CIA, "Libya: Update on Planning and Culpability for Benghazi Attacks," WIRe, March 29, 2013.
[98] Ibid; SSCI Transcript, *Benghazi Follow Up with Staff*, May 22, 2013, p. 6.

5. Senate Select Committee on Intelligence (1/14/2014)

> <u>**FINDING #5**</u>: **There were "tripwires" designed to prompt a reduction in personnel or the suspension of operations at the Mission facility in Benghazi and although there is evidence that some of them had been crossed, operations continued with minimal change. Some nations closed their diplomatic facilities in Benghazi as the security conditions deteriorated during the summer of 2012, but other nations stayed along with the United States, contrary to some public reports and statements that the U.S. was the last country represented in Benghazi.**

State Department documents indicate that its Bureau of Near Eastern Affairs was aware of the fact that many of the tripwires had indeed been crossed and discussed suspending operations, but never did. Given these developments and the available intelligence at the time, the Committee believes the State Department should have recognized the need to increase security to a level commensurate with the threat, or suspend operations in Benghazi. However, operations continued with minimal improvements in security and personnel protections. Although some countries and international organizations had reduced their presence in Benghazi, the United States maintained a diplomatic presence there similar to the UN, the European Union, and other Western countries such as Italy, France, Turkey, and Malta.[99]

There were plans to co-locate the Mission facility and the Annex starting in 2013, but no changes were made before the September 11, 2012, attacks. The Chief of Base stated that there had been discussions with Ambassador Stevens about co-locating the Annex and the State Department compound at the same facility. "We had been actively looking," he said. "We had had our officers come out there to survey different locations in Benghazi to look for a location that we could co-locate with the State Department, and we were planning to do that before the end of this [2012] calendar year. So there was absolutely a plan to do that."[100]

> <u>**RECOMMENDATION**</u>: **Where adequate security is not available, the Department of State should be prepared to evacuate or close diplomatic facilities under the highest threat, as it has in recent years in Sana'a, Yemen, and Damascus, Syria.**

---

[99] Email from U.S. Department of State, Office of Legislative Affairs to SSCI staff, December 6, 2013, 5:00 p.m.
[100] SSCI Transcript, *Member and Staff Interview of former Chief of Base*, December 20, 2012, p. 7.

5. Senate Select Committee on Intelligence (1/14/2014)

> **RECOMMENDATION:** The Committee supports the recommendations of
> the Accountability Review Board to bring greater collaboration and
> connectivity between the State Department's Bureau of Diplomatic Security
> and the Intelligence Community.[101] The Department of State must pay special
> attention to the "on the ground" assessments of IC and State personnel in the
> field and IC analytic products about assessed risks to specific U.S. facilities
> overseas.

Response During the Attacks

> **FINDING #6:** The State Department personnel at the Temporary Mission
> Facility in Benghazi relied on the security officers at the CIA Annex as a last
> resort for security in the event of an attack.

Although there was no formal written agreement about how security should
be handled between the two facilities in Benghazi, there was a common
understanding that each group would come to the other's aid if attacked, which is
what happened the night of September 11, 2012.[102] IC personnel immediately
came to the aid of their colleagues at the Temporary Mission Facility, and fought
bravely to secure TMF personnel and their own Annex facility. The Committee
interviewed U.S. personnel in Benghazi that night, and they credited their lives
being saved to the personnel who responded to the attacks.

With respect to the role of DoD and AFRICOM in emergency evacuations
and rescue operations in Benghazi, the Committee received conflicting information
on the extent of the awareness within DoD of the Benghazi Annex. According to
U.S. AFRICOM, neither the command nor its Commander were aware of an annex

---

[101] The Committee also supports the "positive changes" noted by the Independent Panel on Best Practices that are
"currently underway or planned within DS, with Department support, for both better intelligence access and
additional intelligence analyst positions. Specifically, liaison representatives from the National Counterterrorism
Center (NCTC), the National Geospatial[-Intelligence] Agency (NGA), and the National Security Agency (NSA)
have been assigned to DS/ITA [Diplomatic Security/Intelligence and Threat Analysis] .... Additionally, nine
positions for overseas deployed Intelligence Research Analysts have been approved for Fiscal Year (FY) 2014."
U.S. Department of State, *Report of the Independent Panel on Best Practices,* August 29, 2013, p. 18.
[102] SSCI Transcript, *Member and Staff Interview of former Chief of Base,* December 20, 2012, p. 6. The Chief of
Base said: "We had a 100 percent unwritten plan to go to their aid in the case of an emergency. But there was
nothing written."

in Benghazi, Libya.[103] However, it is the Committee's understanding that other DoD personnel were aware of the Benghazi Annex.

RECOMMENDATION: There should be more specific information exchanged between DoD and the IC, through the appropriate channels, to make regional Combatant Commanders aware of the general presence of Intelligence Community personnel in their areas of responsibility for the purposes of emergency evacuations and rescue. This information could have been helpful to the Commander of AFRICOM and should have been more easily available to him.

FINDING #7: There were no U.S. military resources in position to intervene in short order in Benghazi to help defend the Temporary Mission Facility and its Annex on September 11 and 12, 2012.

DoD moved aerial assets, teams of Marines, and special operations forces toward Libya as the attacks were ongoing, but in addition to the seven-man reinforcement team from Tripoli, the only additional resources that were able to arrive on scene were unmanned, unarmed aerial surveillance assets. The unmanned aerial vehicle that flew to Benghazi that night ███████████████ ████████████████████████████████████ when he could not be found at the Temporary Mission Facility.[104]

According to Major General Darryl Roberson, Vice Director of Operations for the Joint Staff:

> There were no ships available to provide any support that were anywhere close to the facility at Benghazi. The assets that we had available were Strike Eagles loaded with live weapons that could have responded, but they were located in Djibouti, which is the equivalent of the distance between here [Washington D.C.] and Los Angeles. The other fighters that might have been available were located in Aviano, Italy. They were not loaded with weapons. They were not on an alert status. We would've had to build weapons, load weapons, get tankers to support it, and get it there. There was

---

[103] Email from Office of the Chairman of the Joint Chief of Staff for Legislative Affairs to SSCI staff, August 15, 2013, 5:14 p.m.
[104] SSCI Transcript, *Member and Staff Interview of former Chief of Base*, December 20, 2012, pp. 63-64.

no way that we were going to be able to do that. Unfortunately, there was not a carrier in the Mediterranean that could have been able to support; the assets that we mobilized immediately were the only assets we had available to try to support.[105]

The Committee has reviewed the allegations that U.S. personnel, including in the IC or DoD, prevented the mounting of any military relief effort during the attacks, but the Committee has not found any of these allegations to be substantiated. The following assets were deployed or in the process of deploying in response to the Benghazi attacks (based on a review of DoD documents and testimony before the Committee):

- The six-man CIA security team (plus an interpreter) left from the Annex to respond to the Temporary Mission Facility soon after it came under attack. The CIA security team did not make it in time to save Ambassador Stevens and Sean Smith, but they successfully evacuated the other Americans at the Mission facility to the Annex.

- As noted, one unarmed Predator was diverted to provide surveillance coverage of the Temporary Mission Facility as it was being attacked. This Predator was subsequently replaced by another unarmed Predator to enable the first Predator to return to base for refueling.

- A seven-person security team (consisting of two DoD personnel, four CIA personnel, and a linguist) flew from the U.S. Embassy in Tripoli to Benghazi and successfully helped evacuate the Americans from the Annex to the airport. It is important to clarify that, at the time of the attacks in Benghazi, there were six DoD personnel assigned to Embassy Tripoli. Four employees were under Special Operations Command Africa (SOC-AFRICA) and reported through a similar, but separate, chain of command within AFRICOM. The other two individuals from that team were DoD personnel working ███████ (based on a memorandum of understanding) under a separate special operations task force. According to the DoD, the four staff under SOC-AFRICA were told by their command to stay to protect Embassy Tripoli due to concerns of a similar attack in Tripoli.[106]

---

[105] SSCI Transcript, *Hearing on the Attacks in Benghazi*, November 15, 2012, pp. 68-69.
[106] SSCI Transcript, *Benghazi Follow Up with Staff*, May 22, 2013, pp. 42-45.

- Sometime between midnight and 2:00 a.m. Benghazi time, Secretary of Defense Leon Panetta verbally ordered two Marine Fleet Antiterrorism Security Teams (or "FAST platoons") to deploy from their base in Rota, Spain, to Libya.

  - One team was to go to Benghazi to respond to the attack on the Temporary Mission Facility.

  - One team was to deploy to Tripoli to protect the Embassy if it was attacked.

  - The first FAST platoon would take ▮ hours to be airborne. As Major General Roberson testified, "whenever they got the notification, ▮ hours later they are supposed to be airborne and moving to wherever they need to."[107] The second FAST platoon would have taken 96 hours to deploy, according to Roberson.[108]

  - Because all Americans were evacuated from Benghazi before the first FAST platoon could arrive, it was diverted to protect the U.S. Embassy in Tripoli and arrived at 8:56 p.m. Tripoli time, on September 12, 2012.[109]

- Sometime between midnight and 2:00 a.m. Benghazi time, Secretary Panetta also ordered two teams of special operations forces to Benghazi, but like the FAST platoons, neither made it to Libya before the Americans had already evacuated the next morning after the attack.

  - One special operations force—which was training in Croatia—was ordered to prepare to deploy to an intermediate NATO staging base in Sigonella, Italy.

  - The other special operations force—based in the United States— was ordered to deploy to the intermediate NATO staging base at Sigonella.

---

[107] SSCI Transcript, *Hearing on the Attacks in Benghazi*, November 15, 2012, p. 146.
[108] Ibid.
[109] DoD, *Timeline of Department of Defense Actions on September 11-12, 2012*, p. 2.

- o The first special operations force would take ▮ hours to be airborne. As Major General Roberson testified: "The CIF [Commanders In-Extremis Force] in Croatia is on an ▮▮▮▮▮," meaning it would take ▮ hours of preparation time before it could begin the flight from Croatia to Benghazi.[110] The CIF from Croatia only made it to the staging base at Sigonella by 7:57 p.m. Benghazi time, on September 12, almost 10 hours after all Americans were evacuated from Benghazi.[111]

  - o The other special operations force—from the United States—did not arrive at the staging base at Sigonella until 9:28 p.m. Benghazi time, on September 12.[112]

- There have been congressional and public questions about why military assets were not used from the U.S. military base in Souda Bay, Crete. The Chairman of the Joint Chiefs of Staff, General Martin Dempsey, testified before the Senate Armed Services Committee on February 7, 2013, that (1) the military asset in Souda Bay, Crete, "wasn't the right tool for the particular threat we faced;" (2) "…the aircraft were not among the forces that we had at heightened alert;" and (3) the "boots-on-the-ground capabilities" that DoD deployed would have arrived too late, so they did not deploy to Benghazi.[113]

  - o Two months after the attacks in Benghazi, DoD moved a FAST platoon from Rota, Spain, to Souda Bay, Crete, reducing its preparation time to ▮▮▮▮▮▮.[114]

> **RECOMMENDATION:** It is imperative that the State Department, DoD, and the IC work together to identify and prioritize the largest gaps in coverage for the protection of U.S. diplomatic, military, and intelligence personnel in the North Africa region and other high-threat posts around the world. The small number of U.S. military resources devoted to the vast and

---

[110] SSCI Transcript, *Hearing on the Attacks in Benghazi*, November 15, 2012, p. 146.

[111] DoD, *Timeline of Department of Defense Actions on September 11-12, 2012*, p. 2.

[112] Ibid.

[113] Martin Dempsey, Chairman of the Joint Chiefs of Staff General, *Testimony before the Senate Armed Services Committee during Hearing on the Terrorist Attacks on U.S. Facilities in Benghazi, Libya*, February 7, 2013.

[114] SSCI Transcript, *Hearing on the Attacks in Benghazi*, November 15, 2012, p. 152.

FINDING #8: Unarmed U.S. military surveillance assets were not delayed
when responding to the attack, and they provided important situational
awareness for those under siege during the attacks against the Temporary
Mission Facility and the Annex on September 11 and 12, 2012.

At the direction of AFRICOM, at 10 p.m. Benghazi time, DoD moved a
remotely piloted, unarmed surveillance aircraft, which was already conducting a
separate intelligence mission over Darnah, to airspace above the Mission facility.
It arrived at approximately 11:10 p.m. Benghazi time, shortly before the U.S.
security personnel evacuated to the Annex. A second remotely piloted, unarmed
surveillance aircraft relieved the first, and monitored the eventual evacuation of
personnel from the Annex to the Benghazi airport later on the morning of
September 12, 2012. According to a CIA cable which served as the joint report
from Tripoli Station and Benghazi Base on the attacks: "ISR coverage was [a]
crucial resource ███████████████████ . . . . ISR was also crucial to provide
situational awareness to Benghazi Base and Team Tripoli efforts on the ground."[115]

The Intelligence Picture After the Attacks

FINDING #9: In finished reports after September 11, 2012, intelligence
analysts inaccurately referred to the presence of a protest at the Mission
facility before the attack based on open source information and limited
intelligence, but without sufficient intelligence or eyewitness statements to
corroborate that assertion. The IC took too long to correct these erroneous
reports, which caused confusion and influenced the public statements of
policymakers.

---

[115] CIA TRIPOLI 27900, September 19, 2012, p. 9.

In the immediate aftermath of the attacks, the IC received numerous reports, both classified and unclassified, which provided contradictory accounts that there were demonstrations at the Temporary Mission Facility. In some cases, these intelligence reports—which were disseminated widely in the Intelligence Community—contained references to press reports on protests that were simply copied into intelligence products. Other reporting indicated there were no protests. For example, the IC obtained closed circuit television video from the Mission facility ███████████████████████████, and there were credible eyewitness statements of U.S. personnel on the ground that night, which the FBI began to collect from interviewing survivors starting on September 15, 2012, in Ramstein Air Base, Germany.

The IC also had information that there were no protests outside the Temporary Mission Facility prior to the attacks, but did not incorporate that information into its widely circulated assessments in a timely manner. Contrary to many press reports at the time, eyewitness statements by U.S. personnel indicate that there were no protests at the start of the attacks. For example, on September 15, 2012, the CIA's Chief of Station in Tripoli sent to the then-Deputy Director of the CIA and others at the CIA an email that reported the attacks were "not/not an escalation of protests."[116] Yet, the CIA's January 4, 2013, Analytic Line Review downplays the importance of this email, noting, ". . . as a standard practice, we do not base analysis on e-mails and other informal communications from the field because such accounts often change when formalized as disseminated intelligence reports."[117]

Moreover, it appears this reporting from those present during the attacks did not make its way into assessments at CIA Headquarters, as the Deputy Director of the Middle East and North Africa Analysis Office at CIA wrote an internal email, dated September 16, 2012, that mentioned "protestors that preceded the violence."[118] On September 18, 2012, the FBI and CIA reviewed the closed circuit television video from the Mission facility that showed there were no protests prior to the attacks. Although information gathered from interviews with U.S. personnel who were on the ground during the attacks was shared informally between the FBI

---

[116] CIA, *Analytical Line Review of the Benghazi Attacks*, January 4, 2013, p. 7.
[117] Ibid., p. 8.
[118] Email from ██████████████ to ███████████, "FW: DCIA/DDCIA Memo as sent to DD/DI ██████," September 16, 2012, 4:08 p.m., p. 1.

and CIA, it was not until two days later, on September 20, 2012, that the FBI disseminated its intelligence reports detailing such interviews.[119]

A dearth of clear and definitive HUMINT or eyewitness reporting led IC analysts to rely on open press reports and limited SIGINT reporting that incorrectly attributed the origins of the Benghazi attacks to "protests," over first-hand accounts from U.S. officials on the ground. CIA's January 4, 2013, Analytic Line Review found that "[a]pproximately a dozen reports that included press accounts, public statements by AAS members, HUMINT reporting, DOD reporting, and signals intelligence all stated or strongly suggested that a protest occurred outside of the Mission facility just prior to the attacks."[120]

Of the 11 reports cited by the CIA's Analytic Line Review, six were press articles, two were the public statements of Ansar al-Sharia, and the three others were intelligence reports. Specific open source reports and intelligence on which analysts appear to have based their judgments include the public statements by Ansar al-Sharia that the attacks were a "spontaneous and popular uprising."[121] Also, there was protest activity in Egypt and approximately 40 other cities around the world and violent attacks against U.S. diplomatic facilities in Tunisia, Yemen, and Egypt from September 11-20, 2012. In addition, there were intelligence reports in the days following the Benghazi attacks that al-Qa'ida-associated terrorists hoped to take advantage of global protests for further attacks.[122]

As a result of evidence from closed circuit videos and other reports, the IC changed its assessment about a protest in classified intelligence reports on September 24, 2012, to state there were no demonstrations or protests at the Temporary Mission Facility prior to the attacks. This slow change in the official assessment affected the public statements of government officials, who continued to state in press interviews that there were protests outside the Mission compound. The IC continues to assess that although they do not think the first attack came out of protests, the lethality and efficacy of the attack "did not require significant

---

[119] ODNI, *Intelligence Community Response: Fact-Based & Substantive Review Only Regarding SSCI Report of Terrorist Attacks on U.S. Facilities in Benghazi*, August 30, 2013, p. 15.

[120] CIA, *Analytical Line Review of the Benghazi Attacks*, January 4, 2013, p. 4.

[121] ODNI, *The Benghazi Intelligence Review*, October 22, 2012, translated transcript of an open source YouTube video: "Libya: Ansar Al-Shari'ah Video Statement on US Consulate Attack in Benghazi," September 12, 2012, p. 2.

[122] NCTC, "Libya: Variety of Extremists Participated in Benghazi Attacks," NCTC Current, September 15, 2012.

amounts of preplanning."[123] The IC continues to review the amount and nature of any preplanning that went into the attacks.[124]

RECOMMENDATION: Intelligence analysts should more aggressively request and integrate eyewitness reporting—especially from U.S. Government personnel—in the aftermath of a crisis. The IC should establish a process or reevaluate its current procedures to improve the speed and process with which operational reporting (for example, eyewitness reporting) and raw collection make it into disseminated intelligence products.

RECOMMENDATION: The IC must act quickly to correct the written record and address misperceptions in its finished analytical products. The IC should avoid repeating erroneous information in its intelligence products as analysts continued to do when they wrote there were "protests" at the Temporary Mission Facility, which then made its way into reports disseminated to U.S. policymakers and Congress.

FINDING #10: The State Department Bureau of Intelligence and Research (INR) did not disseminate any independent analysis in the year following the Benghazi attacks.

Based on the Committee's review, the State Department's INR disseminated no intelligence products related to the Benghazi attacks in the year following the attacks. Considering the attacks began on a State Department facility, involved the deaths of two State Department personnel, and were an important indication of escalating threats against U.S. facilities and personnel in the region, the Committee finds it unsettling that INR chose not to, or was unable to, disseminate any analysis related to the attacks or the implications of the attacks.

INR witnesses told Committee staff that its staff resources were scarce, but also said that "…unless we have something that is unique analysis that is really going to change things we feel that we're better off coordinating on what the IC says then briefing within our building."[125]

---

[123] SSCI Transcript, *Benghazi Follow Up with Staff,* May 22, 2013, p. 82.
[124] Ibid.
[125] SSCI Transcript, *Staff Briefing: U.S. Department of State Bureau of Intelligence and Research Re: Benghazi,* February 1, 2013, p. 47.

5. Senate Select Committee on Intelligence (1/14/2014)

Yet, INR officials have access to State Department information and perspectives that many in the Intelligence Community do not; therefore, INR should play a more active—not just a coordinating—role in analysis for the IC and not just the State Department. The State Department's Inspector General went even further and found that INR should be the office to produce a comprehensive security assessment for each post based on all available diplomatic and intelligence sources.[126]

In response to inquiries by Members of Congress about the intelligence reporting before, during, and after the Benghazi attacks, the DNI's office stated that all intelligence reports on Benghazi would be assembled by AIS and those hundreds of documents would be provided to the congressional intelligence committees as part of an official "Benghazi Intelligence Review" (BIR).

The BIR documents were delivered on October 22, 2012, but were not a complete set of intelligence reporting related to the Benghazi attacks. The Committee found that there was significant confusion within AIS about their

---

[126] U.S. Department of State, Office of Inspector General, *Special Review of the Accountability Review Board Process*, September 2013, p. 30.
[127] U.S. Department of State, *Report of the Independent Panel on Best Practices*, August 29, 2013, p. 20.

efforts to bring together documents for the BIR. Although the review was
presented to the Committee as comprehensive, it was not even thorough. The
Committee found that AIS believed it was tasked to find some illustrative
documents (that may not have been verified by analysts as significant or priority
documents), as opposed to providing all Benghazi documents to Congress. The
Committee is concerned that AIS, the office within the Intelligence Community
charged with setting and evaluating the standards for analysis, could perform so
poorly in responding to a request from the Committee.

The Talking Points

On September 15, 2012, the CIA provided to the House and Senate
Intelligence Committees a set of unclassified talking points at the request of the
House Permanent Select Committee on Intelligence. The talking points and the
emails, in redacted form, detailing their coordination are now available to the
public and the Committee encourages the public to review them. Members of the
Committee have differing views on the substance of, and circumstances
surrounding, the CIA's talking points that are addressed in the Additional Views of
this report. A detailed timeline of the different versions of the talking points is in
Appendix I of this report.

> **RECOMMENDATION: In responding to future requests for unclassified
> talking points from Congress, the Intelligence Community should simply tell
> Congress which facts are unclassified and let Members of Congress provide
> additional context for the public.**

Lessons Learned After the Attacks to Improve the Interaction between the State Department's Bureau of Diplomatic Security and the IC

The Benghazi attacks demonstrate that U.S. facilities are at risk of being
attacked at any time, without specific tactical warning; therefore, security at all
high-risk overseas U.S. Government facilities must be improved and reevaluated
on an ongoing basis as threats change and emerge. The IC is playing a key role in
that review process by helping to evaluate the threats and strengthen the security of
its own facilities. The State Department and the IC should share best practices
whenever possible to improve security to high-risk, high-threat posts. As noted,

additional security measures were implemented in a timely manner by the CIA at the Annex, yet not at the Temporary Mission Facility.

The Department of State has missed opportunities to draw lessons from past events that could improve security programs and enhance security for the entire foreign affairs community, according to the September 2013 "Special Review of the Accountability Review Board Process," by the State Department's Inspector General.[128]

FINDING #12: **The co-location of IC and diplomatic personnel in Benghazi could have enhanced security; but co-location often presents tradeoffs that should be carefully evaluated in high-threat environments.**

Keeping intelligence facilities separate from State Department compounds can provide important operational advantages. According to the Chief of Base: "We had the luxury that the Mission didn't have of keeping our compound very low-profile and making our movements—we used very good ▮▮▮▮▮▮▮▮▮▮ protocol movements, and our vehicular moves were very much low-profile. So we had a security advantage, I guess you could say, over our State colleagues." A June 12, 2012, CIA cable from Benghazi Base came to a similar conclusion, finding: "…as a direct result of a concerted effort to build and maintain a low profile we believe that the locals for the most part do not know we are here and housed/officed in a separate stand alone facility from our [United States Government] USG counterparts."[129]

RECOMMENDATION: **The Committee agrees that IC and diplomatic personnel should generally be co-located overseas except where the IC determines that, for operational reasons, co-location is not helpful in meeting mission objectives or that it poses a security risk. In those limited instances, the IC should work with the State Department in light of Chief of Mission authorities. However, the Committee does not believe that co-location decisions should be subjected to a broader interagency approval process.**

---

[128] U.S. Department of State, Office of the Inspector General, *Special Review of the Accountability Review Board Process*, September 2013, p. 1; *see also* U.S. Department of State, Office of Inspector General, *Audit of Department of State Compliance With Physical and Procedural Security Standards at Selected High Threat Level Posts*, June 2013.
[129] CIA BENGHAZI 14986, June 12, 2012, p. 2.

> **FINDING #13:** The primary source of security for the Temporary Mission Facility, local Libyan militia members, failed to provide any significant defense of the compound from the attack.

Video footage shows—and the ARB also found—that, at 9:42 p.m. Benghazi time, a local police vehicle stationed outside the Mission facility withdrew as soon as armed attackers advanced toward the U.S. compound. In addition, the TMF in Benghazi had been vandalized and attacked in the months prior to the September 11-12 attacks by some of the same guards who were there to protect it.[130]

Local security guards, especially security guards who are not operated and overseen by the host government, are an inherently less reliable security force than security provided by U.S. forces or the military or police forces of a host government. According to the State Department, the Mission facility did not store classified information, and therefore no Marine contingent was present.[131] Although U.S. Government security forces are always preferred, the CIA and State determined that local militias would provide the so-called "least bad option" in post-revolutionary Libya. The former Chief of Base stated: "There was no alternative. You know, there really is no functioning government there. And the militia groups that both we, and the State Department, depended on were in fact kind of the de facto government there in Benghazi."[132]

The Government of Libya lacked the capacity to respond to the crisis militarily or with law enforcement personnel. Its governance over the entire Benghazi area was also extremely limited, which further constrained its ability to respond. The ineffectiveness of the Libyan government in its ability to respond to emergencies and control areas like Benghazi was well-known to the U.S. Government and Ambassador Stevens prior to the attacks. In fact, on August 29, 2012, the CIA published an intelligence report entitled, "Libya: Struggling to

---

[130] Classified Report of the ARB, December 18, 2012, Appendix 26.

[131] Also, according to the official website of the U.S. Marine Corps: "The primary mission of the Marine Security Guard (MSG) is to provide internal security at designated U.S. diplomatic and consular facilities in order to prevent the compromise of classified material vital to the national security of the United States." *See* www.mcesg.marines.mil, accessed December 5, 2013.

[132] SSCI Transcript, *Member and Staff Interview of former Chief of Base*, December 20, 2012, p. 20.

Create Effective Domestic Security System" that highlighted the Libyan Government's inability to prevent or respond to security incidents.[133]

Bringing the Attackers to Justice

FINDING #14: More than a year after the Benghazi attacks, the terrorists who perpetrated the attacks have still not been brought to justice. The IC has identified several individuals responsible for the attacks. Some of the individuals have been identified with a strong level of confidence. However, insight into the current whereabouts and links between these individuals in some cases is limited due in part to the nascent intelligence capabilities in the region.

Individuals affiliated with terrorist groups, including AQIM, Ansar al-Sharia,[134] AQAP, and the Mohammad Jamal Network, participated in the September 11, 2012, attacks. Intelligence suggests that the attack was not a highly coordinated plot, but was opportunistic; however, well-armed attackers easily overwhelmed the Libyan security guards and the five U.S. Diplomatic Security agents present at the Temporary Mission Facility. It remains unclear if any group

---

[133] CIA, "Libya: Struggling To Create Effective Domestic Security System," WIRe, August 29, 2012.
[134] After the Benghazi attacks, the IC began to distinguish Ansar al-Sharia into two groups: (1) AAS-Benghazi; and (2) AAS-Darnah.

or person exercised overall command and control of the attacks or whether extremist group leaders directed their members to participate. Some intelligence suggests the attacks were likely put together in short order, following that day's violent protests in Cairo against an inflammatory video, suggesting that these and other terrorist groups could conduct similar attacks with little advance warning.

The FBI's investigation into the individuals responsible for the Benghazi attacks has been hampered by inadequate cooperation and a lack of capacity by foreign governments to hold these perpetrators accountable, making the pursuit of justice for the attacks slow and insufficient. As a result, key information gaps remain about the potential foreknowledge and complicity of Libyan militia groups and security forces, the level of pre-planning for the attacks, the perpetrators and their involvement in other terrorist activities, and the motivation for the attacks.

The Libyan Government has not shown the political incentive or will within its own country to seek out, arrest, and prosecute individuals believed to be associated with the attacks. Furthermore, the security environment in Benghazi remains extremely dangerous for individuals wishing to work with the U.S. Government on its investigation into the attacks. In testimony before the Senate Appropriations Subcommittee on Commerce, Justice, Science, and Related Agencies, then-FBI Director Robert Mueller noted that as many as 15 individuals supporting the investigation or otherwise helpful to the United States have been killed in Benghazi since the attacks, underscoring the lawless and chaotic circumstances in eastern Libya. It is unclear whether their killings were related to the Benghazi investigation.[135]

> **RECOMMENDATION**: **The U.S. Government must swiftly bring the attackers to justice, in spite of the unwillingness or lack of capacity of the Libyan government to assist in this effort.**

---

[135] Robert S. Mueller III, Director of the FBI, *Testimony before the Senate Appropriations Subcommittee on Commerce, Justice and Science*, May 16, 2013.

V. CONCLUSION

In the year since Chris Stevens, Sean Smith, Tyrone Woods, and Glen Doherty were killed during the terrorist attacks on U.S. facilities in Benghazi, Libya, the Senate Intelligence Committee has worked to understand the events leading up to, during, and after these attacks. Although this report does not attempt to address every aspect of this tragedy, we believe it identifies important findings and recommendations that will improve our intelligence analysis, priorities, and capabilities and help ensure the future safety of U.S. personnel serving overseas.

We recognize, particularly in this post-9/11 era, that the risk to U.S. diplomatic, military, and intelligence officials around the world remains high. We cannot eliminate this risk, but we can and must do more to minimize the potential harm to the men and women who, understanding and accepting this risk, have chosen to serve the United States abroad. Unfortunately, as we learned in Benghazi, the tactical intelligence that can warn of an imminent threat is not always present. This cannot be an excuse for inaction, however. It is imperative that the Intelligence Community position itself to anticipate, rather than just react to, potential terrorism hotspots and changing dynamics on the ground, and that U.S. personnel and facilities overseas are equipped to immediately defend against and withstand any potential attack. It is also imperative that those in decision-making positions in Washington, D.C. heed the concerns and wisdom of those on the front lines and make resource and security decisions with those concerns in mind. The United States government did not meet this standard of care in Benghazi, but we believe this report's findings and recommendations will help avoid similar tragedies.

The Committee honors the lives and sacrifices of the four American heroes who died in Benghazi on September 11, 2012. We also recognize those who came to their aid or mobilized assistance in their defense. This report cannot in any way compensate for the sacrifices of these individuals, but it is our hope that we can, as a nation, resolve to do all that is needed to protect the lives and well-being of every American citizen serving this country abroad.

APPENDIX I: The Benghazi Talking Points

On September 15, 2012, the CIA provided the HPSCI and the SSCI with unclassified talking points for Members' use in media and public statements regarding the September 11, 2012, terrorist attacks in Benghazi, Libya. The talking points were requested by the HPSCI during a meeting with then-CIA Director Petraeus on Friday, September 14, 2012. As made clear by 100 pages of emails released by the Obama Administration on May 15, 2013,[136] the talking points were then also provided to U.S. Ambassador to the UN, Susan Rice, in her appearances on several television talk shows on Sunday, September 16, 2012. The contents of the talking points and Rice's comments in her public appearances generated significant controversy, including in Congress. As discussed in more detail below, the SSCI devoted considerable staff time and held three closed briefings for Members to address the Benghazi talking points issue.

The final, unclassified version of the CIA talking points, as provided to HPSCI on September 15, 2012, read as follows:

—The currently available information suggests that the demonstrations in Benghazi were spontaneously inspired by the protests at the US Embassy in Cairo and evolved into a direct assault against the US diplomatic post in Benghazi and subsequently its annex. There are indications that extremists participated in the violent demonstrations.

—This assessment may change as additional information is collected and analyzed as currently available information continues to be evaluated.

—The investigation is ongoing and the US Government is working with Libyan authorities to bring to justice those responsible for the deaths of US citizens.

---

[136] ABC News. "White House Benghazi Emails." accessed December 3, 2013. http://abcnews.go.com/images/Politics/white-house-benghazi-emails.pdf

5. Senate Select Committee on Intelligence (1/14/2014)

SSCI Actions to Review the Talking Points

The SSCI conducted two closed, on-the-record sessions and one unrecorded session regarding the Benghazi talking points with the General Counsel of the ODNI, Robert Litt. Two similar on-the-record sessions occurred on January 3, 2013, the first with Litt and Chairman Feinstein and the second with Litt and Vice Chairman Chambliss, due to scheduling conflicts. Limited IC and SSCI staff were present at each session, but the transcript was made available to all SSCI members and staff. During the January 3 sessions, Litt went through the evolution of what he said were eleven different drafts of the talking points, starting on September 14 through the final version on September 15, 2012. He provided a summary document he created showing the changes made to each draft, without email time stamps and sender/recipient information because the Administration, claiming privilege, would not provide the Committee the opportunity to look at the actual emails. Members were not allowed to keep that handout, but staff were allowed to take notes.

A third Members-only session with Litt, which was not recorded, took place on February 26, 2013. During that session, Litt shared with Members copies of nearly 100 pages of emails associated with the interagency coordination process that took place in drafting the talking points. (Redacted versions of these emails were then made public by the Administration on May 15, 2013.) Litt also shared details about which individuals or agencies made changes to the points, when those changes occurred, and the nature of the changes. Members had to return the copies of the emails to Litt at the end of the briefing. Staff access to this briefing was strictly limited to both the Majority and Minority Staff Directors plus one additional staffer per side.

Members also asked questions about the talking points in open and closed hearings of the SSCI on multiple occasions, and staff submitted several formal questions for the record and informal inquiries to the IC about the issue. In some cases, the testimony of senior IC officials about the talking points was poorly informed or confusing, creating further uncertainty among Members and staff. Chairman Feinstein and Vice Chairman Chambliss also wrote to the DNI on two occasions—December 4, 2012, and January 30, 2013—specifically requesting full documentation on the changes made to the talking points.

This Committee faced significant resistance from the Administration in getting access to the emails and documentation that Mr. Litt ultimately provided on February 26, 2013, and that were then made public—in redacted form—on May 15, 2013. This resistance was apparently based, in part, on Executive branch concerns related to executive privilege and the deliberative process which appeared to evaporate when the emails were made public. However, it also served to exacerbate the controversy surrounding the talking points, prolonged media and public speculation, and raised questions of trust of the IC as Members attempted to extract information. This matter could have been mitigated much sooner if the Executive branch had promptly provided the email documentation that was ultimately given to SSCI on February 26th and made public on May 15th.

Analysis of the Talking Points

Below is the timeline of the twelve changes to the CIA talking points, as assembled from the 100 pages of emails made public by the Administration on May 15, 2013.[137] The timeline is in 12-point font to facilitate comparison to the publicly available summary document about the creation of the CIA talking points, which was created by Robert Litt.[138]

1) Fri., Sept. 14th 2012, 11:15 a.m.—written by Director, CIA Office of Terrorism Analysis

- We believe based on currently available information that the attacks in Benghazi were spontaneously inspired by the protests at the US Embassy in Cairo and evolved into a direct assault against the US Consulate and subsequently its annex.
- The crowd almost certainly was a mix of individuals from across many sectors of Libyan society. That being said, we do know that Islamic extremists with ties to al-Qa'ida participated in the attack.
- Initial press reporting linked the attack to Ansar al-Sharia. The group has since released a statement that the [sic] its leadership did not order the attacks, but did not deny that some of its members were involved. Ansar al-Sharia's facebook page aims to spread *sharia* in Libya and emphasizes the need for jihad to counter what it views as false interpretations of Islam, according to an open source study.

---

[137] Emails on CIA Talking Points, accessed December 5, 2013, http://abcnews.go.com/images/Politics/white-house-benghazi-emails.pdf
[138] ABC News, "CIA Benghazi Talking Points Timeline," accessed December 5, 2013, http://abcnews.go.com/images/Politics/Benghazi%20Talking%20Points%20Timeline.pdf

- The wide availability of weapons and experienced fighters in Libya almost certainly contributed to the lethality of the attacks.
- Since April, there have been at least five other attacks against foreign interests in Benghazi by unidentified assailants, including the June attack against the British Ambassador's convoy. We cannot rule out that individuals had previously surveilled the US facilities, also contributing to the efficacy of the attacks.
- We are working with Libyan authorities and intelligence partners in an effort to help bring to justice those responsible for the deaths of US citizens.

2) 12:23 p.m.—addition made by CIA's Office of General Counsel

- We believe based on currently available information that the attacks in Benghazi were spontaneously inspired by the protests at the US Embassy in Cairo and evolved into a direct assault against the US Consulate and subsequently its annex. This assessment may change as additional information is collected and analyzed and currently available information continues to be evaluated.
- The crowd almost certainly was a mix of individuals from across many sectors of Libyan society. That being said, we do know that Islamic extremists with ties to al-Qa'ida participated in the attack.
- Initial press reporting linked the attack to Ansar al-Sharia. The group has since released a statement that the [sic] its leadership did not order the attacks, but did not deny that some of its members were involved. Ansar al-Sharia's facebook page aims to spread *sharia* in Libya and emphasizes the need for jihad to counter what it views as false interpretations of Islam, according to an open source study.
- The wide availability of weapons and experienced fighters in Libya almost certainly contributed to the lethality of the attacks.
- Since April, there have been at least five other attacks against foreign interests in Benghazi by unidentified assailants, including the June attack of the British Ambassador's convoy. We cannot rule out that individuals had previously surveilled the US facilities, also contributing to the efficacy of the attacks.
- We are working with Libyan authorities and intelligence partners in an effort to help bring to justice those responsible for the deaths of US citizens.

3) 4:42 p.m.—edits made by CIA's (1) Office of Public Affairs & (2) Congressional Affairs

- The ~~We believe based on~~ currently available information suggests that the ~~demonstrations~~ ~~attacks~~ in Benghazi were spontaneously inspired by the protests at the US Embassy in Cairo and evolved into a direct assault against the US Consulate and subsequently its annex. This assessment may change as additional information is collected and analyzed and currently available information continues to be evaluated. On 10 September we warned of social media reports calling for a demonstration in front of the Embassy and that jihadists were threatening to break into the Embassy.

- The crowd almost certainly was a mix of individuals from across many sectors of Libyan society. The investigation is on-going as to who is responsible. That being said, we do know that Islamic extremists ~~with ties to al-Qa'ida~~ participated in the ~~attack~~ violent demonstrations.
- Initial press reporting linked the attack to Ansar al-Sharia. The group has since released a statement that ~~the~~ its leadership did not order the attacks, but did not deny that some of its members were involved. Ansar al-Sharia's Facebook page aims to spread sharia in Libya and emphasizes the need for jihad to counter what it views as false interpretations of Islam, according to an open source study.
- The wide availability of weapons and experienced fighters in Libya almost certainly contributed to the lethality of the attacks.
- The Agency has produced numerous pieces on the threat of extremists linked to al-Qaeda in Benghazi and eastern Libya. These noted that, since April, there have been at least five other attacks against foreign interests in Benghazi by unidentified assailants, including the June attack against the British Ambassador's convoy. We cannot rule out that individuals had previously surveilled the US facilities, also contributing to the efficacy of the attacks.
- The US Government is ~~We are~~ working with Libyan authorities and intelligence partners in an effort to help bring to justice those responsible for the deaths of US citizens.

4) 5:09 p.m.—edits made by CIA Deputy Director Mike Morell before being sent outside CIA for first time

- The currently available information suggests that the demonstrations in Benghazi were spontaneously inspired by the protests at the US Embassy in Cairo and evolved into a direct assault against the US Consulate and subsequently its annex. This assessment may change as additional information is collected and analyzed and currently available information continues to be evaluated. On 10 September we warned of social media reports calling for a demonstration in front of the Embassy and that jihadists were threatening to break into the Embassy.
- The crowd almost certainly was a mix of individuals from across many sectors of Libyan society. The investigation is on-going as to who is responsible for the violence. That being said, we do know that Islamic extremists participated in the violent demonstrations.
- Initial press reporting linked the attack to Ansar al-Sharia. The group has since released a statement that its leadership did not order the attacks, but did not deny that some of its members were involved. Ansar al-Sharia's Facebook page aims to spread sharia in Libya

and emphasizes the need for jihad to counter what it views as false interpretations of Islam, according to an open source study.

- The wide availability of weapons and experienced fighters in Libya almost certainly contributed to the lethality of the attacks.
- The Agency has produced numerous pieces on the threat of extremists linked to al-Qaeda in Benghazi and eastern Libya. These noted that, since April, there have been at least five other attacks against foreign interests in Benghazi by unidentified assailants, including the June attack against the British Ambassador's convoy. We cannot rule out that individuals had previously surveilled the US facilities, also contributing to the efficacy of the attacks.
- The US Government is working with Libyan authorities and intelligence partners in an effort to help bring to justice those responsible for the deaths of US citizens.

5) 6:21 p.m.—edit made by Tommy Vietor, Spokesman for the National Security Staff

- The currently available information suggests that the demonstrations in Benghazi were spontaneously inspired by the protests at the US Embassy in Cairo and evolved into a direct assault against the US Consulate and subsequently its annex. This assessment may change as additional information is collected and analyzed and currently available information continues to be evaluated. On 10 September we warned of social media reports calling for a demonstration in front of Embassy Cairo and that jihadists were threatening to break into the Embassy.
- The crowd almost certainly was a mix of individuals from across many sectors of Libyan society. The investigation is on-going as to who is responsible for the violence. That being said, we do know that Islamic extremists participated in the violent demonstrations.
- Initial press reporting linked the attack to Ansar al-Sharia. The group has since released a statement that its leadership did not order the attacks, but did not deny that some of its members were involved. Ansar al-Sharia's Facebook page aims to spread sharia in Libya and emphasizes the need for jihad to counter what it views as false interpretations of Islam, according to an open source study.
- The wide availability of weapons and experienced fighters in Libya almost certainly contributed to the lethality of the attacks.
- The Agency has produced numerous pieces on the threat of extremists linked to al-Qaeda in Benghazi and eastern Libya. These noted that, since April, there have been at least five other attacks against foreign interests in Benghazi by unidentified assailants, including the June attack against the British Ambassador's convoy. We cannot rule out that individuals had previously surveilled the US facilities, also contributing to the efficacy of the attacks.

- The US Government is working with Libyan authorities and intelligence partners in an effort to help bring to justice those responsible for the deaths of US citizens.

6) 6:41 p.m.—edits made by Shawn Turner, ODNI Spokesman

- The currently available information suggests that the demonstrations in Benghazi were spontaneously inspired by the protests at the US Embassy in Cairo and evolved into a direct assault against the US Consulate and subsequently its annex. This assessment may change as additional information is collected and analyzed and currently available information continues to be evaluated. On 10 September we notified Embassy Cairo ~~warned~~ of social media reports calling for a demonstration and encouraging ~~in front of the Embassy Cairo and that~~ jihadists ~~were threatening~~ to break into the Embassy.
- The crowd almost certainly was a mix of individuals from across many sectors of Libyan society. The investigation is on-going as to who is responsible for the violence. That being said, we do know that Islamic extremists participated in the violent demonstrations.
- Initial press reporting linked the attack to Ansar al-Sharia. The group has since released a statement that its leadership did not order the attacks, but did not deny that some of its members were involved. Ansar al-Sharia's Facebook page aims to spread sharia in Libya and emphasizes the need for jihad to counter what it views as false interpretations of Islam, according to an open source study.
- The wide availability of weapons and experienced fighters in Libya almost certainly contributed to the lethality of the attacks.
- The Agency has produced numerous pieces on the threat of extremists linked to al-Qaeda in Benghazi and eastern Libya. These noted that, since April, there have been at least five other attacks against foreign interests in Benghazi by unidentified assailants, including the June attack against the British Ambassador's convoy. We cannot rule out that individuals had previously surveilled the US facilities, also contributing to the efficacy of the attacks.
- The US Government is working with Libyan authorities and intelligence partners in an effort to help bring to justice those responsible for the deaths of US citizens.

7) 6:52 p.m.—edits made by Tommy Vietor on behalf of Assistant to the President for Homeland Security and Counterterrorism, John Brennan

- The currently available information suggests that the demonstrations in Benghazi were spontaneously inspired by the protests at the US Embassy in Cairo and evolved into a direct assault against the US Consulate and subsequently its annex. This assessment may change as additional information is collected and analyzed and currently available information continues to be evaluated. On 10 September we notified Embassy Cairo of

5. Senate Select Committee on Intelligence (1/14/2014)

social media reports calling for a demonstration and encouraging jihadists to break into the Embassy.

- ~~The crowd almost certainly was a mix of individuals from across many sectors of Libyan society.~~ The investigation is on-going as to who is responsible for the violence, although the crowd almost certainly was a mix of individuals. ~~That being said,~~ We do know that Islamic extremists participated in the violent demonstrations.
- Initial press reporting linked the attack to Ansar al-Sharia. The group has since released a statement that its leadership did not order the attacks, but did not deny that some of its members were involved. Ansar al-Sharia's Facebook page aims to spread sharia in Libya and emphasizes the need for jihad to counter what it views as false interpretations of Islam, according to an open source study.
- The wide availability of weapons and experienced fighters in Libya almost certainly contributed to the lethality of the attacks.
- The Agency has produced numerous pieces on the threat of extremists linked to al-Qaeda in Benghazi and eastern Libya. These noted that, since April, there have been at least five other attacks against foreign interests in Benghazi by unidentified assailants, including the June attack against the British Ambassador's convoy. We cannot rule out that individuals had previously surveilled the US facilities, also contributing to the efficacy of the attacks.
- The US Government is working with Libyan authorities and intelligence partners in an effort to help bring to justice those responsible for the deaths of US citizens.

8) 8:58 p.m.—first two edits suggested by FBI, all made by CIA's Office of Public Affairs

- The currently available information suggests that the demonstrations in Benghazi were spontaneously inspired by the protests at the US Embassy in Cairo and evolved into a direct assault against the US Consulate and subsequently its annex. This assessment may change as additional information is collected and analyzed and currently available information continues to be evaluated. On 10 September ~~the Agency~~ we notified Embassy Cairo of social media reports calling for a demonstration and encouraging jihadists to break into the Embassy.
- The investigation is on-going as to who is responsible for the violence, although the crowd almost certainly was a mix of individuals. That being said, there are indications ~~we do know~~ that Islamic extremists participated in the violent demonstrations.
- ~~Initial press presorting linked the attack to Ansar al-Sharia. The group has since released a statement that its leadership did not order the attacks, but did not deny that some of its members were involved. Ansar al-Sharia's Facebook page aims to spread sharia in Libya and emphasizes the need for jihad to counter what it views as false interpretations of Islam, according to an open source study.~~

- The wide availability of weapons and experienced fighters in Libya almost certainly contributed to the lethality of the attacks.
- The Agency has produced numerous pieces on the threat of extremists linked to al-Qaeda in Benghazi and eastern Libya. ~~These noted that,~~ Since April, there have been at least five other attacks against foreign interests in Benghazi by unidentified assailants, including the June attack against the British Ambassador's convoy. We cannot rule out that individuals had previously surveilled the US facilities, also contributing to the efficacy of the attacks.
- The US Government is working with Libyan authorities and intelligence partners in an effort to help bring to justice those responsible for the deaths of US citizens.

9) Saturday, Sept. 15th 9:45 a.m.—edits made by CIA Deputy Director Mike Morell

- The currently available information suggests that the demonstrations in Benghazi were spontaneously inspired by the protests at the US Embassy in Cairo and evolved into a direct assault against the US Consulate and subsequently its annex.
- This assessment may change as additional information is collected and analyzed and currently available information continues to be evaluated. ~~On 10 September the Agency notified Embassy Cairo of social media reports calling for a demonstration and encouraging jihadists to break into the Embassy.~~
- The investigation is on-going. and ~~as to who is responsible for the violence, although the crowd almost certainly was a mix of individuals. That being said, there are indications that Islamic extremists participated in the violent demonstrations.~~
- ~~The wide availability of weapons and experienced fighters in Libya almost certainly contribute to the lethality of the attacks.~~
- ~~The Agency has produced numerous pieces on the threat of extremists linked to al-Qaeda in Benghazi and eastern Libya. Since April, there have been at least five other attacks against foreign interests in Benghazi by unidentified assailants, including the June attack against the British Ambassador's convoy. We cannot rule out that individuals had previously surveilled the US facilities, also contributing to the efficacy of the attacks.~~ the US Government is working with Libyan authorities and ~~intelligence partners in an effort~~ to ~~help~~ bring to justice those responsible for the deaths of US citizens.

10) 11:08 a.m.—edits made by CIA Deputy Director Mike Morell

- The currently available information suggests that the demonstrations in Benghazi were spontaneously inspired by the protests at the US Embassy in Cairo and evolved into a direct assault against the US Consulate and subsequently its annex. There are indications that extremists participated in the violent demonstrations.

- This assessment may change as additional information is collected and analyzed and as currently available information continues to be evaluated.
- The investigation is on-going, and the US Government is working with Libyan authorities to bring to justice those responsible for the deaths US citizens.

11) 11:25 a.m.—edits made by Deputy National Security Adviser Ben Rhodes

- The currently available information suggests that the demonstrations in Benghazi were spontaneously inspired by the protests at the US Embassy in Cairo and evolved into a direct assault against the US diplomatic post in Benghazi ~~Consulate~~ and subsequently its annex. There are indications that extremists participated in the violent demonstrations.
- This assessment may change as additional information is collected and analyzed and as currently available information continues to be evaluated.
- The investigation is on-going, and the US Government is working with Libyan authorities to bring to justice those responsible for the deaths US citizens.

12) 11:26 a.m.—edits made by State Department official Jake Sullivan

- The currently available information suggests that the demonstrations in Benghazi were spontaneously inspired by the protests at the US Embassy in Cairo and evolved into a direct assault against the US diplomatic post in Benghazi and subsequently its annex. There are indications that extremists participated in the violent demonstrations.
- This assessment may change as additional information is collected and analyzed and as currently available information continues to be evaluated.
- The investigation is on-going, and the US Government is working with Libyan authorities to bring to justice those responsible for the deaths of US citizens.

APPENDIX II: Unclassified Timeline of the Benghazi Attacks

There were effectively <u>three different phases/attacks</u> against the U.S. Temporary Mission Facility and the CIA Annex in Benghazi on September 11-12, 2012, as described below.[139]

1. Attack on the U.S. Temporary Mission Facility at Approximately 9:40 p.m.

9:42 p.m.   Video footage shows—and the Accountability Review Board also found—that, at 9:42 p.m., <u>a local police vehicle stationed outside the Temporary Mission Facility withdrew</u> as soon as armed attackers advanced toward the U.S. compound.

Dozens of attackers easily gained access to the TMF by scaling and then opening the front vehicle gate.

(Over the course of the entire attack on the Mission facility, <u>at least 60 different attackers entered the U.S. compound</u>.)

Ambassador Chris Stevens was in the residence of the Main Building ("Building C"), along with a Diplomatic Security agent, and Information Management Officer Sean Smith. The three of them proceeded to the "safe area" in the building.

DS personnel contacted CIA personnel at the Annex to ask for assistance.

9:45 p.m.   After entering the Mission facility, the attackers used diesel fuel to set fire to the barracks/guard house of the Libyan 17th February Brigade militia, which served as a security force provided by the host nation for the Mission compound, and then proceeded towards the main buildings of the compound.

The attackers then used diesel fuel to set the Main Building ablaze where Ambassador Stevens was secured in the "safe area." Thick smoke rapidly filled the entire structure. The attackers moved unimpeded throughout the compound, entering and exiting buildings at will.

---

[139] Times are approximate and local to Libya.

5. Senate Select Committee on Intelligence (1/14/2014)

10:00 p.m.	A DS agent began leading the Ambassador and Sean Smith toward the emergency escape window to escape the smoke. Nearing unconsciousness himself, the agent opened the emergency escape window and crawled out. He then realized he had become separated from the Ambassador and Sean Smith in the smoke, so he reentered and searched the building multiple times.
	The DS agent, suffering from severe smoke inhalation, climbed a ladder to the roof where he radioed the other DS agents for assistance.
10:03 p.m.	The CIA security team left the Annex for the Mission compound after team members secured heavy weapons.
10:10 p.m.	Security team members started arriving at the Mission facility and made their way onto the compound in the face of enemy fire.
10:30 p.m.	In their armored vehicle, other DS agents drove from Building B to assist the agent on the roof of Building C who had searched for the Ambassador and Mr. Smith. After numerous attempts, they found Mr. Smith, who was deceased.
	The CIA security team from the Annex and some 17th February Brigade members pushed back the attackers and secured a perimeter around the Main Building, and the security team joined in the search for the Ambassador.
11:10 p.m.	An unarmed, unmanned DoD surveillance aircraft arrived over the Mission compound and soon after detected a roadblock several blocks east of the Mission facility. During this time, State and CIA personnel re-entered the burning compound numerous times in an attempt to locate Ambassador Stevens, but to no avail.
11:15 p.m.	The combined CIA and DS security team made a final search for the Ambassador before leaving for the Annex in two

separate armored vehicles. One vehicle encountered heavy fire
as it ran a roadblock several blocks east of the Mission
compound.

11:30 p.m.   All U.S. personnel, except for the missing U.S. Ambassador,
arrived at the CIA Annex, which was approximately two
kilometers away. Sean Smith's body was also taken to the
Annex.

2. Attack on the CIA Annex from Approximately 11:56 p.m. until 1:00 a.m.

11:56 p.m.   Sporadic arms fire and rocket-propelled grenades (RPGs) were
fired at the Annex. Over the next hour, the Annex took
sporadic small arms fire and RPG rounds, the security team
returned fire, and the attackers dispersed.

1:00 a.m.   Local Libyans found the Ambassador at the Mission Facility
and brought him to a local hospital. Despite attempts to revive
him, Ambassador Stevens had no heartbeat and had perished
from smoke inhalation.

1:15 a.m.   A seven-man reinforcement team of additional U.S. security
personnel from Tripoli landed at the Benghazi airport and
began to negotiate with the local Libyan militias for
transportation and a security convoy to the Annex.

4:30 a.m.   The security team from Tripoli departed the airport for the
Annex after more than three hours of negotiations and
communications with Libyan officials.

3. Final Attack on the CIA Annex at Approximately 5:15 a.m.

5:04 a.m.   The security team from Tripoli arrived at the Annex.

5:15 a.m.   Mortar rounds, small-arms fire, and RPGs began to hit the
Annex. Tyrone Woods and Glen Doherty were killed when
they took direct mortar fire as they engaged the enemy from the
roof of the Annex. The mortar fire also seriously injured one

5. Senate Select Committee on Intelligence (1/14/2014)

other security officer and one DS special agent, necessitating the evacuation of the Annex. That attack lasted only 11 minutes, then dissipated.

6:00 a.m.   A heavily-armed Libyan militia unit arrived to help evacuate the Annex of all U.S. personnel to the airport.

6:33 a.m.   U.S. personnel left the Annex for the airport.

7:30 a.m.   The first plane of U.S. personnel evacuated from Benghazi to Tripoli.

10:00 a.m.   The second plane of U.S. personnel evacuated from Benghazi to Tripoli. This flight included the bodies of the four dead Americans.

APPENDIX III: Locations of Temporary Mission Facility & Annex

Source: NGA, November, 2012

5. Senate Select Committee on Intelligence (1/14/2014)

APPENDIX IV: Map from September 5, 2012, AFRICOM Report

(U) Report Title: *"Libya: Extremism in Libya Past, Present, and Future."*

5. Senate Select Committee on Intelligence (1/14/2014)

This page intentionally left blank.

5. Senate Select Committee on Intelligence (1/14/2014)

ADDITIONAL VIEWS

Overview

The Majority[140] believes that the terrorist attacks against U.S. personnel at the Temporary Mission Facility and the Annex in Benghazi, Libya, on September 11 and 12, 2012, were likely preventable based on the known security shortfalls at the U.S. Mission and the significant strategic (although not tactical) warnings from the Intelligence Community (IC) about the deteriorating security situation in Libya. The Majority also believes, however, that the Benghazi attacks have been the subject of misinformed speculation and accusations long after the basic facts of the attacks have been determined, thereby distracting attention from more important concerns: the tragic deaths of four brave Americans, the hunt for their attackers, efforts by the U.S. Government to avoid future attacks, and the future of the U.S.-Libya relationship.

The Majority would like to commend our Republican colleagues on the Committee who supported this report for their earnest and thorough efforts with us to find out what really happened in Benghazi before, during, and after the attacks, despite the swirling controversy and pressures. To produce this report, we worked together on a bipartisan basis to dispel the many factual inaccuracies and conspiracy theories related to the Benghazi attacks so that the public would have a fair and accurate accounting of the events.

We would also like to express our appreciation for the dedication and professionalism of the workforce of the IC which, as noted in a key finding in this report, provided strategic warning about the deteriorating security situation in Libya and the threat to U.S. interests there in the months prior to the attacks in Benghazi.

The Talking Points Controversy

Perhaps no issue related to Benghazi has been as mischaracterized as the unclassified talking points prepared by the Central Intelligence Agency (CIA) at the request of the House Permanent Select Committee on Intelligence (HPSCI) and provided to HPSCI, this Committee, and Administration officials on September 15,

---

[140] For the purposes of this report, and this Committee, the Majority includes Independent Senator Angus King.

2012. The Majority notes that the controversy over the CIA talking points consumed a regrettable and disproportionate amount of time and energy during the Committee's substantive review of the Benghazi attacks.

1. *The Talking Points Were Flawed But Mostly Accurate*

The Majority believes that the CIA talking points were flawed but—as discussed in the report—painted a mostly accurate picture of the IC's analysis of the Benghazi attacks **at that time, in an unclassified form and without compromising the nascent investigation of the attacks** by the Federal Bureau of Investigation (FBI). In retrospect, the talking points could have and should have been clearer. As discussed below, omissions and wording choices contributed to significant controversy and confusion, as did an erroneous reference to "demonstrations." In addition, the Administration was slow to provide details explaining the drafting and editing process that produced the talking points. Speculation and conspiracy theories about the details could have been mitigated if the factual record of how the talking points were produced was provided sooner to this Committee and to the public.

Officials in the Executive Branch and Members of Congress also added to the confusion in the days after September 11, 2012, by inconsistently characterizing the events in Benghazi, even though the President referred to them as "attacks" and "acts of terror" on September 12, 2012.[141] Administration officials provided vague and sometimes conflicting characterizations of the events in some instances. Members of Congress also lent support to the narrative of a protest gone awry for days following the attack. For example, in a September 22, 2012, resolution honoring the four Americans who died, the Senate unanimously adopted the narrative that the violence in Benghazi "coincided with an attack on the United States Embassy in Cairo, Egypt, which was **also** swarmed by an angry mob of protesters on September 11, 2012."[142]

2. *Confusion from Use of the Term "Terrorists" vs. "Extremists"*

A key point of contention was that the final talking points referred to "extremists" rather than "terrorists." IC analysts and senior leaders such as former

---

[141] "Remarks by the President on the Deaths of U.S. Embassy Staff in Libya." The Rose Garden, September 12. 2012.
[142] S. Res. 588 (2012). Emphasis added.

CIA Director David Petraeus testified to the Committee that when describing attackers, the word "extremist" was meant to imply that terrorist groups were involved – and, in fact, elements of the IC routinely use the term "Islamist extremists" when referring to al-Qaida and similar groups.[143] However, the assumption that these two terms would be seen by the public as interchangeable proved to be incorrect. "Extremists" and "terrorists" are not interchangeable terms. Some in the public, Congress, and the press interpreted the use of the word "extremist" as an attempt to downplay the role of terrorists in the Benghazi attacks. Through the course of our review, however, we found no evidence of any effort to downplay the role of terrorists in the Benghazi attacks.

3. The CIA Dropped the Term "Al-Qa'ida"

It is important to reiterate that the reference to "al-Qa'ida" included in early drafts of the talking points was removed by CIA staff, **not** by the White House or the FBI, as was incorrectly alleged by some members of Congress and the press. The reference was removed in an internal CIA draft **prior** to dissemination to the interagency process and prior to senior CIA leadership viewing the draft. These facts are corroborated by emails provided to the Committee on a "read and return" basis on February 26, 2013, and made public on May 15, 2013.

According to testimony before the Committee by General Counsel for the Director of National Intelligence (DNI) Robert Litt on February 26, 2013, the reference to "al-Qa'ida" was removed to protect intelligence sources and methods. This rationale was neither confirmed nor refuted in the emails provided. However, according to testimony by former CIA Director David Petraeus, when the talking points were drafted, classified sources and methods did exist that linked a specific terrorist group to the attack, but the IC did not yet have an unclassified factual basis for connecting the attacks to any group formally affiliated with or self-affiliated with al-Qa'ida.[144] In addition, the CIA staff who edited the points made changes eliminating "al-Qa'ida" and "Ansar al-Sharia" to ensure that the points contained no information that could either: (1) reveal intelligence sources and methods or (2) compromise the FBI investigation by prematurely attributing responsibility for the attacks to any one person or group, thereby pre-judging a

---

[143] Statement by David Petraeus, Former CIA Director, *Hearing with General David Petraeus Re. His Knowledge of the Attacks on U.S. Facilities in Benghazi, Libya*, November 16, 2012, p. 17, SSCI Document Tracking System.
[144] Ibid, p. 16-17.

5. Senate Select Committee on Intelligence (1/14/2014)

potential prosecution and making it harder to charge other perpetrators in the future.[145]

4. There Were No Protests in Benghazi

We now know that the CIA's September 15, 2012, talking points were inaccurate in that they wrongly attributed the genesis of the Benghazi attacks to protests that became violent. However, as stated in the report, this characterization reflected the assessment by the IC of the information available at that time, which lacked sufficient intelligence and eyewitness statements to conclude that there were no protests. Further, it is important to remember that this early assessment was made in the context of approximately 40 protests around the globe against U.S. embassies and consulates in response to an inflammatory film. There were also other violent attacks against U.S. embassies and consulates in Egypt, Tunisia, Yemen and other cities around the world on or after September 11. According to CIA emails dated September 16, 2012, the then-Deputy Director of the CIA requested further information from CIA staff at Embassy Tripoli about whether there was countervailing evidence of protests that occurred prior to the attacks in Benghazi. It was not until September 24, 2012—eight days later—that the IC revised its assessment that there were no protests leading up to the attacks (*see* discussion in the main report under Finding #9 for bipartisan Committee views on the development of the intelligence picture after the attacks).

5. The Talking Points Went Through the Normal Interagency Coordination Process

The Majority concludes that the interagency coordination process on the talking points followed normal, but rushed coordination procedures and that there were no efforts by the White House or any other Executive Branch entities to

---

[145] According to the CIA, the talking points editors at the Agency were influenced by an email from an officer in the National Clandestine Service saying that the part of the original talking points stating that "we do know that Islamic extremists with ties to al-Qa'ida participated in the attack" implied complicity in the deaths of the Americans and therefore could compromise the FBI investigation. The CIA employee who drafted the first version of the points therefore agreed that because it was still unknown precisely who was responsible for the Benghazi attacks, the language of the third version of the talking points should be changed to say "we know that they [Islamic extremists] participated in the protests." Although the CIA personnel editing points did not make this change, "attack" in the second bullet was changed to "violent demonstrations," effectively accomplishing the same purpose. In addition, the word "attacks" in the first bullet of the talking points was changed to "demonstrations." The CIA staff editing the talking points also then deleted the mention in the second bullet of the extremists who participated having "ties to al-Qa'ida." *See* report from Michael J. Morell, "Lessons Learned from Formulation of Unclassified Talking Points re the Events in Benghazi, 11-12 September 2012," August 6, 2013, p. 4.

"cover-up" facts or make alterations for political purposes. Indeed, former CIA Director David Petraeus testified to the Committee on November 16, 2012, "They went through the normal process that talking points—unclassified public talking points—go through."[146] In fact, the purpose of the National Security Council (NSC) is to coordinate the many national security agencies of the government, especially when information about a terrorist attack is flowing in and being analyzed quickly—and the NSC used this role appropriately in the case of the talking points coordination. Furthermore, such coordination processes were also standardized, often at the urging of Congress, following the September 11, 2001, terrorist attacks with the explicit goal of reducing information "stovepipes" between and among agencies.

6. *Conclusion*

The Majority agrees that the process to create the talking points was not without problems, so we join our Republican colleagues in recommending—as we do in the report—that in responding to future requests for unclassified talking points from Congress, the IC should simply tell Congress which facts are unclassified and let Members of Congress provide additional context for the public. However, we sincerely hope that the public release of the emails on May 15, 2013, that describe the creation of the talking points, and the evidence presented in this report, will end the misinformed and unhelpful talking points controversy once and for all.

DIANNE FEINSTEIN
JOHN D. ROCKEFELLER IV
RON WYDEN
BARBARA A. MIKULSKI
MARK UDALL
MARK WARNER
MARTIN HEINRICH
ANGUS KING

---

[146] Statement by David Petraeus, Former CIA Director, *Hearing with General David Petraeus Re: His Knowledge of the Attacks on U.S. Facilities in Benghazi, Libya*, November 16, 2012, p. 24.

5. Senate Select Committee on Intelligence (1/14/2014)

ADDITIONAL VIEWS OF SENATORS CHAMBLISS, BURR, RISCH, COATS, RUBIO, AND COBURN

Over a year has passed since the terrorist attacks on U.S. facilities in Benghazi, Libya, claimed the lives of four brave Americans—Glen Doherty, Sean Smith, Christopher Stevens, and Tyrone Woods. The Senate Select Committee on Intelligence endeavored to conduct a thorough and bipartisan review of the events and circumstances surrounding these attacks. The Committee's report, the *SSCI Review of Terrorist Attacks on U.S. Facilities in Benghazi, September 11-12, 2012,* offers findings and recommendations that we hope will improve intelligence collection and analysis, information sharing, and the physical security for Americans serving overseas in our diplomatic and intelligence facilities.

While the Committee has completed its report, important questions remain unanswered as a direct result of the Obama Administration's failure to provide the Committee with access to necessary documents and witnesses. We believe the Administration's lack of cooperation is directly contrary to its statutory obligation to keep the congressional intelligence committees fully and currently informed and has effectively obstructed the Committee's efforts to get to the ground truth with respect to these remaining questions. Too often, providing timely and complete information to Congress is viewed by the Administration as optional or an accommodation, rather than compliance with a statutory requirement. It is our view that the Committee should have held a vote to exercise its subpoena power to end this obstruction, once and for all, in the early stages of the review.

As we prepared these Additional Views, the Executive branch still has not provided all relevant documents to the Committee. Other documents have been provided to the Committee on a "read only" basis, meaning that the Committee was only permitted to view them for a limited period of time, while being supervised by the coordinating agency, and had to rely upon our notes when preparing the report. Significantly, key Executive branch witnesses who were directly involved in decisions that affected the ability of the United States to defend or respond to these attacks have declined our invitations to be interviewed by the Committee, even after being returned to full duty by the State Department. In other cases, the testimony provided to the Committee contradicted written documents we reviewed, or—as with some of the testimony by the Under Secretary of State for Management, Patrick Kennedy—was particularly specious.

1

We understand that mistakes can be made during the back-and-forth of oral testimony, but when that occurs, the Intelligence Community (IC) and the Executive branch have historically been quick to correct the record. Yet, we are still waiting for some of these troubling contradictions to be resolved. Further, in what is becoming an habitual refrain, the Administration has made repeated and spurious claims of the "executive" and "deliberative process" privileges, serving to deny information to the Committee that was otherwise relevant to our review. Similarly, information has been withheld from the Committee because of the "ongoing criminal investigation" into the attacks, in an apparent effort to shield certain government agencies from congressional oversight or potential embarrassment. We have also learned that the Federal Bureau of Investigation has developed significant information about the attacks and the suspected attackers that is not being shared with Congress, even where doing so would not in any way impact an ongoing investigation.

Complete Absence of Accountability

In the course of this review, we have come to the unavoidable conclusion that, for an event marked by significant failures, one of the biggest failures is the Administration's complete refusal or inability to attain accountability—from the attackers themselves and from those U.S. Government officials who made poor management decisions relating to the Benghazi facilities. This is not a charge we bring lightly, but it is one clearly substantiated by the facts. We recognize that sometimes circumstances are simply beyond our control, but the Benghazi attacks do not fall into this category of chance. Prior to the attacks, senior U.S. Government officials were aware of the deteriorating security situation and tenuous physical security of the Temporary Mission Facility in Benghazi, but did little, if anything, of consequence about it. The U.S. government personnel on the ground in Benghazi raised constant alarms in the months before September 2012. The combination of these alarms with the multitude of prior attacks in the Benghazi area should have spurred swift action by State Department officials in Washington. It did not. Many times, the lack of congressional funding is used by an Administration to downplay its own role or minimize responsibility; but in this case, this excuse simply cannot justify highly questionable management decisions. To date, in spite of legitimate questions about the actions of these senior officials raised by our own review, the reviews of other congressional committees, and the Accountability Review Board, not one person has faced disciplinary action of any consequence.

We believe the background of one senior State Department official made him uniquely situated to anticipate the potential for a terrorist attack on the Benghazi facilities. Prior to the 1998 East Africa Embassy bombings which killed 12 Americans, Under Secretary Kennedy was serving as the Assistant Secretary of State for Administration, and concurrently served as the Acting Assistant Secretary of State for Diplomatic Security. Coincidentally, some of the same failures identified by the report of the Accountability Review Board following the 1998 Embassy bombings were noted by the Benghazi Accountability Review Board. Mr. Kennedy later served in key positions in Iraq, in the immediate aftermath of the toppling of Saddam Hussein, and in the IC. The threat of terrorism, including against U.S. facilities, was not new to him, and given the security situation in Benghazi, the attacks could have been foreseen. Given the threat environment, Mr. Kennedy should have used better judgment and should be held accountable.

We are equally disturbed by the Administration's ongoing failure to secure justice and accountability for those responsible for these attacks. Despite the President's promise, not a single suspected attacker is in custody. Ahmed Abu Khattala, whom the press reports has been charged by the United States for his lead role in the attacks, continues to live freely in Libya while giving taunting interviews to major media outlets. Yet, inexplicably, U.S. diplomacy cannot seem to secure his capture so he can be detained and fully interrogated before any criminal proceedings are initiated. Other leading suspects, such as Faraj al-Chalabi and Ali Ani al-Harzi, also remain free, including after failed diplomatic efforts by the Secretary of State relating to al-Harzi's capture and interrogation. As we discuss later in these views, the President's failure to develop a clear, cogent detention and interrogation policy and his refusal to yield on sending new terrorists to Guantanamo Bay have had—and will continue to have—far-reaching consequences for our national security, as exemplified by the events relating to Benghazi. There simply is no justification, not even an ill-conceived campaign promise, for not doing more to capture and interrogate terrorists who caused the deaths of four Americans. The United States can and should do better. We have heard the excuse that these terrorists cannot be captured because Libya is a dangerous operating environment. Yet, the same Administration offering this excuse somehow managed to recently capture al-Qa'ida operative Abu Anas al-Libi in Tripoli, briefly interrogate him, and bring him to the United States for prosecution for his role in the 1998 Embassy bombings. We believe a similar result is possible here, but only if the U.S. Government more aggressively pursues justice for these attacks against our nation.

Manipulating the Facts

When American citizens are murdered in terrorist attacks against our nation, we believe the Executive branch has a particular obligation, beyond statutory requirements, to openly and fully cooperate with congressional efforts to investigate and understand these matters, no matter how potentially embarrassing or inconvenient. That certainly has not been the case here. From the beginning, the Administration's handling of the Benghazi attacks has been a source of confusion to Congress, the American people, other nations, and—most significantly—the families of those killed in Benghazi. From the refusal to clearly explain the decisions by, and interactions of, the President, the Secretary of Defense, and the Secretary of State on the night of the attacks to the talking points fiasco, the Administration's response has been notable for its deficiencies. Many of us were frustrated and astounded by the great pains the Administration took after the attacks to avoid the clear linkage of what happened in Benghazi to the threat of international terrorism. Contrary to the long-standing commitment of the Office of the Director of National Intelligence (ODNI) and the Central Intelligence Agency (CIA) to provide timely information to the Committee following any terrorist attack or attempted attack, we were given neither prompt nor adequate information about the Benghazi attacks. Instead, we were subjected to Sunday news programs, carefully crafted speeches, and delayed briefings—all designed to label the terrorist attacks as violent demonstrations spontaneously inspired by an obscure anti-Muslim film that has long since been forgotten.

Maybe we would be less skeptical if there were not so many examples of this Administration downplaying the very real threat of international terrorism. The Fort Hood terrorist attack by Nidal Hasan was labeled "workplace violence," despite Hasan's email communications with al-Qa'ida in the Arabian Peninsula cleric, Anwar al-Aulaqi, in the months before he opened fire, killing 13 and wounding 32 military and civilian personnel in 2009. Another Aulaqi protégé, Umar Farouk Abdulmutallab, was treated as an ordinary criminal and given *Miranda* warnings, despite being captured after failing to detonate plastic explosives on a Northwest Airlines flight over Detroit on December 25, 2009. Then there was Faisal Shahzad, the incompetent Times Square bomber, whose car bomb failed to detonate in May 2010. The Administration tried to spin Shahzad as

4

a one-off lone wolf until the media discovered he had traveled to Pakistan for five months and trained with the Pakistani Taliban. As with Benghazi, the Administration's obligation to provide information to Congress about those cases seemed to be superseded by a desire to script the message that al-Qa'ida had been decimated or to protect a criminal investigation in spite of equally vital intelligence prerogatives.

The Talking Points

The obstruction faced by the Committee during its review is epitomized by the months-long saga involving the CIA's Benghazi talking points. In the immediate aftermath of September 11th, the Committee began asking the IC who was likely responsible for the attacks and what the intelligence was indicating. At the same time, the House Permanent Select Committee on Intelligence requested unclassified talking points from the CIA that could be used by Members in responding to press inquiries. Rather than simply provide Congress with the best intelligence and on-the-ground assessments, the Administration chose to try to frame the story in a way that minimized any connection to terrorism. Before the Benghazi attacks—in the lead-up to the 2012 presidential election, the Administration had continued to script the narrative that al-Qa'ida had been decimated and was on the run. The Benghazi terrorist attacks inconveniently, and overwhelmingly, interfered with this fictitious and politically-motivated storyline. Thus, the story as told through the talking points and repeated on the Sunday talk shows became one of a protest or demonstration gone awry, rather than an act of terrorism against the United States by individuals with ties to al-Qa'ida. Until the forthright testimony of the Director of the National Counterterrorism Center (NCTC) on September 19, 2012,[147] no one in the Administration—from the President[148] on down—had publicly called Benghazi the terrorist attack it clearly was. Yet, when the Administration was questioned after the NCTC Director's

---

[147] Matthew G. Olsen, Director of NCTC, *Testimony before the Senate Homeland Security and Governmental Affairs Committee during Hearing on Homeland Threats and Agency Responses*, September 19, 2012.
[148] In his Rose Garden speech the day after the Benghazi attacks, the President passed up at least ten opportunities to clearly identify the Benghazi attacks as terrorist attacks. Instead, he chose to use the following: "killed in an attack," "outrageous and shocking attack," "killers who attacked," "this type of senseless violence," "these brutal acts," "this attack," "fought back against the attackers," "this attack in Benghazi," "this terrible act," and "those of their attackers." His statement—"No acts of terror will ever shake the resolve of this great nation"—does nothing to resolve this shortcoming, as its placement in this speech simply creates ambiguity in whether it refers to the previously cited terrorist attacks on September 11, 2001, or is meant to include the Benghazi terrorist attacks as well.

testimony, IC officials, including the Director and Deputy Director of the CIA, said they knew instantly during the attacks that it was terrorism.[149]

As the Committee began to receive intelligence relating to the attacks, it became clear that the narrative conveyed through the talking points and during the Sunday talk shows did not stand up to scrutiny. We now know that the talking points, as originally drafted by the CIA, included the words "al-Qa'ida," "Ansar al-Sharia," and "attacks," and spoke of other attacks against foreign interests in Benghazi. There was no mention of a protest gone awry outside the Temporary Mission Facility. Yet, through an "interagency process" that specifically included coordination with and by the White House, the message was recast to downplay or eliminate these references and minimize any potential embarrassment to the State Department for its failure to heed earlier security warnings.

Rather than openly engage with the Committee on how the talking points were drafted, the Administration resisted repeated Committee efforts to learn who was involved and what changes were made, including by imposing unreasonable restrictions on Member and staff access to the same information about the talking points that would eventually be released to the public. Not until the nomination of John Brennan to be the next Director of the CIA was pending before the Committee, did the Administration even consider addressing the Committee's requests, albeit still with resistance. In response to specific requests by the Committee for the full paper trail, the emails documenting the changes in the talking points drafts, they chose to provide a re-creation of the drafts by the ODNI and simply on a "read only" basis. These conditions meant there was no opportunity for in-depth, ongoing exploration by Members or staff of the paper trail. As the Administration well knows, the "read only" practice is often used to "check the box" on providing information to Congress, but to do so in a way that is simply not helpful to congressional oversight as it denies ready and complete access to documents. It took seven months before these emails were finally disclosed in full to Congress, and to the public in redacted form.

Compounding this resistance, no effort was made to correct the record when, during testimony before the Committee in late 2012, the Acting Director of the CIA emphatically stated that the talking points were sent to the White House "for

---

[149] See, e.g., SSCI Transcript, *Hearing on the Attacks in Benghazi*, November 15, 2012, pp. 55, 62, 65, and 116-118; and SSCI Transcript, *Hearing with General David Petraeus Re: His Knowledge of the Attacks on U.S. Facilities in Benghazi, Libya*, November 16, 2012, pp. 17 and 83-84.

5. Senate Select Committee on Intelligence (1/14/2014)

their awareness, not for their coordination."[150] The emails, which the Committee received later, clearly show that the White House was, from the earliest moments, asked to "coordinate" on the talking points.[151] This may seem, to some, like a distinction without a difference, but in the world of Federal government interactions, "coordination" carries with it a level of involvement and responsibility to overrule or influence that is not present when information is conveyed simply "for awareness." The measure of White House influence can be seen in a September 15, 2012, email[152] from then-CIA Director David Petraeus acknowledging that, in spite of his own misgivings, the final content of the talking points was the "[National Security Staff's] call, to be sure." In contrast, the Acting Director's testimony perpetuated the myth that the White House played no part in the drafting or editing of the talking points. Today, it remains unclear exactly what was discussed during the Deputies Committee meeting that resulted in the final version of the talking points—or even who was present besides the Acting Director of the CIA, who actually made the edits. These are basic questions that should have been readily answered in the interests of transparency and accountability.

Disturbing Lack of Cooperation by the State Department

As the Committee attempted to piece together key events before, during, and after the attacks, we faced the most significant and sustained resistance from the State Department in obtaining documents, access to witnesses, and responses to questions. The Committee does, on occasion, deal with "jurisdictional" obstacles that bureaucratically arise when we seek information relevant to an intelligence matter, simply because the holder of the information is not an element of the IC. Our review of the Benghazi attacks was no different. Even though the attacks involved IC employees and the CIA Annex and it was CIA personnel who came to the aid of the personnel at the Temporary Mission Facility, the State Department swiftly asserted questionable jurisdictional objections and resisted full cooperation with our review. We surmise that this lack of forthrightness stems from a desire to protect individual political careers, now and in the future, and the Department's reputation, at the expense of learning all the facts and apportioning responsibility.

---

[150] SSCI Transcript, *Hearing on the Attacks in Benghazi*, November 15, 2012, p. 54 .

[151] *See* Jonathan Karl and Chris Good, "The Benghazi Emails: Talking Points Changed at State Dept.'s Request," *ABC News*, May 15, 2013, abcnews.go.com/Politics/Benghazi-emails-talking-points-changed-state-depts-request/story?id=19187137 (provides a link to the declassified and redacted emails at abcnews.go.com/images/Politics/white-house-benghazi-emails.pdf, p. 9).

[152] Ibid., p. 95.

Ironically, the State Department was not shy about voicing its concerns and objections to the Committee's draft report. In written comments, State made a concerted effort to downplay the Department's responsibility for ensuring the physical security of its employees and facilities overseas. For example, State repeatedly attempted to minimize its own culpability for the lack of security precautions by pointing to the fact that the same number of people died at the CIA Annex as at the Temporary Mission Facility and, therefore, CIA should be equally criticized for its own security at the Annex.[153] The logic is remarkable for its boldness, but neither helpful nor persuasive. The two security officers who were killed at the Annex were on the roof, in the act of defending the Annex, when they were struck by mortars. It is likely no amount of added physical security at the Annex would have prevented their deaths. Conversely, the Ambassador and Sean Smith were killed at the Temporary Mission Facility by attackers who easily gained unfettered access to the compound. There is a tremendous difference between a fortified facility that suffers a fatal blow from a mortar attack and a porous compound that yields to a basic ground assault. Yet, in an attempt to absolve itself of responsibility, State absurdly equated these scenarios. Moreover, this simplistic "numbers" argument fails to account for the likelihood that there would have been more American casualties, but for the successful rescue efforts by the Annex personnel.

Failures in Leadership—State Department

While many individuals with information relevant to our review were more than forthcoming with the Committee, we are particularly disappointed that Charlene Lamb, who was the Deputy Assistant Secretary for International Programs, has refused to explain to the Committee why certain decisions were made concerning enhanced security at the Temporary Mission Facility and who ultimately was responsible for those decisions. The Committee extended invitations to Ms. Lamb on three occasions prior to and after her reinstatement—each time, she refused to meet with the Committee.[154] Unfortunately, even after Ms. Lamb was returned to full duty, the State Department did not make her available to the Committee, something we believe should have been a priority for both Ms. Lamb and the State Department. Based on what we have learned during the Committee's review, we believe Ms. Lamb's testimony is critical to

---

[153] "Intelligence Community Response, Fact-Based & Substantive Review Only Regarding SSCI Report of Terrorist Attacks on U.S. Facilities in Benghazi," August 30, 2013.
[154] The Committee extended invitations to Ms. Lamb through State on November 19, 2012, July 12, 2013, and August 20, 2013.

determining why the leadership failures in the State Department occurred and the specific extent to which these failures reached into its highest levels.

We know from the testimony of Eric Nordstrom, who served as the Regional Security Officer in Libya until shortly before the attacks, that Ms. Lamb and other senior State Department officials were unreceptive to repeated requests from the Libyan mission regarding security personnel in both Tripoli and Benghazi. According to Mr. Nordstrom, the previous U.S. Ambassador to Libya, Gene Cretz, and his Deputy Chief of Mission (DCM), Joan Polaschik, traveled to Washington in mid-February 2012 to specifically ask for additional security personnel.[155] In addition to meeting with Ms. Lamb, they met separately with Mr. Kennedy and other senior officials. Yet, when the Libyan mission transmitted its official request for additional security personnel on March 28, 2012, the pushback from Ms. Lamb's office was swift and significant. While the request, which included five temporary duty Diplomatic Security agents in Benghazi, was clearly reasonable, one of Ms. Lamb's subordinates asked Mr. Nordstrom why the official cable sought "the sun, the moon, and the stars." When Mr. Nordstrom stated that he did not understand why this was an issue, the response from Ms. Lamb's office was telling: "Well, you know, this is a political game. You have to not make us look bad here, that we're not being responsive."[156] In a disturbingly prophetic e-mail to DCM Polaschik following this exchange, Mr. Nordstrom wrote:

> I doubt we will ever get [Diplomatic Security] to admit in writing what I was told [in] reference [to] Benghazi that DI/[International Programs] was directed by Deputy Assistant Secretary Lamb to cap the agents in Benghazi at 3, and force post to hire local drivers. This is apparently a verbal policy only but one which DS/IP/[Near Eastern Affairs] doesn't plan to violate. I hope that nobody is injured as a result of an incident in Benghazi, since it would be particularly embarrassing to both DS and DAS [Lamb] if it was a result of some sort of game they are playing.[157]

According to Mr. Nordstrom, Ms. Lamb was also vocal about her unwillingness to provide additional security personnel, including support of an extension of the Department of Defense (DoD) Site Security Team. Mr.

---

[155] SSCI Transcript, *Member and Staff Interview of Eric Nordstrom*, June 27, 2013, pp. 5 and 26.
[156] Ibid., p. 28.
[157] *See* ibid., pp. 24-25.

Nordstrom told the Committee that Ms. Lamb claimed it would be embarrassing and give Libya more security agents than in Yemen and Pakistan.[158] In reality, as Mr. Nordstrom explained to both Ms. Lamb and the Committee, the Embassies in Sana'a and Islamabad actually complied with the Overseas Security Policy Board security standards and had security systems in place. On July 9, 2012, the Libyan mission sent another formal request for additional security personnel. The State Department never responded to this request in the form of a cable. According to Mr. Nordstrom, Ms. Lamb said that a response had been drafted, but was "lost in the shuffle."[159] Mr. Nordstrom's testimony does not stand alone. We heard of similar difficulties with Ms. Lamb from Gregory Hicks, the former DCM who arrived in Tripoli just over one month before the attacks. In a May 2012 briefing with Ms. Lamb as he prepared for his new assignment, he pushed back on the proposed security complement, but "did not get a favorable response" from Ms. Lamb.[160]

While Ms. Lamb should be held accountable for her actions in failing to provide better security in Benghazi, we believe that Mr. Kennedy, as the Under Secretary for Management, bears a specific responsibility for these lapses. According to DCM Hicks, the Libyan mission had a very unique status in that it was effectively on "ordered departure" status at all times. DCM Hicks also told the Committee that Mr. Kennedy approved every person who went to Libya and received a daily report on the number of personnel, their names, and their status.[161] Moreover, while Mr. Kennedy never responded to the Libyan mission's request for additional security personnel, he did specifically decline an offer from Lieutenant General Robert Neller, U.S. Marine Corps, Director of Operations, J3, the Joint Staff, to sustain or provide additional DoD security personnel in Libya by extending the deployment of the DoD Site Security Team in Tripoli, transitioning to a Marine Security Detachment, or deploying a U.S. Marine Corps Fleet Antiterrorism Security Team.[162] In short, he had direct insight into the security situation at all times, had received DoD offers of assistance, and affirmatively declined to improve the Libyan mission's security posture.

---

[158] Ibid., pp. 4 and 32.

[159] Ibid., p. 60.

[160] SSCI Transcript, *Member and Staff Interview of Gregory Hicks and Mark Thompson*, June 12, 2013, p. 10.

[161] SSCI Transcript, *Member and Staff Interview of Gregory Hicks*, June 19, 2013, p. 5.

[162] Email from Lieutenant General Robert B. Neller, U.S.M.C., JCS J3, to Patrick Kennedy, July 11, 2012, 2:46 PM; email from Patrick Kennedy to Lieutenant General Neller, July 13, 2012, 6:31 PM ("We are not/not requesting an extension of the team; and deeply appreciate the support we have had. We have finally been able to obtain weapons permits for the 11 new locally engaged Embassy bodyguards late last week and are in the process of integrating them into our operations.").

Ultimately, however, the final responsibility for security at diplomatic facilities lies with the former Secretary of State, Hillary Clinton. Because the Temporary Mission Facility in Benghazi did not meet the security standards set by the State Department, it would have required a waiver to be occupied. Although certain waivers of the standards could have been approved at a lower level, other departures, such as the co-location requirement, could only be approved by the Secretary of State.[163] At the end of the day, she was responsible for ensuring the safety of all Americans serving in our diplomatic facilities. Her failure to do so clearly made a difference in the lives of the four murdered Americans and their families.

The State Department's inordinate effort to minimize management failures contrasts sharply with its public commitment to accountability. At the same time, a strong case can be made that State engaged in retaliation against witnesses who were willing to speak with Congress. No reasonable explanation accounts for the State Department's unacceptable treatment of these witnesses, at the same time it returned to active duty witnesses such as Ms. Lamb who were shielded from, or actively avoided, Committee requests for interviews.

Failures in Leadership—General Dempsey

The failures in leadership relating to Benghazi were not limited to the State Department. The tenure of the Chairman of the Joint Chiefs of Staff, General Martin Dempsey, has been marked by what we view as significant deficiencies in command. From Syria to Benghazi, there has been either a profound inability or clear unwillingness to identify and prevent problems before they arise. Given the known operating environment in Benghazi, much less North Africa, a strong military leader would have ensured there was a viable plan in place to rescue Americans should the need arise. We understand the Department of Defense cannot plan for a rescue operation of every Embassy or diplomatic facility across the globe, but Benghazi was different given its hostile environment and lack of host nation security and support. Yet, there was no such plan. General Dempsey's attempts to excuse inaction by claiming that forces were not deployed because they would not have gotten there in time does not pass the common sense test. No one knew when the attacks against our facilities in Benghazi would end, or how aggressive the attacks would be. That is the whole point of a pre-established

---

[163] SSCI Transcript, *Member and Staff Interview of Eric Nordstrom*, June 27, 2013, pp. 36-37.

emergency rescue plan—so that the length of the attack alone does not dictate the rescue or survival of Americans. Understanding that the State Department bears ultimate responsibility for the safety of Americans serving in diplomatic facilities abroad, General Dempsey should have ensured that plan was in place, but he failed to do so.

A strong military leader would also have ensured that his commanders in the field were fully aware of all United States personnel, including CIA personnel, who were located within their areas of responsibility. Yet, the Committee has confirmed that General Carter Ham, as the Commander of U.S. Africa Command, was not even aware there was a CIA annex in Benghazi at the time of the attacks. We are puzzled as to how the military leadership expected to effectively respond and rescue Americans in the event of an emergency when it did not even know of the existence of one of the U.S. facilities. The fate of United States personnel serving in dangerous areas of the world should not rest on *ad hoc* rescue operations, no matter how heroic, simply because the United States Government and its civilian and military leaders have failed in their collective responsibilities to provide security and potentially life-saving assistance.

Continued Fall-out from No Detention Policy

As we learn from the errors and failures surrounding Benghazi, we believe one critical area of national security policy must be reexamined and changed by this Administration. President Obama and his Administration must end their efforts to close the detention facility at Guantanamo Bay and must develop a clear, cogent policy for the detention and interrogation of suspected terrorists. Since the President ordered Guantanamo's closure in 2009, we have witnessed a dangerous tendency to either not detain terrorism suspects or to conduct all-too-brief intelligence interrogations, followed by the inevitable reading of *Miranda* rights and appointment of counsel which often ends the interrogation. Amazingly, the same Administration that has demanded the closure of the state-of-the-art detention facility at Guantanamo has vigorously embraced the use of floating prisons for conducting brief intelligence interrogations overseas. This approach is not only at odds with the spirit of the Geneva Conventions, but it fails to recognize how good intelligence collection can work if given the time to do so.

Intelligence collection and criminal prosecutions can work hand-in-hand, but we should not sacrifice intelligence collection simply because of the political unwillingness to detain a terrorist without criminal charges. Detaining and interrogating terrorism suspects—such as those believed to be involved in Benghazi—at Guantanamo Bay or other viable facilities outside the United States, as the law clearly provides, would ensure that we are maximizing the collection of vital intelligence, while still preserving the option to bring criminal charges. Instead, this Administration has chosen to return to a pre-9/11 mindset in which criminal charges take precedence over intelligence collection. As we saw with the 1998 Embassy bombings, the bombing of the USS Cole in 2000, and the September 11, 2001, terrorist attacks, this approach did not work then, and it does not work today. It is the perpetuation of this mindset that we believe is directly responsible for the Administration's failure to secure justice for those suspected of involvement in the attacks. If this Administration were serious about holding terrorists accountable for causing the deaths of American citizens, Khattala, al-Chalabi, and al-Harzi would today be at Guantanamo, instead of being free to continue to threaten Americans. We have heard the statistics about successful criminal prosecutions of terrorists; but at the end of the day, if we are not gathering the intelligence needed to prevent attacks and capture terrorists before they harm us, those statistics will neither help us protect this country nor provide much comfort to the families of those whose fate may be prematurely determined by terrorist attacks.

Aside from enabling key intelligence collection, long-term detention serves another invaluable function—it keeps dangerous terrorists behind bars. As the Committee's report notes, in the months leading up to the Benghazi terrorist attacks, the IC provided multiple warnings about terrorist activities in the region, including by al-Qa'ida and its affiliates. As press reports prior to and after the attacks indicate, there was particular concern about the rise of Ansar al-Sharia, the group involved in the Benghazi attacks that, according to public reports, was founded by former Guantanamo detainee Sufian bin Qumu.

Following the 2009 Executive order to close Guantanamo, there has been a concerted effort by this Administration to downplay the recidivist activities of former Guantanamo detainees in support of its overtly political goal to transfer as many detainees as possible to foreign countries and even to the United States. Listening to supporters of this ill-advised Executive order, one would believe that former detainees have universally rejected their terrorist associations and are now living peaceably throughout the world. The facts say otherwise. The recidivism rate among all former detainees is now over 29% and rising consistently. We

5. Senate Select Committee on Intelligence (1/14/2014)

know that al-Qa'ida in the Arabian Peninsula has counted former detainees among its leaders and members. Yet, the Administration continues to press for the release of more detainees, even to locations plagued by terrorism and amidst evidence that they will not be effectively monitored by host countries. Not every detainee must be held indefinitely, but not one should be released unless it is absolutely clear that he will no longer pose a threat to the United States or our interests. We simply cannot risk another Sufian bin Qumu being involved in terrorist activities that result in the deaths of American citizens.

Unanswered Questions

We believe the Committee's report has adequately reviewed and reported on the actions by the IC relating to Benghazi. Due to the issues outlined above, however, this review did not exhaust every question or provide every answer relating to these attacks. There remain important issues that should be addressed by congressional committees with express jurisdiction over these matters. It is our hope that the Committee's report and these Additional Views will assist in the eventual disclosure of those facts necessary to determine why our personnel and facilities in Benghazi were so vulnerable to attack. For example, we believe the issues of accountability and retaliation within the State Department must be fully explored by a committee that can and will use its subpoena authority to obtain information from an uncooperative State Department. It is wholly unsatisfactory that no one has borne responsibility for the poor policy decisions regarding the security of the Benghazi facility that appear to have been made at the highest levels of the Department. As we noted, the ultimate accountability lies with the former Secretary of State, and we believe there should be a full examination of her role in these events, including on the night of the attacks.

Questions also remain about who took the deployment of the Foreign Emergency Support Team (FEST) "off the table" and why this decision was made. The Committee has been told that this decision was made during a meeting that included Mr. Kennedy, the Secretary of State, and the Secretary of Defense. While we believe the military should have been the first response, the FEST's terrorism response mission—and previous deployments following the 1998 East Africa Embassy bombings and the 2000 USS Cole bombing, should have put them squarely in play. Yet, in what seems to be an unwillingness by State Department leadership to acknowledge that Benghazi was a terrorist incident, the decision was made to not deploy the FEST. The Committee interviewed Mark Thompson,

Deputy Coordinator for Operations at the State Department, who believed that the FEST option was taken off the table because of safety concerns. As Mr. Thompson testified before the Committee, this rationale did not make sense, given that the discussion was about sending the FEST to Tripoli or a nearby country, not to Benghazi.[164]

Similarly, there must be a full examination of our military response, or lack thereof. The CIA and other elements of the IC do, and must continue to, gather intelligence in dangerous areas of the world, as they did in Benghazi. Once they are asked to do so, however, we must do more to keep them safe. We appreciate that steps have been taken to ensure that U.S. assets can be deployed more quickly in the future, but the Benghazi families are entitled to understand the full facts surrounding response decisions made during the attacks. Only with the airing of these facts can supposition and conjecture be put to rest, and be replaced with full accountability.

Recently, new questions surfaced regarding the accuracy of information provided to Congress by the CIA about nondisclosure agreements signed by security officers who were present during the attacks. We have heard and understand the CIA's oral and written explanations for why these new agreements were needed, but are troubled by the lack of clarity in their initial response and the fact that this discrepancy had to be pointed out by personnel formerly associated with the CIA. As with other matters in this review, the Administration's lack of transparency and candor is raising more questions than the underlying discrepancy itself. At the same time, the Committee has learned that the CIA Inspector General did not investigate complaints relating to the Benghazi attacks from CIA whistleblowers. Whether these complaints are ultimately substantiated or dismissed is irrelevant. On a matter of this magnitude involving the deaths of four Americans, the Inspector General has a singular obligation to take seriously and fully investigate any allegation of wrongdoing. His failure to do so raises significant questions that we believe the Committee must explore more fully.

Finally, we believe the role of the White House must be fully explored. As we write these Additional Views, we are still without a full understanding of the substance of the Deputies Committee meeting that resulted in the final changes to the talking points, and we have yet to receive a clear explanation of the specific

---

[164] SSCI Transcript, *Member and Staff Interview of Gregory Hicks and Mark Thompson*, June 12, 2013, pp. 32 and 38.

interactions among the President, the Secretary of Defense, and the Secretary of
State on the night of the attacks. This is not a call for Situation Room photos. It is
a demand for the truth that is owed the American people.

Conclusion

The failures of Benghazi can be summed up this way: the Americans
serving in Libya were vulnerable; the State Department knew they were
vulnerable; and no one in the Administration really did anything about it. The
Intelligence Community does not collect intelligence about threats to our security
in dangerous place so it can be ignored by senior decisionmakers. Nor should a
Regional Security Officer's repeated warnings go unheeded. Yet, the intelligence
and warnings from the field were met by this Administration with a deafening
silence. The four Americans who perished in Benghazi deserved better from their
country. Their families, who have been waiting over a year for promised justice
and answers, are entitled to know the truth about what happened and why. It is our
intent that the findings and recommendations outlined in this report will facilitate
and inform other reviews, especially those conducted by congressional committees
with specific jurisdiction over the State Department. We stand ready to assist
those reviews in every way possible. Ultimately, we must ensure that all the facts
about our government's actions prior to, during, and after the attacks are brought to
light for the American people to judge for themselves. The families of those
murdered in Benghazi deserve the truth, and all of our intelligence, military, and
diplomatic professionals who serve overseas in dangerous places are entitled to
have confidence that the errors of Benghazi will not be repeated.

SAXBY CHAMBLISS
RICHARD BURR
JAMES E. RISCH
DAN COATS
MARCO RUBIO
TOM COBURN, M.D.

ADDITIONAL VIEWS OF SENATOR COLLINS

The Senate Select Committee on Intelligence (SSCI) "Review of Terrorist Attacks on U.S. Facilities in Benghazi, September 11-12, 2012," represents the most extensive review to date of the actions and analysis of the Intelligence Community (IC) leading up to, during, and after the attacks in Benghazi. I commend the SSCI leaders and staff for drafting a report that joins the only one other Senate report on Benghazi, "Flashing Red: A Special Report on the Terrorist Attack at Benghazi," an analysis that Joseph Lieberman, the former Chairman of the Senate Homeland Security and Governmental Affairs Committee (HSGAC), and I authored and issued in December 2012. Our Homeland Security Committee conducted the first bipartisan investigation of what took place during the terrorist attack that cost four Americans their lives. Although hampered by time constraints and insufficient cooperation by the Administration, our report is an indictment of the State Department's failure to adequately secure the Benghazi compound despite numerous indications of an extremely dangerous threat environment.

Like our report, the SSCI report joins an increasing number of analyses to reach the sobering verdict that the State Department could have and should have done much more to prepare for the terrorist attack in Benghazi. The critical findings of this and previous reports regarding the judgments, actions, and management processes at the Department of State beg for accountability, and yet, more than a year after the attack, no one has been held responsible for the critical management failures that contributed to the vulnerability of the American personnel and facilities in Benghazi.

The SSCI report, while adding considerably to our knowledge, would have been strengthened if it had placed greater emphasis on the lack of accountability for the broader management failures at the State Department. It would have been premature for earlier reports published in the months immediately following the attack, such as the Accountability Review Board and the "Flashing Red" report, to reach final judgments with respect to the State Department's personnel actions because the contributing factors to the vulnerability of the facility were still being pieced together. This report could have more fully evaluated the accountability issues because sufficient time had elapsed for the State Department to demonstrate whether or not decision-makers would be held accountable for poor judgments, refusals to tighten security, and misinformation.

For example, Under Secretary of State for Management Patrick Kennedy testified before the Homeland Security and Governmental Affairs Committee in 2012 that the threat environment in Benghazi was "flashing red," yet our investigation found that Under Secretary Kennedy, and other State Department officials, failed to ensure that a facility he personally approved in December 2011 had the necessary security to match the heightened threat environment.

The SSCI report describes many of the management deficiencies that contributed to the inadequate security posture: excessive confusion in the State Department's security decision-making process, uncertainty regarding the facility's future, and the absence of sufficient communication at State Department headquarters. As referenced in the report, the State Department Office of Inspector General (OIG) also found that the Department lacks a conceptual framework and process for risk management, and the Independent Best Practices panel found that security standards waivers for overseas facilities are commonplace. Of the 29 Accountability Review Board (ARB) recommendations, fully 26 relate to systemic management reforms in the Department according to the OIG.

Furthermore, this report, as well as other reports examining Benghazi, has found that the State Department failed to act upon some of the lessons learned from previous attacks. The State Department OIG's September 2013 audit of the ARB process listed four pages of recommendations by the Benghazi ARB that mirror similar recommendations from the report of the ARBs following the 1998 East Africa embassy bombings nearly fourteen years earlier. The OIG blamed this outcome, in part, on the absence of sustained oversight among Department principals, who are defined as the Secretary, deputy secretaries, and under secretaries.

A broken system overseen by senior leadership contributed to the vulnerability of U.S. diplomats and other American personnel in one of the most dangerous cities in the world. This is unacceptable, and yet the Secretary of State has not held anyone responsible for the system's failings. This leads to a perception that senior State Department officials are exempt from accountability because the Secretary of State has failed to hold anyone accountable for the systemic failures and management deficiencies that contributed to the grossly inadequate security for the Benghazi facility.

To be clear, the responsibility for the attack lies with the attackers themselves. Unfortunately, the promises of the President and other senior Administration officials to bring any of the attackers to justice have ringed hollow thus far. The report finds that more than a year after the attack, the terrorists who perpetrated the attack have still not been brought to justice. The report includes an important recommendation I requested, in consultation with the Chairman and Vice Chairman, that the U.S. government must bring the attackers to justice in spite of the unwillingness or lack of capacity of the Libyan government to assist in this effort. Failure to do so would be to repeat one of the mistakes that contributed to the lethality of the attack, which was the excessive reliance on a local Libyan security force that lacked the capacity or willingness to defend the compound.

The failure to follow through on this promise undermines the credibility of the United States, diminishes the commitments made to the families who lost loved ones that night, and ignores the fact that our adversaries pay very close attention to our response to terrorist attacks. In general, inaction has not made the United States any safer. The failure of the United States to respond meaningfully, in the view of our adversaries, to attacks prior to 9/11/01, such as the 1998 al Qaeda attack against U.S. embassies in Kenya and Tanzania and the 2000 USS Cole bombing, served only to embolden the terrorists to plan and execute larger and more deadly attacks.

Finally, the report does not go far enough to address the Administration's failure to correctly label the incident as a deliberate and organized terrorist attack in the days following the attack. As our "Flashing Red" report found, there was never any doubt among key officials, including officials in the IC and the Department of State, that the attack in Benghazi was an act of terrorism. Yet, high-ranking Administration officials, including the President himself, repeatedly cast doubt on the nature of the attack, at times attributing it to the reaction to an anti-Islamic video and to a spontaneous demonstration that escalated into violence.

The SSCI report accurately describes that the IC moved too slowly to correct errors about a protest that never happened, and describes eyewitness testimony that should have been made available or pursued by the intelligence community more aggressively. The report does not, however, describe all of the operational reporting that should have been available to the IC after the attack.

3

The "Flashing Red" report identified two emails from the State Department Diplomatic Security Operations Center on the day of the attack, September 11, and the day after, September 12, 2012, which characterized the attack as an "initial terrorism incident" and as a "terrorist event." In addition to the eyewitness testimony and the State Department reports, agencies and offices responsible for terrorism, including the National Counterterrorism Center (NCTC), the CIA's Office of Terrorism Analysis, and the FBI's Counterterrorism Division, were immediately involved with gathering information about the attack. Indeed, how could there have been any doubt in anyone's mind that, when a large number of armed men break into a U.S. diplomatic facility, set fire to its building, and fire mortars at Americans, that is by definition a terrorist attack?

Despite the fact that the September 11, 2012 attacks in Benghazi were recognized as terrorist attacks by the Intelligence Community and personnel at the Department of State from the beginning, Administration officials were inconsistent and at times misleading in their public statements and failed for days to make clear to the American people that the deaths in Benghazi were the result of a terrorist attack. It took eight days before the Administration communicated clearly and unequivocally to the American people and to Congress regarding this fact through testimony by NCTC Director Matthew Olsen before the Senate Homeland Security and Governmental Affairs Committee on September 19, 2012.

Even after the Administration finally published the complete timeline of the changes made to the talking points, it is baffling how a fundamental, unclassified fact that was known to the IC from the beginning was only communicated clearly to the American people by the Administration after the issue had already been sufficiently muddled to result in confusion.

While I support the SSCI report and appreciate its thorough analysis of much of what went wrong, I believe that more emphasis should have been placed on the three issues I have discussed: (1) the Administration's initial misleading of the American people about the terrorist nature of the attack, (2) the failure of the Administration to hold anyone at the State Department, particularly Under Secretary Kennedy, fully accountable for the security lapses, and (3) the unfulfilled promises of President Obama that he would bring the terrorists to justice.

SUSAN COLLINS